Visual Motion of Curves and Surfaces

Visual Motion of Curves and Surfaces

Roberto Cipolla
University of Cambridge

Peter Giblin
University of Liverpool

CAMBRIDGE
UNIVERSITY PRESS

CAMBRIDGE UNIVERSITY PRESS
Cambridge, New York, Melbourne, Madrid, Cape Town, Singapore, São Paulo, Delhi

Cambridge University Press
The Edinburgh Building, Cambridge CB2 8RU, UK

Published in the United States of America by Cambridge University Press, New York

www.cambridge.org
Information on this title: www.cambridge.org/9780521118187

First published 2000
Reprinted 2001
This digitally printed version 2009

A catalogue record for this publication is available from the British Library

ISBN 978-0-521-63251-5 hardback
ISBN 978-0-521-11818-7 paperback

Contents

Preface   *page* vii

1   Introduction   1

2   Differential Geometry of Curves and Surfaces   5
2.1   Curves and their tangents   5
2.2   Surfaces: the parametric form   7
2.3   Monge form   13
2.4   Implicit form   15
2.5   First fundamental form for surfaces   18
2.6   Curvature of curves   21
2.7   Three surface types   25
2.8   Second fundamental form and curvatures: parametrized surfaces   27
2.9   Second fundamental form and curvatures: Monge form of surface   39
2.10 Special Monge form   41
2.11 Second fundamental form: implicit form of surface   45
2.12 Special curves on a surface   45
2.13 Contact   48

3   Views of Curves and Surfaces   54
3.1   Camera models: parallel (orthographic) projection   54
3.2   Perspective projection   55
3.3   Opaque vs. semi-transparent surfaces   59
3.4   Static properties of contour generators and apparent contours   59
3.5   Properties: orthogonal projection   61
3.6   Properties: perspective projection   66
3.7   Methods of proof: Monge–Taylor proofs   72
3.8   Monge–Taylor proofs: orthogonal projection   72
3.9   Monge–Taylor proofs: perspective projection   74
3.10 Vector proofs: orthogonal projection   76

3.11   Vector proofs: perspective projection   77
3.12   Methods of proof: pure geometric proofs   78

4   Dynamic Analysis of Apparent Contours   79
4.1   Orthogonal projection   80
4.2   Epipolar parametrization: orthogonal case   84
4.3   Perspective projection   85
4.4   Epipolar parametrization: perspective case   89
4.5   Surface curvatures using the epipolar parametrization   94
4.6   Degeneracies of the epipolar parametrization   95
4.7   Visual events: swallowtail, lips and beaks   96
4.8   Frontiers (epipolar tangencies)   97
4.9   Following cusps   105
4.10   Formulae for K and H by following cusps   105
4.11   Image velocity of a cusp point   108
4.12   Envelopes of surfaces and apparent contours   109

5   Reconstruction of Surfaces from Profiles   114
5.1   Localization and tracking of apparent contours   114
5.2   Camera model for perspective projection onto image plane   119
5.3   Camera model for weak perspective and orthographic projection   123
5.4   Camera calibration   124
5.5   Epipolar geometry   126
5.6   Epipolar geometry from projection matrices   129
5.7   Reconstruction of surfaces   131

6   Recovery of Viewer Motion from Profiles   139
6.1   The fundamental matrix from point correspondences   139
6.2   Recovery of the projection matrices and viewer motion   142
6.3   Recovery of the projection matrices for uncalibrated cameras   144
6.4   Frontier points and epipolar tangencies   147
6.5   Recovery of motion under pure translation   149
6.6   General motion   151
6.7   Weak perspective   155
6.8   Circular motion   158
6.9   Envelope of apparent contours under circular motion   165

Afterword   173
Bibliography   174
Index   179

Preface

Computer Vision is the automatic analysis of sequences of images for the purpose of recovering three-dimensional surface shape. In recent years, several branches of mathematics, both ancient and modern, have been applied to computer vision. Projective geometry, which in its mathematical form dates back at least two centuries, is used to describe the relationship between points and lines in different images of the same object. Differential geometry, which is even older, though it received its definitive modern look in the first half of the nineteenth century, is used to describe the shape of curves and surfaces. More recently developments in singularity theory have enriched the field of geometry by making possible a wealth of detail only dreamed of fifty years ago. Likewise, developments in the speed and power of computers over the last decade have turned other dreams into reality, and made possible real-world applications of mathematical theory.

The goal of this book is to reconstruct surfaces from their 'apparent contours', that is the outlines which they present to us when we view them from a distance. It is not obvious that these apparent contours contain enough information to reconstruct an unmarked smooth surface at all. It is even less obvious that without accurate knowledge of the observer's motion they contain this information; in fact, at the time of writing, we do not know in generality whether this is true. We have, however, successfully implemented the reconstruction when the observer's motion is only partly known – that is, when it is constrained to be of a special kind called circular motion. Other work on more general motion is in progress.

Chapter 1 is introductory, and Chapters 2 to 4 introduce the mathematical ideas and techniques necessary to the study of surfaces and their apparent contours under viewer motion. In Chapters 5 and 6 we bring the mathematics to life with the latest techniques in photogrammetry and computer vision. We describe the real-time implementation of the theory with real image sequences. We show that in practice apparent contours can be used effectively to reconstruct both motion and surface shape.

Acknowledgements

Chapters 2 and 3 owe a great deal to Andrew Zisserman, who collaborated on an earlier version. We are particularly grateful to him for help in proof-reading and many valuable comments.

Several students have helped in producing figures. Gordon Fletcher was instrumental in creating many of the figures from Chapters 2, 3 and 4, using the 'Liverpool Surfaces Modelling Package' written by Richard Morris. Paulo Mendonca and Kenneth Wong have helped in the real-time implementation of the theory and in obtaining the results described in Chapters 5 and 6.

The first author acknowledges the support of the Engineering and Physical Science Research Council. The second author acknowledges the hospitality of the Mathematics Department of Brown University, where some of this book was written, and also the Fulbright Commission for a Senior Fulbright Scholarship 1997/8. He also acknowledges the European grants VIVA and VANGUARD.

The front cover is based on a reconstruction of Benvenuto Cellini's bronze sculpture, Perseus, which is undergoing restoration at the Uffizi Gallery in Florence. We are very grateful to Dr Francesca d'Uva and Dr Tina Guiducci of Burson Marsteller and Cassa di Risparmio di Firenze and to Francesco Porta of Datanord Multimedia for supplying the images.

1

Introduction

We have tried to make our book self-contained. The underlying differential geometry and singularity theory is explained with minimal prerequisites in Chapter 2. We hope that this chapter will prove of value to anyone who wishes to apply differential geometry to vision problems. To follow the main thrust of this chapter the reader only needs a working knowledge of calculus and linear algebra. Most of the material is quite well known, but the slant given here is towards applications, and we have tried to illustrate the material with many examples and figures. In particular, we study curvature of surfaces and special curves on surfaces such as parabolic and flecnodal curves. We make much use of the idea of contact, between surfaces and lines or planes. It is this idea which links classical differential geometry with modern singularity theory, where geometrical properties are studied by means of functions or mappings which in turn measure contact.

In Chapter 3 we introduce the main character in our story, the apparent contour. Apparent contours are the outlines or profiles of curved surfaces. An example is shown in Figure 1.1. We describe apparent contours under orthographic projection and for perspective projection, and we describe in detail the singularities which a single apparent contour can be expected to have. We also obtain geometrical information about surfaces from a single apparent contour, though this is necessarily limited. Initially results are stated, but we give three different approaches to proofs, 'Monge–Taylor proofs', which rely on special coordinate systems which are very powerful for proving results about surfaces; 'vector proofs', which are coordinate-free but require more experience to use effectively; and 'pure geometric proofs', which are more like thought experiments but can sometimes yield the greatest intuition.

An excellent modern reference for applications of projective geometry to computer vision is O.D. Faugeras' *Three-Dimensional Computer Vision*. On the differential geometry side, another book from which we, and others, have drawn inspiration is J.J. Koenderink's now classic *Solid Shape*, published in 1990. Koenderink's book is replete with geometric proofs and statements, but sometimes lacks mathematical detail. We have tried to supply some of this detail in Chapters 2 and 3 of our book.

In Chapter 4 we introduce dynamic contours. That is, we progress from a single view of a surface to multiple views, from which we can expect to derive much more information. In fact, in principle, a complete reconstruction of a surface is possible from a family of apparent contours obtained by circumnavigating a surface. (Unfortunately in practice some parts of a surface may be occluded by other parts, and in addition apparent contours may be hard to track.) The 'in principle' reconstruction was first established for orthographic projection in Giblin and Weiss (1987), and this was generalized and placed in a better mathematical framework by Cipolla and Blake (1990 and 1992).

We describe the dynamic analysis for orthographic and perspective projection, and introduce the important idea of an epipolar parametrization. We also give a brief introduction to circular motion, which will play a major role in the last chapters of the book. The epipolar parametrization breaks down in certain circumstances, one of which is the 'epipolar tangency' situation. This is bad news for reconstruction but, surprisingly, very good news for determining motion. In fact the so-called frontier points which arise from epipolar tangency are instrumental in giving us information about the motion of the observer, something we exploit in Chapter 6. Other breakdowns of the epipolar parametrization are caused by degeneracies of the apparent contour – the 'visual events' which we observe when moving our viewpoint – and we list the possible cases and explain their geometrical significance.

In Chapter 5 we bring the mathematical techniques to life and describe the implementation of algorithms to reconstruct a surface from the image sequence of outlines. Details of every stage in the reconstruction, from raw pixel intensities to a stable description of the three-dimensional surface, are given. These include the calibration of cameras, localization and tracking of outlines, epipolar geometry and stereo reconstruction.

In Chapter 6 we address the more difficult problem of recovering the observer's motion from the apparent contours in different views. The recovery of the three-dimensional configuration of points and the motion compatible with their views (known as structure from motion) has been an active area of research in computer vision over the last two decades and a large number of algorithms and working systems already exist. We review the key results in the literature, in many cases providing simple geometric and algebraic proofs. Finally we show how the motion of the viewer can be computed

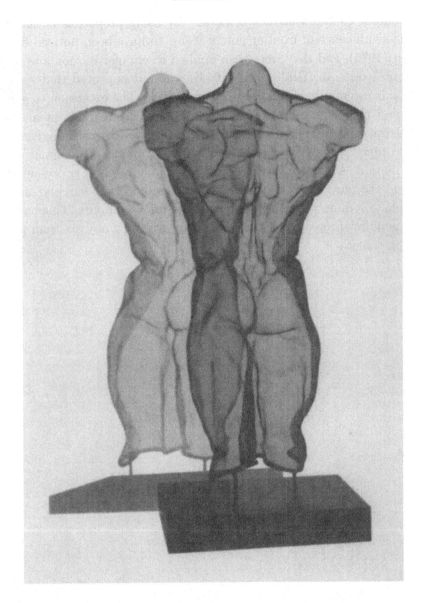

Fig. 1.1 Two views of a semi-transparent surface (sculpture) by David Begbie. For curved surfaces, the dominant image feature is the apparent contour or outline. This is the projection of the locus of points on the surface which separate visible and occluded parts. The apparent contours are rich sources of geometric information. In particular, their deformation under viewer motion can be used to recover the geometry of the visible surface. The geometry of the viewpoints can also be inferred.

from apparent contours instead of points, by using properties of the frontier. The significance of frontier points seems to have been noticed first by J. Rieger (1986), and they were then applied to circular motion and orthographic projection in (Giblin et al. 1994), where it is proved that recovery of motion is essentially unique in this simple case. The extension to general motion and perspective projection was presented by (Cipolla et al. 1995) and (Aström et al. 1996 and 1999), where an iterative algorithm gives good results in many cases. We present the latest techniques for estimating the camera motion. A particularly simple and reliable method is presented for recovering the motion of objects on turntables, known as circular motion. This exploits symmetry of the envelope of apparent contours. This has been used to acquire three-dimensional models of arbitrary objects from an uncalibrated camera.

2

Differential Geometry of Curves and Surfaces

In this chapter we aim to introduce the reader to all the differential geometry of curves and surfaces in 3-space needed for a full understanding of the remainder of the book, and of the literature on apparent contours and their applications in computer vision. Our aim is to give all the useful formulae and to make the concepts and results clear. We give several methods of proof, and in some cases apply all these methods to the same problem, to give a flavour of the strengths and weaknesses of the different techniques available. We begin with 'first-order properties', that is properties which depend only on first derivatives, and work up to those depending on second or higher derivatives.

2.1 Curves and their tangents

A curve in 3-dimensional space is nearly always represented by a parametrization

$$\mathbf{r} : I \to \mathbf{R}^3,$$

where I is some interval $a < t < b$ of real numbers (a could be $-\infty$ or b could be ∞, or both). Also I could be a circle for parametrizing a closed curve, in which case the components of $\mathbf{r}$ will be functions of $\sin t$ and $\cos t$. Writing $\mathbf{r}(t) = (X(t), Y(t), Z(t))$ the curve is *regular* provided the *velocity vector* $\mathbf{r}'(t) = (X'(t), Y'(t), Z'(t))$ is never the zero vector. (Here the prime $'$ stands for $\frac{d}{dt}$. We might also use a suffix: $\mathbf{r}_t = \mathbf{r}'$, although we normally reserve suffixes for partial derivatives where there is more than one variable.) The *unit tangent vector* $\mathbf{T}(t)$ is the unit vector in the direction of the velocity, namely

$$\mathbf{T}(t) = \frac{\mathbf{r}'(t)}{||\mathbf{r}'(t)||}.$$

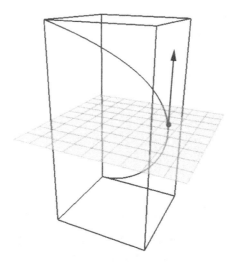

Fig. 2.1. A normal plane and tangent vector of a space curve.

The denominator, $||\mathbf{r}'(t)||$, is called the *speed* of the curve; *unit speed* means that $||\mathbf{r}'(t)|| = 1$ for all t. The curve has a *normal plane* at any point $\mathbf{r}(t_0)$, namely the plane through this point perpendicular to the tangent vector. See Figure 2.1. This plane has equation $(\mathbf{x} - \mathbf{r}(t_0)) \cdot \mathbf{r}'(t_0) = 0$.

The *arclength* $s = l(t)$ of the curve between $\mathbf{r}(t_0)$ and $\mathbf{r}(t)$ is given by

$$s = l(t) = \int_{t_0}^{t} ||\mathbf{r}'(t)|| \, dt, \tag{2.1}$$

that is, the integral of the speed. We deduce from (2.1) that $\frac{ds}{dt} = ||\mathbf{r}'(t)||$. In particular if the parameter t is s itself, then $||\mathbf{r}'(s)|| = 1$: using arclength as the parameter, the curve is automatically of unit speed. In order that changing from t to s is a valid change of parameter we need to know that $\frac{ds}{dt}$ is never zero. Thus every *regular* curve can be re-parametrized to be unit speed. This is often useful when doing calculations. An example of a non-regular curve is given by $\mathbf{r}(t) = (t^2, t^3, 0)$, which is a curve in the x, y-plane with a cusp at the origin. The speed is zero precisely for $t = 0$.

Example 2.1.1 Helix

Let $\mathbf{r}(t) = (\cos t, \sin t, t)$, which has $\frac{ds}{dt} = ||\mathbf{r}'(t)|| = \sqrt{2}$ for all t. Thus $s = \sqrt{2}t + \text{constant}$ and, making $s = 0$ when $t = 0$, the reparametrized curve

$$\mathbf{R}(s) = \left(\cos \frac{s}{\sqrt{2}}, \sin \frac{s}{\sqrt{2}}, \frac{s}{\sqrt{2}} \right)$$

is unit speed. □

2.2 Surfaces: the parametric form

With a *surface* the matter is quite different. There is no natural concept of 'unit speed'. The geometry of surfaces is also much richer than that of curves, and it is well worth having several representations of a surface available for different purposes. We shall describe three of these.

We take a plane—the *parameter plane*—with coordinates (u, v) and an open and connected region U of this plane. Then we can parametrize a surface by

$$\mathbf{r}(u, v) = (X(u, v), Y(u, v), Z(u, v)),$$

where X, Y, Z are functions with sufficiently many continuous derivatives (at least two and often infinitely many). The condition corresponding to the 'regularity' of a space curve is that, for every $(u, v) \in U$, the *Jacobian matrix*

$$\begin{pmatrix} X_u & X_v \\ Y_u & Y_v \\ Z_u & Z_v \end{pmatrix}$$

(where suffixes stand for partial derivatives) should have rank 2. The content of this is that the rank should not drop *below* 2. If it does drop, the two columns $\mathbf{r}_u$ and $\mathbf{r}_v$ are parallel (or zero) as vectors in $\mathbf{R}^3$. Note that

$$\mathbf{r}_u, \ \mathbf{r}_v \text{ are parallel or zero } \Leftrightarrow \mathbf{r}_u \wedge \mathbf{r}_v = \mathbf{0}.$$

In fact $\mathbf{r}_u$, evaluated at (u, v_0), is the tangent vector to the space curve $\mathbf{r}(u, v_0)$ where v has a fixed value v_0, and similarly $\mathbf{r}_v$ is the tangent vector to the space curve $\mathbf{r}(u_0, v)$. If these two vectors are parallel then the perpendicular coordinate curves $u = u_0, v = v_0$ are transformed into tangential curves by $\mathbf{r}$, which is not allowable.

When the Jacobian matrix always has rank 2, i.e. $\mathbf{r}_u \wedge \mathbf{r}_v$ is never the zero vector, we say that the map $\mathbf{r}$ is an *immersion*, and that $\mathbf{r}$ defines an *immersed surface*, namely $M = \mathbf{r}(U)$. The surface M has a *tangent plane* at $\mathbf{r}(u, v)$ for every parameter point (u, v), namely the plane through $\mathbf{r}(u, v)$ spanned by the vectors $\mathbf{r}_u$ and $\mathbf{r}_v$. This is a genuine 2-dimensional plane by the immersion condition. So an immersed surface can be thought of as one where, corresponding to every parameter point (u, v), there is a definite tangent plane at $\mathbf{r}(u, v)$.

All surfaces will be assumed immersed unless the contrary is stated.

Note that $\mathbf{r}_u$ and $\mathbf{r}_v$ are not perpendicular in general. The normal to the tangent plane is also called the *normal* to the surface and is in the direction $\mathbf{r}_u \wedge \mathbf{r}_v$. See Figure 2.2. The *unit surface normal* $\mathbf{n}$ determined by the ordering

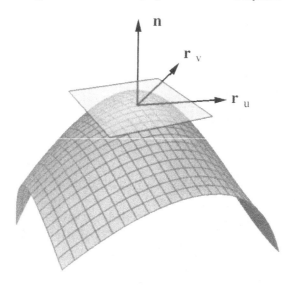

Fig. 2.2 Surface normal and tangent vectors $\mathbf{r}_u, \mathbf{r}_v$. Note that the lines drawn are not u, v coordinate curves; they just give a shape to the surface.

u, v of the parameters is

$$\mathbf{n} = \frac{\mathbf{r}_u \wedge \mathbf{r}_v}{||\mathbf{r}_u \wedge \mathbf{r}_v||}.$$

Note that interchanging u and v takes $\mathbf{n}$ into $-\mathbf{n}$, and that the normal depends only on first derivatives of the parametrization.

Sometimes it is convenient to use a slightly different parameter space, for example where one, or both, of the parameters is naturally taken to be an angle. (Formally we would say the parameter space was the product of a circle and a line, or of two circles.)

Example 2.2.1 Sphere

A unit sphere, centre $(0,0,0)$, minus the north pole $(0,0,1)$ can be parametrized by *stereographic projection* as

$$\mathbf{r}(x,y) = \left(\frac{4x}{x^2 + y^2 + 4}, \frac{4y}{x^2 + y^2 + 4}, \frac{x^2 + y^2 - 4}{x^2 + y^2 + 4} \right)$$

where (x, y) ranges over the whole plane. Here, the point $(x, y, -1)$ in the plane $z = -1$ is joined to the point $(0, 0, 1)$ and this segment meets the sphere again at $\lambda(x, y, -1) + (1 - \lambda)(0, 0, 1)$ where $\lambda = 4/(x^2 + y^2 + 4)$. See Figure 2.3. It can be shown that $\mathbf{r}_x \wedge \mathbf{r}_y$ is never zero, so this $\mathbf{r}$ is an immersion.

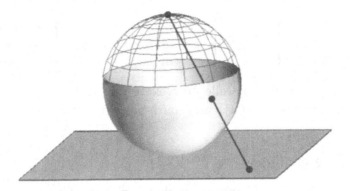

Fig. 2.3 Stereographic parametrization of a sphere minus the north pole. Note that the sphere is cut away simply to show the line from the north pole penetrating the sphere; the whole sphere minus the north pole is covered.

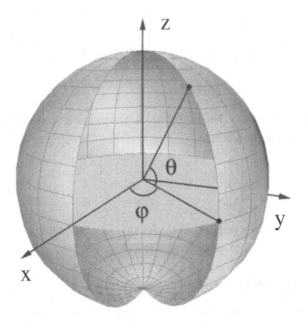

Fig. 2.4 Cut away picture of θ (latitude) and ϕ (longitude) coordinates on the sphere minus north and south poles.

A sphere, radius ρ, minus the north and south poles, can be parametrized by spherical polar coordinates as $\mathbf{r}(\theta, \phi) = (\rho \cos \theta \cos \phi, \rho \cos \theta \sin \phi, \rho \sin \theta)$ where $-\frac{\pi}{2} < \theta < \frac{\pi}{2}$, $0 \leq \phi < 2\pi$. (Here, ϕ is regarded as an angle parameter which covers a whole circle.) See Figure 2.4. The tangent vectors and unit normal are

$$
\mathbf{r}_\theta = \begin{bmatrix} -\rho\sin\theta\cos\phi \\ -\rho\sin\theta\sin\phi \\ \rho\cos\theta \end{bmatrix} \qquad
\mathbf{r}_\phi = \begin{bmatrix} -\rho\cos\theta\sin\phi \\ \rho\cos\theta\cos\phi \\ 0 \end{bmatrix} \qquad
\mathbf{n} = \begin{bmatrix} -\cos\theta\cos\phi \\ -\cos\theta\sin\phi \\ -\sin\theta \end{bmatrix}.
$$

The normal is (of course!) parallel to $\mathbf{r}$. Note that if $\theta = \pm\frac{\pi}{2}$ then $\mathbf{r}_\phi = \mathbf{0}$; this is why we exclude the north and south poles from the parametrization.
□

Example 2.2.2 Cylinder

A cylinder, radius ρ, with axis along the z-axis, can be parametrized by cylindrical polar coordinates as $\mathbf{r}(\phi, z) = (\rho\cos\phi, \rho\sin\phi, z)$. (Again, ϕ covers a whole circle here.) The tangent vectors and unit normal are

$$
\mathbf{r}_\phi = \begin{bmatrix} -\rho\sin\phi \\ \rho\cos\phi \\ 0 \end{bmatrix} \qquad
\mathbf{r}_z = \begin{bmatrix} 0 \\ 0 \\ 1 \end{bmatrix} \qquad
\mathbf{n} = \begin{bmatrix} \cos\phi \\ \sin\phi \\ 0 \end{bmatrix}.
$$

The normal is orthogonal to the cylinder's axis. □

Example 2.2.3 A non-surface

Let $\mathbf{r}(u, v) = (u + 2v, 2u + 4v, 3u + 6v)$. Although $\mathbf{r}$ is parametrized by two parameters, the tangent vectors

$$
\mathbf{r}_u = \begin{bmatrix} 1 \\ 2 \\ 3 \end{bmatrix} \qquad
\mathbf{r}_v = \begin{bmatrix} 2 \\ 4 \\ 6 \end{bmatrix}
$$

are parallel, so a surface normal is undefined. In fact this $\mathbf{r}$ gives a curve—indeed a straight line—not a surface. □

Example 2.2.4 Almost an immersed surface: the crosscap

A less drastic failure—which we include here simply to show what the immersion definition allows—is $\mathbf{r}(u, v) = (u, v^2, uv)$. Here, $\mathbf{r}_u = (1, 0, v)^\top, \mathbf{r}_v = (0, 2v, u)^\top$ and these are parallel (vector product zero) if and only if $u = v = 0$. So excluding the origin $(0, 0)$ from the parameter plane, $\mathbf{r}$ gives an immersed surface. See Figure 2.5. The surface is called a 'crosscap' or 'Whitney umbrella'[1] and has a line of self-intersection corresponding to $u = 0$: we have $\mathbf{r}(0, v) = \mathbf{r}(0, -v)$ for all v. Thus at points $(0, v^2, 0)$ $(v \neq 0)$ there are

---

[1] The handle of the umbrella is actually the negative y-axis, which is not present in this parametrized form but is present in the 'equation' form $x^2 y = z^2$.

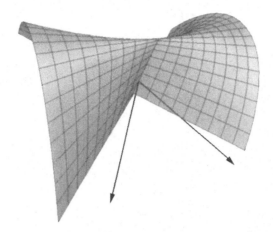

Fig. 2.5 A crosscap or Whitney umbrella (Example 2.2.4), showing the normals to the two sheets at a point along the self-intersection line. In this picture, the origin is at the pinch point near the top and the positive y-axis points downwards along the self-intersection line. The x-axis lies on the surface and is nearly horizontal left to right.

two normals, corresponding to the two 'sheets' of the surface which cross at that point. Note that the two parameter points $(0, v)$ and $(0, -v)$ are distinct, for $v \neq 0$. This means that each different *parameter point* (u, v) *does* give a definite tangent plane.

The (non-unit) normal at a general point works out to be $(-2v^2, -u, 2v)$, so that at $(0, v^2, 0)$ the normals are in the direction $(\pm v, 0, 1)$. At $u = v = 0$, which is the origin, these two normals have coincided in $(0, 0, 1)$ but at this point the Jacobian matrix actually fails to have rank 2, and the surface is not immersed. (Note that the normal at $\mathbf{r}(u, 0)$, say, is in direction $(0, -1, 0)$ for $u \neq 0$ so the limit of these normals is not the same as the limit of normals as we approach the origin along $\mathbf{r}(0, v)$. At the origin there is no normal even in a limiting sense.) $\square$

In practice the surfaces which arise in computer vision do not have self-intersections such as those on the crosscap, and from now on we shall stick to surfaces where two distinct parameter points never give the same surface point, so tangent planes and normals to the surface M in $\mathbf{R}^3$ are uniquely defined.

Example 2.2.5 Surface of revolution

Let $\mathbf{p}(t) = (X(t), Y(t))$ be a regular *plane* curve, which we place in the x, y-plane of x, y, z-space. We assume that the curve does not cross the x-axis

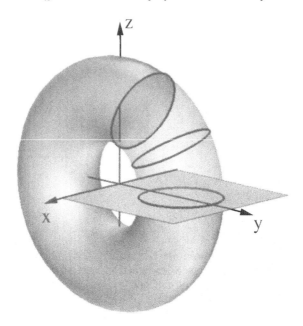

Fig. 2.6. A torus generated by rotating a circle about a line (the x-axis) in space.

($Y(t)$ never zero), and rotate about this axis to give the surface

$$\mathbf{r}(t, \theta) = (X(t), Y(t) \cos \theta, Y(t) \sin \theta),$$

where θ is an angle parameter covering a whole circle. Using $'$ for $\frac{d}{dt}$ the vectors

$$\mathbf{r}_t = (X', Y' \cos \theta, Y' \sin \theta) \quad \text{and} \quad \mathbf{r}_\theta = (0, -Y \sin \theta, Y \cos \theta)$$

are independent since Y is never zero and X', Y' are never both zero, so the surface is immersed and has a well-defined tangent plane at each point, spanned by $\mathbf{r}_t$ and $\mathbf{r}_\theta$.

For example, taking $\mathbf{p}(t) = (\cos t, \sin t + 2)$, which is a circle of radius 1 centred at $(0, 2, 0)$ in 3-space, the surface is a *torus*. See Figure 2.6.

As another example, take $X(t) = t$, $Y(t) = 1$: rotating this line gives a *cylinder*. The vectors $\mathbf{r}_t$ and $\mathbf{r}_\theta$ are $(1, 0, 0)$, $(0, -\sin \theta, \cos \theta)$ and the normal is $(0, -\cos \theta, -\sin \theta)$. This particular normal points inwards. $\square$

The above is an example of a 'global parametrization': the whole surface of revolution is given by $\mathbf{r}$, which is always an immersion ($\mathbf{r}_t, \mathbf{r}_\theta$ independent). On the other hand for the sphere in Example 2.2.1 either the north pole or the north and south poles are missing if we want a well-behaved parametriza-

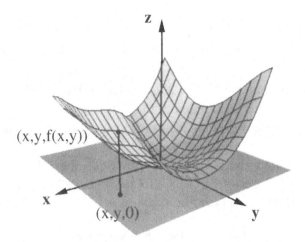

Fig. 2.7 A Monge patch in which the tangent plane at one point is the plane $z = 0$.

tion. This is the more typical case: parametrizations tend to cover parts of whole surfaces.

2.3 Monge form

In the Monge form (named after Gaspard Monge, 1746–1818) the surface (now called a *Monge patch*) is written as the graph of function: $z = f(x, y)$. We can regard the Monge form as a special kind of parametrization:

$$\mathbf{r}(x, y) = (x, y, f(x, y)), \quad \mathbf{r}_x = (1, 0, f_x), \quad \mathbf{r}_y = (0, 1, f_y).$$

Note that $\mathbf{r}_x \wedge \mathbf{r}_y$ is never $\mathbf{0}$, so this $\mathbf{r}$ is always an immersion. (Furthermore we never have two distinct parameter points giving the same surface point.) We have

$$\text{non-unit normal } \tilde{\mathbf{n}} = \mathbf{r}_x \wedge \mathbf{r}_y \;=\; (-f_x, -f_y, 1);$$

$$\text{unit normal } \mathbf{n} \;=\; \frac{(-f_x, -f_y, 1)}{\sqrt{f_x^2 + f_y^2 + 1}}. \tag{2.2}$$

Note that the normal is never 'horizontal', that is, never parallel to the x, y-plane.

We often use a special Monge form in which, at $x = y = 0$, f, f_x and f_y are all zero. Then at $x = y = 0$ the normal is $(0, 0, 1)$ and the tangent plane to the surface at the origin is the x, y-plane. See Figure 2.7.

In that case the equation of the surface can be written in the 'special

Monge form'

$$z = \frac{1}{2}(a_{20}x^2 + 2a_{11}xy + a_{02}y^2) + \frac{1}{6}(a_{30}x^3 + 3a_{21}x^2y + 3a_{12}xy^2 + a_{03}y^3) + \cdots.$$
$$(2.3)$$

Binomial denominators $2 = 2!, 6 = 3!$ are inserted here, and coefficients are named to reflect the powers of x and y in the terms of the Taylor expansion. In special applications we might choose to abandon one or both of these conventions.

By a rotation about the z-axis, that is by replacing x by $x\cos\theta + y\sin\theta$ and y by $-x\sin\theta + y\cos\theta$ for a suitable θ, the xy-term in (2.3) can be eliminated. The coefficient of xy becomes

$$\frac{1}{2}(a_{20} - a_{02})\sin 2\theta + a_{11}\cos 2\theta.$$

If θ makes this zero so does $\theta + \frac{\pi}{2}$, and there are always at least two values of θ in $0 \leq \theta < \pi$. When there is no xy-term, we shall say later (Definition 2.8.8) that the x and y-axes are in *principal directions* at the origin. (Note that in this context a positive or negative axis is regarded as giving the same 'direction'. Really 'principal line' would be a better term but 'principal direction' is traditional.) Since the two values of θ differ by $\frac{\pi}{2}$, the second θ gives the same pair of principal directions but they are interchanged.

When the xy-term is eliminated then of course all the other coefficients in (2.3) change, but terms of a particular degree stay of the same degree—for example, the new cubic terms of (2.3) will depend only on the original cubic terms and θ.

Example 2.3.1 Monge form of a sphere

A sphere of radius $\rho > 0$ centred at $(0, 0, \rho)$ is tangent to the x, y-plane at the origin. The equation is $x^2 + y^2 + (z - \rho)^2 = \rho^2$; if we want the part of the sphere near the origin we must take the negative square root when finding z, to give $z = \rho - \sqrt{\rho^2 - x^2 - y^2}$. Thus the Monge form starts out with

$$z = \frac{1}{2\rho}(x^2 + y^2) + \frac{1}{8\rho^3}(x^4 + 2x^2y^2 + y^4) + \cdots, \qquad (2.4)$$

on expanding the square root by the binomial theorem. □

Notice that in this case, which is typical, the Monge form does not give us the whole sphere. In fact just the sphere below the equator will be covered by (2.4). For this reason, the phrase *Monge patch* is sometimes used. See Figure 2.8. To obtain the upper hemisphere (which does not pass through the origin) we need to take the + sign in front of the square root above.

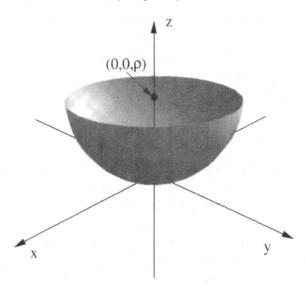

Fig. 2.8. Monge patch for a sphere.

The equator, itself, where the normal is horizontal (parallel to the x, y-plane) cannot be part of any parametrization as the graph of a function $z = f(x, y)$.

If a surface or a surface patch is in Monge form, then the intersection of the surface with its tangent plane at the origin is simply the curve $f(x, y) = 0$ in the plane $z = 0$. For example the surfaces $z = x^2 + y^2$, $z = x^2 - y^2$ and $z = x^2 + y^3$ meet their tangent plane at the origin in respectively a point, two intersecting lines and a cusped curve. See Figure 2.14.

2.4 Implicit form

The Monge form, or indeed any graph $z = f(x, y)$, is a special case of a surface given 'implicitly' by an *equation* $F(x, y, z) = 0$. This is the most 'global' of the three representations. A unit sphere centred at the origin is given completely by the equation $x^2 + y^2 + z^2 - 1 = 0$, for example. But the implicit form is often the hardest to handle, and we shall not often have occasion to use it.

The *normal* vector is easy to obtain, however: it is along the gradient of the function F, that is along (F_x, F_y, F_z). Notice that for this to be nonzero, we need at least one of the partial derivatives to be nonzero. But in fact this is also the condition for the surface given by $F = 0$ to be free from singularities such as self-crossings, cuspidal edges, etc. The condition that

F, F_x, F_y, F_z are never all zero at the same point (x, y, z) is also expressed by saying that 0 is a 'regular value' of the function F. See for example (Bruce and Giblin 1992, Ch. 4). The equation of the tangent plane at (x_0, y_0, z_0), where $F(x_0, y_0, z_0) = 0$, is

$$(x - x_0)F_x + (y - y_0)F_y + (z - z_0)F_z = 0.$$

Example 2.4.1 Quadric surfaces

A quadric surface M is a surface in x, y, z-space given by an equation containing only terms of degree 0, 1 and 2 in the variables x, y and z. They are of interest in the general context of this book since they have very simple 'contour generators'. The contour generator of any surface M relative to a point $\mathbf{c}$ in space is the curve of points on M where the tangent plane passes through $\mathbf{c}$. Equivalently, consider the cone of rays through $\mathbf{c}$ which are tangent to M; the contour generator is the curve on M along which this cone is tangent to M. From Chapter 3 onwards we shall call $\mathbf{c}$ the 'camera centre'. See Figure 3.4.

When M is a quadric surface it can be represented as $\mathbf{X}^\top \mathbf{Q} \mathbf{X} = 0$ where $\mathbf{X}$ is a 4-vector, $\mathbf{X} = (x, y, z, 1)^\top$, and $\mathbf{Q}$ is a 4×4 symmetric matrix. The matrix $\mathbf{Q}$ is partitioned as

$$\mathbf{Q} = \begin{bmatrix} \mathbf{Q}_3 & \mathbf{q} \\ \mathbf{q}^\top & Q_{44} \end{bmatrix}$$

where $\mathbf{Q}_3$ is a (symmetric) 3×3 matrix, $\mathbf{q}$ a 3×1 column vector and Q_{44} a real number. For a quadric centred at $(0,0,0)$, that is, for which (x, y, z) lies on the quadric if and only if $(-x, -y, -z)$ does, we have $\mathbf{q} = \mathbf{0}$, and the quadric is then often written as $\mathbf{x}^\top \mathbf{Q}_3 \mathbf{x} = $ constant, where $\mathbf{x} = (x, y, z)^\top$. The quadric is nonsingular—that is, it is not a cone or a plane pair—if and only if the matrix $\mathbf{Q}$ is nonsingular.

We go on to explore a little further properties of quadric surfaces which depend only on tangents. Given a point $\mathbf{c} = (c_1, c_2, c_3)$ in 3-space, write $\mathbf{C}$ for the column 4-vector[1] $(c_1, c_2, c_3, 1)^\top$.

Definition 2.4.2 Polar plane

The equation $\mathbf{X}^\top \mathbf{Q} \mathbf{C} = 0$, being linear in x, y, z, defines a *plane*. This plane is called the *polar plane of* $\mathbf{c}$ with respect to the quadric. See Figure 2.9.

When the quadric is nonsingular and $\mathbf{c}$ is outside, we show below that the polar plane contains the points of contact of the cone of rays through $\mathbf{c}$

---

[1] This is essentially passing to 'homogeneous coordinates'. We shall use these again in Chapter 5.

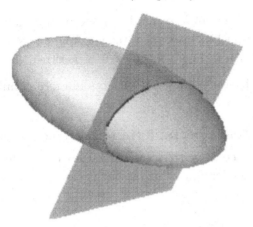

Fig. 2.9. Polar plane of a quadric surface with respect to a point outside it.

tangent to the quadric—the 'contour generator' for camera centre $\mathbf{c}$ as we call it later. As $\mathbf{c}$ approaches the quadric the cone of rays becomes more and more planar, and in the limit when $\mathbf{c}$ is on the quadric, the cone of rays and the polar plane both become the tangent plane to the quadric at $\mathbf{c}$.

For a sphere of radius a centred at $(0, 0, b)$ the quadric matrix has the form

$$\mathbf{Q} = \begin{bmatrix} 1 & 0 & 0 & 0 \\ 0 & 1 & 0 & 0 \\ 0 & 0 & 1 & -b \\ 0 & 0 & -b & b^2 - a^2 \end{bmatrix}$$

for which $\mathbf{X}^\top \mathbf{Q} \mathbf{X} = x^2 + y^2 + (z - b)^2 - a^2$. The polar plane of the origin is the plane $\mathbf{X}^\top \mathbf{Q} (0, 0, 0, 1)^\top = 0$, that is the plane $z = (b^2 - a^2)/b$. If $b = \pm a$ we obtain the tangent plane at the origin, the plane $z = 0$.

Proof of the above property of the polar plane
Taking $\mathbf{x} = (x, y, z)^\top$ on the quadric, any point on the line l joining $\mathbf{x}$ to $\mathbf{c}$ is (writing $\mathbf{c}$ as a column vector) $\mathbf{v} = \lambda \mathbf{c} + (1 - \lambda)\mathbf{x}$. Let $\mathbf{V}$ be the column 4-vector $(\mathbf{v}^\top, 1)^\top$, so that we have $\mathbf{V} = \lambda \mathbf{C} + (1 - \lambda)\mathbf{X}$. The condition for $\mathbf{v}$ to lie on the quadric, namely $\mathbf{V}^\top \mathbf{Q} \mathbf{V} = 0$, gives a quadratic equation for λ:

$$(\lambda \mathbf{C}^\top + (1 - \lambda)\mathbf{X}^\top)\mathbf{Q}(\lambda \mathbf{C} + (1 - \lambda)\mathbf{X}) = 0.$$

When this quadratic equation is multiplied out, there are three terms, involving λ^2, λ and a constant term. The constant term is $\mathbf{X}^\top \mathbf{Q} \mathbf{X}$, and this is zero by definition of $\mathbf{x}$, since $\mathbf{x}$ lies on the quadric. Thus one solution of the quadratic equation is $\lambda = 0$. The coefficient of λ is

$$\mathbf{C}^\top \mathbf{Q} \mathbf{X} + \mathbf{X}^\top \mathbf{Q} \mathbf{C} - 2\mathbf{X}^\top \mathbf{Q} \mathbf{X} = 2(\mathbf{X}^\top \mathbf{Q} \mathbf{C} - \mathbf{X}^\top \mathbf{Q} \mathbf{X}) = 2(\mathbf{X}^\top \mathbf{Q} \mathbf{C}).$$

In the first equality we use the fact that, since $\mathbf{C}^\top \mathbf{Q} \mathbf{X}$ is a 1×1 matrix, it is equal to its transpose $\mathbf{X}^\top \mathbf{Q}^\top \mathbf{C}$, which in turn is equal to $\mathbf{X}^\top \mathbf{Q} \mathbf{C}$ since $\mathbf{Q}$ is symmetric.

The condition for the coefficient of λ to vanish is the condition that *both* roots of the quadratic for λ are zero, which means that the line from $\mathbf{c}$ to $\mathbf{x}$ is *tangent* to the quadric at $\mathbf{x}$. This condition is simply $\mathbf{X}^\top \mathbf{QC} = 0$, as asserted. □

We shall study contact between lines and surfaces in more detail in §2.13.

2.5 First fundamental form for surfaces

Consider a curve on a surface M with parametrization $\mathbf{r}(t) = \mathbf{r}(u(t), v(t))$, where t is the curve parametrization, which is not necessarily arclength. By the chain rule,

$$\mathbf{r}'(t) = \mathbf{r}_u u' + \mathbf{r}_v v',$$

and

$$
\begin{aligned}
||\mathbf{r}'(t)||^2 &= \begin{bmatrix} u' & v' \end{bmatrix} \begin{bmatrix} \mathbf{r}_u \cdot \mathbf{r}_u & \mathbf{r}_u \cdot \mathbf{r}_v \\ \mathbf{r}_v \cdot \mathbf{r}_u & \mathbf{r}_v \cdot \mathbf{r}_v \end{bmatrix} \begin{bmatrix} u' \\ v' \end{bmatrix} \\
&= \begin{bmatrix} u' & v' \end{bmatrix} \begin{bmatrix} E & F \\ F & G \end{bmatrix} \begin{bmatrix} u' \\ v' \end{bmatrix} \\
&= Eu'^2 + 2Fu'v' + Gv'^2.
\end{aligned}
$$

Note that

$$E = \mathbf{r}_u \cdot \mathbf{r}_u, \quad F = \mathbf{r}_u \cdot \mathbf{r}_v \text{ and } G = \mathbf{r}_v \cdot \mathbf{r}_v \tag{2.5}$$

are functions defined on M via its parametrization.

First fundamental form The quadratic form $Eu'^2 + 2Fu'v' + Gv'^2$ (or $Edu^2 + 2Fdudv + Gdv^2$) is called the first fundamental form of the surface. If a vector on the tangent plane has components (ξ, η), so that the vector is $\xi\mathbf{r}_u + \eta\mathbf{r}_v$, then the form assigns its length as

$$||\xi\mathbf{r}_u + \eta\mathbf{r}_v||^2 = E\xi^2 + 2F\xi\eta + G\eta^2. \tag{2.6}$$

Thus the form is a *metric* for the surface. We can also interpret this as saying that an 'infinitesimal segment' given by du, dv in the parameter space becomes, on the surface, an 'infinitesimal curve element' of length $Edu^2 + 2Fdudv + Gdv^2$.

The dot product (inner product) $\mathbf{a}_1 \cdot \mathbf{a}_2$ of two tangent vectors $\mathbf{a}_1 = \xi_1\mathbf{r}_u + \eta_1\mathbf{r}_v$ and $\mathbf{a}_2 = \xi_2\mathbf{r}_u + \eta_2\mathbf{r}_v$ at the same point $\mathbf{r}(u, v)$ can be written in the form

$$I(\mathbf{a}_1, \mathbf{a}_2) = \begin{bmatrix} \xi_1 & \eta_1 \end{bmatrix} \begin{bmatrix} E & F \\ F & G \end{bmatrix} \begin{bmatrix} \xi_2 \\ \eta_2 \end{bmatrix}.$$

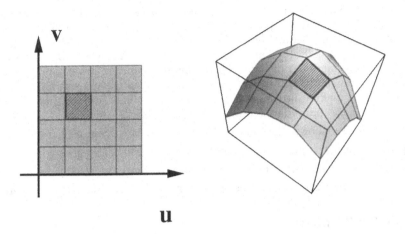

Fig. 2.10. An infinitesimal surface element.

The 2×2 matrix occurring here and above is called the *matrix of the first fundamental form* I relative to the given parametrization. This matrix is often called I, too, pronounced 'one' and not to be confused with the identity matrix I, pronounced 'eye'! In fact on the rare occasions when we mention the identity matrix we shall call it 'id.' to avoid confusion. The first fundamental form *is* the identity when $\mathbf{r}_u$ and $\mathbf{r}_v$ are perpendicular unit vectors.

Notice that this version of the first fundamental form is a bilinear form on the tangent plane to the surface at a point: it associates with each pair of tangent vectors a number, namely their dot (inner) product. Sometimes I is used also for the quadratic form given by putting $\mathbf{a}_1 = \mathbf{a}_2 :$ $I(\mathbf{a}) = ||\mathbf{a}||^2$.

Note that $EG - F^2 = (\mathbf{r}_u \wedge \mathbf{r}_v) \cdot (\mathbf{r}_u \wedge \mathbf{r}_v) = ||\mathbf{r}_u \wedge \mathbf{r}_v||^2 > 0$, since $\mathbf{r}_u$ and $\mathbf{r}_v$ cannot be parallel, by the immersion condition (§2.2).

Remark 2.5.1 Area and invariance

(i) The *area* of a region of surface is given by

$$A = \int ||\mathbf{r}_u \wedge \mathbf{r}_v|| \, dudv = \int \sqrt{EG - F^2} \, dudv. \qquad (2.7)$$

Note, the term $(EG - F^2)$ is the determinant of the first fundamental form matrix, and arises from the Jacobian of the transformation from (u, v) to $\mathbf{r}$. Again, we can say that an 'infinitesimal rectangle' of area $dudv$ in the parameter space becomes, on the surface, an 'infinitesimal surface element' of area $\sqrt{EG - F^2} dudv$. See Figure 2.10.

(ii) The first fundamental form does not change if the surface is bent without stretching. An example is developable surfaces, which are ruled surfaces formed as envelopes of planes in space. Developable surfaces are of three kinds, cones, cylinders and 'tangent developables' of space curves—that is, for a given space curve we take the union of all the (infinite) tangent lines of the curve. See (Bruce and Giblin 1992, pp. 178–182) and Figure 2.18 below. A developable surface can be formed from a flat sheet of paper by rolling and bending it without stretching or tearing. The tangent plane at any point along a given 'generator', that is one of the straight lines making up the surface, is the same. This implies that all points of these surfaces are 'parabolic' (compare Property 2.8.14).

In fact it can be shown that two surface patches are *isometric* (related by a smooth invertible map with smooth inverse which takes each curve to a curve of the same length, rather like bending one surface to form the other) if and only if they can be parametrized to have the same first fundamental form everywhere. □

Example 2.5.2 Sphere

For the parametrization of the sphere minus two points in Example 2.2.1 the first fundamental form is given by

$$I = \begin{bmatrix} \rho^2 & 0 \\ 0 & \rho^2 \cos^2 \theta \end{bmatrix}.$$

Clearly, the coordinate curves are orthogonal since $F = 0$. The length (2.6) of an infinitesimal curve element has the familiar form $dr^2 = \rho^2 d\theta^2 + \rho^2 \cos^2 \theta d\phi^2$. The area (2.7) of an infinitesimal element is $dA = \rho^2 \cos \theta d\theta d\phi$. □

Example 2.5.3 Cylinder

The first fundamental form for the parametrization in Example 2.2.2 is given by

$$I = \begin{bmatrix} \rho^2 & 0 \\ 0 & 1 \end{bmatrix}.$$

The coordinate curves are orthogonal and the length (2.6) of an infinitesimal curve element has the form $dr^2 = \rho^2 d\phi^2 + dz^2$. The area (2.7) of an infinitesimal element is $dA = \rho d\phi dz$. □

Example 2.5.4 Graph of a function, $z = f(x, y)$

When a surface is given as the graph of a function, then we can parametrize it by $\mathbf{r}(x, y) = (x, y, f(x, y))$ and the matrix of I becomes

$$I = \begin{bmatrix} 1 + f_x^2 & f_x f_y \\ f_x f_y & 1 + f_y^2 \end{bmatrix}.$$

When $f_x = f_y = 0$ at some point (horizontal tangent plane) this is the identity matrix. We then say that the surface is given in 'special Monge form'. We shall make much use of this form later in the chapter, especially when $f_x = f_y = 0$ at $x = y = 0$.

2.6 Curvature of curves

We turn now to properties of curves, and later of surfaces, which depend on second derivatives: 'second-order properties'.

Let C be a regular space curve, parametrized by $\mathbf{r}(t)$, where $\mathbf{r}'(t)$ is never zero. The *curvature* $\kappa(t)$ of C is measured by the rate at which the *unit* tangent vector turns. The curve is naturally oriented by increasing values of t and the unit (oriented) tangent is $\mathbf{T} = \mathbf{r}'/\|\mathbf{r}'\|$ (recall §2.1). The formula $\mathbf{T}' = \kappa\mathbf{N}\|\mathbf{r}'\|$ defines the real number $\kappa \geq 0$ and, so long as $\kappa \neq 0$, the unit vector $\mathbf{N}$, which is called the 'principal normal'. Note that $\mathbf{N}$ is perpendicular to $\mathbf{T}$, since the derivative of a unit vector is always perpendicular to that vector. In fact in a precise sense 'most' space curves have no zeroes of curvature (Bruce and Giblin 1992, Ch. 9).

Writing s for arclength we have $s' = \|\mathbf{r}'\|$ from (2.1), and

$$\mathbf{r}' = s'\mathbf{T}, \quad \mathbf{r}'' = s''\mathbf{T} + s'^2\kappa\mathbf{N}.$$

Taking the vector product we have

$$\kappa = \frac{\|\mathbf{r}' \wedge \mathbf{r}''\|}{\|\mathbf{r}'\|^3}$$

so that $\kappa \neq 0$ if and only if $\mathbf{r}'$ and $\mathbf{r}''$ are not parallel. Assuming now that κ is never zero, the plane spanned by $\mathbf{T}$ and $\mathbf{N}$ is the *osculating plane* and is the limit of planes intersecting C at three nearby points. See Figure 2.11. The normal $\mathbf{B} = \mathbf{T} \wedge \mathbf{N}$ to the osculating plane is called the *binormal* of the curve. It is parallel to $\mathbf{r}' \wedge \mathbf{r}''$. See Example 2.6.1 for what happens to the binormals when κ *is* zero at a point.

The circle in the osculating plane with centre $\mathbf{r} + \mathbf{N}/\kappa$ is called the *osculating circle* of C at $\mathbf{r}$. It is in fact the limit of circles through three nearby points of C. See Figure 2.11. Note that if κ is very small the osculating circle is nearly a straight line; in fact zeroes of curvature are sometimes called 'linear points' of a space curve.

The *torsion* of C measures the tendency of the curve to leave its osculating plane: if the torsion is always zero then the curve is actually a plane curve lying in the constant osculating plane. The general formulae are

$$\mathbf{T}' = \kappa\mathbf{N}\|\mathbf{r}'\|, \quad \mathbf{N}' = (-\kappa\mathbf{T} + \tau\mathbf{B})\|\mathbf{r}'\|, \quad \mathbf{B}' = -\tau\mathbf{N}\|\mathbf{r}'\|,$$

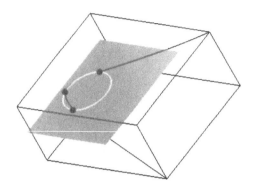

Fig. 2.11 The circle through three neighbouring points on a space curve, and the plane through these points. As the points tend to coincidence, the circle tends to the osculating circle and the plane to the osculating plane.

$$\kappa = \frac{||\mathbf{r}' \wedge \mathbf{r}''||}{||\mathbf{r}'||^3}, \quad \tau = \frac{[\mathbf{r}', \mathbf{r}'', \mathbf{r}''']}{||\mathbf{r}' \wedge \mathbf{r}''||^2}. \tag{2.8}$$

Here, [ ] stands for the triple scalar product of three vectors. Either the equation for $\mathbf{N}'$ or that for $\mathbf{B}'$ can be regarded as providing a *definition* of τ. For more details, see for example (Bruce and Giblin 1992, Ch. 2). Note that $||\mathbf{r}'|| = 1$ for a unit speed curve so that some of these formulae simplify considerably.

For a **plane curve** the principal normal $\mathbf{N}$ is just called the *normal* and it can be given a direction: turn anti-clockwise 90° from the oriented tangent. (Note that this does not make sense in $\mathbf{R}^3$: a clockwise turn from one viewpoint is an anti-clockwise turn from another viewpoint.) Then the curvature acquires a sign:

$$\mathbf{T}' = \kappa \mathbf{N} ||\mathbf{r}'|| \tag{2.9}$$

has $\kappa < 0$ when $\mathbf{T}'$ is in the opposite direction to the oriented normal, that is, $\mathbf{T}'$ is 90° clockwise from $\mathbf{T}$. A zero of curvature of a plane curve is called an *inflexion*. The binormal is constant, perpendicular to the plane of the curve, as noted above. Standard formulae for κ are:

For a parametrized plane curve $\mathbf{r}(t) = (X(t), Y(t))$:

$$\kappa = \frac{X'Y'' - X''Y'}{(X'^2 + Y'^2)^{3/2}}.$$

For a curve given implicitly by an equation $f(x, y) = 0$:

$$\kappa = \frac{f_y^2 f_{xx} - 2f_x f_y f_{xy} + f_x^2 f_{yy}}{(f_x^2 + f_y^2)^{3/2}},$$

where the latter is only up to sign since the equation $f = 0$ does not give an orientation to the curve.

It is easy to obtain the 'Taylor expansion' of a space curve about a point $\mathbf{r}(t_0)$ say. Let us assume $\mathbf{r}(t)$ is a unit speed parametrization where $\|\mathbf{r}'(t)\| = 1$ for all t, and use suffix 0 to mean evaluation at t_0. Then

$$\mathbf{r}' = \mathbf{T}, \quad \mathbf{r}'' = \mathbf{T}' = \kappa\mathbf{N}, \quad \mathbf{r}''' = (\kappa\mathbf{N})' = \kappa'\mathbf{N} + \kappa\mathbf{N}' = \kappa'\mathbf{N} + \kappa(-\kappa\mathbf{T} + \tau\mathbf{B}),$$

so

$$
\begin{aligned}
\mathbf{r}(t) &= \mathbf{r}_0 + (t - t_0)\mathbf{r}_0' + \frac{1}{2}(t - t_0)^2\mathbf{r}_0'' + \frac{1}{6}(t - t_0)^3\mathbf{r}_0''' + \cdots, \\
&= \mathbf{r}_0 + (t - t_0)\mathbf{T}_0 + \frac{1}{2}(t - t_0)^2\kappa_0\mathbf{N}_0 \\
&\quad + \frac{1}{6}(t - t_0)^3(\kappa_0'\mathbf{N}_0 - \kappa_0^2\mathbf{T}_0 + \kappa_0\tau_0\mathbf{B}_0) + \cdots \\
&= \mathbf{r}_0 + \mathbf{T}_0\left((t - t_0) - \frac{\kappa_0^2}{6}(t - t_0)^3 + \cdots\right) \\
&\quad + \mathbf{N}_0\left(\frac{1}{2}(t - t_0)^2\kappa_0 + \frac{1}{6}(t - t_0)^3\kappa_0' + \cdots\right) \\
&\quad + \mathbf{B}_0\left(\frac{1}{6}(t - t_0)^3\kappa_0\tau_0 + \cdots\right).
\end{aligned}
$$

In particular this implies that if we project the curve into the plane of $\mathbf{T}_0$ and $\mathbf{B}_0$, and if τ_0 (as well as κ_0) is nonzero, the resulting plane curve is like $(t+\cdots, t^3+\cdots)$ (putting $t_0 = 0$), that is, the curve has an inflexion. Likewise for projection to the $\mathbf{T}_0, \mathbf{N}_0$-plane (the osculating plane) the resulting plane curve is like $(t + \cdots, t^2 + \cdots)$, which does not have an inflexion, and for projection to the $\mathbf{N}, \mathbf{B}$ plane—the normal plane—the result is $(t^2 + \cdots, t^3 + \cdots)$, which has a cusp. These are illustrated in Figure 2.12.

Example 2.6.1 A curve family

Let $\mathbf{r}(t) = (t, t^3, t^4 + ut^2)$ where u is a constant > 0. Note that $\mathbf{r}'(t) = (1, 3t^2, 4t^3 + 2ut)$, $\mathbf{r}''(t) = (0, 6t, 12t^2 + 2u)$, and these can only be parallel if $\mathbf{r}''(t)$ is zero, which requires $t = u = 0$. Applying the formula (2.8) for torsion, there are zeroes of torsion where

$$[\mathbf{r}', \mathbf{r}'', \mathbf{r}'''] = \begin{vmatrix} 1 & 3t^2 & 4t^3 + 2ut \\ 0 & 6t & 12t^2 + 2u \\ 0 & 6 & 24t \end{vmatrix} = 0.$$

This gives $6t^2 = u$ so there are two solutions for t as $u > 0$. When $u \to 0$ the two torsion zeroes approach the same point of the curve given by $t = 0$. If

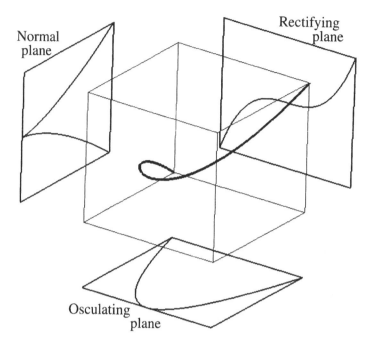

Fig. 2.12 Views of a space curve. The three pictures show 'exploded' projections of the same space curve into three planes. Left: along the **T** direction into the **N,B**-plane (normal plane), giving a cusp; Right: along the **N** direction into the **T,B**-plane (rectifying plane), giving an inflexion; Below: along the **B** direction into the **T,N**-plane (osculating plane), giving an ordinary point. The three planes actually pass through the middle of the cube; exploding them outwards makes for greater clarity. See §2.6.

$u = 0$ then the formula for the curvature κ given above shows that $\kappa(0) = 0$. The binormal at these torsion zeroes, being parallel to $\mathbf{r}' \wedge \mathbf{r}''$, is parallel to

$$\left(-2u^{3/2}, -12u^{1/2}, \pm 3\sqrt{6}\right).$$

When u is small and > 0 these two directions are almost opposite: as t moves along the curve from one torsion zero to the other the binormal violently swings almost through an angle of π. When $u = 0$ the binormal is undefined at $t = 0$ since $\kappa(0) = 0$: the binormal has become discontinuous with a sudden swing of π in direction as t goes through 0. See Figure 2.13.

We now turn to properties of *surfaces* which depend on second derivatives, 'second-order properties'. These tell us not just what the tangent planes are but how the tangent planes are turning as we move around the surface.

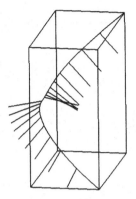

Fig. 2.13 The binormals of a space curve with a zero of curvature. This shows $u = 0$ in Example 2.6.1, where the binormal swings through an angle of π: the binormal is discontinuous.

2.7 Three surface types

We begin with three examples illustrating the different local behaviour of surfaces with respect to their tangent planes at the origin. These examples of surfaces M are all given in Monge form. The terms 'elliptic', 'hyperbolic' and 'parabolic' will be defined formally in a different but equivalent way in Definition 2.8.13 below.

Example 2.7.1 Three behaviours of the tangent plane at a point

(i) *Elliptic point*: M is the paraboloid of revolution, given by $z = x^2 + y^2$. This is 'elliptic' at $\mathbf{O} = (0, 0, 0)$ since the tangent plane $z = 0$ there meets the surface in an isolated point: $x^2 + y^2 = 0$ has only the solution $x = y = 0$. See Figure 2.14, top left.

(ii) *Hyperbolic point*: M is the saddle surface, given by $z = x^2 - y^2$. It is 'hyperbolic' at $\mathbf{O}$ since the tangent plane $z = 0$ there meets the surface in two curves (in this example actually lines) which cross transversally at $\mathbf{O}$. These curves are $x = \pm y$. See Figure 2.14, top right.

(iii) *Parabolic point*: M is given by $z = x^2 + y^3$. The tangent plane $z = 0$ at $\mathbf{O}$ meets the surface in the cuspidal curve $x^2 + y^3 = 0$, and we say that $\mathbf{O}$ is a 'parabolic' point of the surface. See Figure 2.14, centre, for a generic example like this one, and the bottom line of the same figure for non-generic examples. Note that at a generic parabolic point a surface does *not* look like a cylinder: Figure 2.14, centre, is the correct picture to have in mind. $\square$

Algebraically, we shall shortly distinguish the three types by the *Gauss curvature K*, which is > 0 for elliptic points, < 0 for hyperbolic points and $= 0$ for parabolic points (Definition 2.8.13). In §2.8 we give formulae for the case

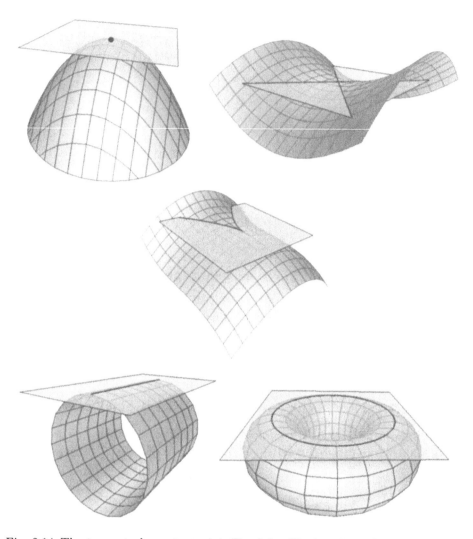

Fig. 2.14 The tangent plane at a point. Top left: elliptic point, where the tangent plane meets the surface (locally) in an isolated point. Top right: hyperbolic point, where the tangent plane meets the surface (locally) in a pair of intersecting curves. Centre: general parabolic point, where the surface meets the tangent plane in a cusp. Bottom: non-generic examples, a cylinder and a torus, where the tangent plane intersects the surface in a single curve.

of a surface in the 'parametrized' form $\mathbf{r}(u,v)$. In §2.9 we give corresponding formulae for a Monge patch and in §2.11 for a surface in 'implicit' form $f(x,y,z) = 0$.

Note that these different contacts with tangent planes are preserved by any smooth invertible transformation of space which sends planes to planes, for example by an *affine transformation*, which is a linear transformation followed (or preceded) by a translation. This necessarily preserves contact between planes and smooth surfaces, and so preserves the notions of elliptic, hyperbolic and parabolic points.

2.8 Second fundamental form and curvatures: parametrized surfaces

We now want to investigate the way in which the tangent plane to a surface patch $M = \mathbf{r}(u, v)$ moves as the point of tangency moves around on the surface. Since tangent planes depend on the first derivatives of $\mathbf{r}$ we can expect to be involved with second derivatives now. We seek ways to encode in a single object all the local variations in the tangent plane. This amounts to describing how the normal $\mathbf{n}$ to M varies as we move away from a given point $\mathbf{p} = \mathbf{r}(u_0, v_0)$ along any curve contained in M. We shall describe two ways to encode the information: via the 'second fundamental form' II and via the 'shape operator' S. Either of these objects captures essentially the local shape of M.

The basic setup then is to have a curve

$$\mathbf{r}(t) = \mathbf{r}(u(t), v(t)) \tag{2.10}$$

on M, given by taking the curve $(u(t), v(t))$ in parameter space and using the parametrization $\mathbf{r}$ to throw this on to M. At any point on the curve $\mathbf{r}(t)$ we can ask how the normal $\mathbf{n}$ (the surface normal, not the curve principal normal) varies in the direction of the velocity vector $\mathbf{r}'(t)$, that is, we can ask for $\mathbf{n}'(t)$, the *derivative of $\mathbf{n}$ along $\mathbf{r}'$*. Since $\mathbf{n}$ is a *unit* vector, its derivative $\mathbf{n}'$ is perpendicular to $\mathbf{n}$, and hence is a tangent vector to M. Every tangent vector is a linear combination of the basis vectors $\mathbf{r}_u$ and $\mathbf{r}_v$, so it is natural to ask how to express $\mathbf{n}'$ as $\xi\mathbf{r}_u + \eta\mathbf{r}_v$ for suitable scalars ξ and η. See Figure 2.15. Recall that $\mathbf{r}_u, \mathbf{r}_v$ are always assumed to be linearly independent (§2.2).

We differentiate $\mathbf{n}(t) = \mathbf{n}(u(t), v(t))$ to obtain (omitting t from the notation)

$$\mathbf{n}' = \mathbf{n}_u u' + \mathbf{n}_v v' \tag{2.11}$$

where $'$ means differentiation with respect to t. (In terms of differentials we can write $d\mathbf{n} = \mathbf{n}_u du + \mathbf{n}_v dv$.) We need to express this in terms of $\mathbf{r}_u$ and $\mathbf{r}_v$ as above.

$$\mathbf{n}' = \mathbf{n}_u u' + \mathbf{n}_v v' = \xi\mathbf{r}_u + \eta\mathbf{r}_v. \tag{2.12}$$

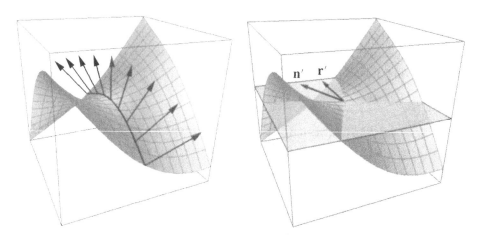

Fig. 2.15 Left: unit surface normals (called $\mathbf{n}(t)$ in the text) along a curve $\mathbf{r}(t)$ on a surface M. Right: $\mathbf{r}'$ is tangent to the curve $\mathbf{r}(t)$ and $\mathbf{n}'$ is also in the tangent plane to M, which in this example meets M in two intersecting curves (hyperbolic point). Note that to avoid cluttering the picture, the curve $\mathbf{r}(t)$ is not drawn again in the right-hand figure.

Taking the dot product of (2.12) with $\mathbf{r}_u$ and $\mathbf{r}_v$:

$$\begin{aligned}
\mathbf{r}_u \cdot \mathbf{n}' &= \mathbf{r}_u \cdot \mathbf{n}_u u' + \mathbf{r}_u \cdot \mathbf{n}_v v' = \xi \mathbf{r}_u \cdot \mathbf{r}_u + \eta \mathbf{r}_u \cdot \mathbf{r}_v = \xi E + \eta F \\
\mathbf{r}_v \cdot \mathbf{n}' &= \mathbf{r}_v \cdot \mathbf{n}_u u' + \mathbf{r}_v \cdot \mathbf{n}_v v' = \xi \mathbf{r}_v \cdot \mathbf{r}_u + \eta \mathbf{r}_v \cdot \mathbf{r}_v = \xi F + \eta G,
\end{aligned}$$

using the notation of (2.5).

We can now write down how to transform the velocity vector (u', v') in parameter space into the corresponding tangent vector to M. In matrix form this transformation is

$$\begin{bmatrix} \xi \\ \eta \end{bmatrix} = -\mathrm{I}^{-1}\mathrm{II} \begin{bmatrix} u' \\ v' \end{bmatrix} \tag{2.13}$$

where II is the matrix of the *second fundamental form* at $\mathbf{r}(u, v)$ with entries L, M, N defined by

$$\mathrm{II} = \begin{bmatrix} L & M \\ M & N \end{bmatrix} = -\begin{bmatrix} \mathbf{r}_u \cdot \mathbf{n}_u & \mathbf{r}_v \cdot \mathbf{n}_u \\ \mathbf{r}_u \cdot \mathbf{n}_v & \mathbf{r}_v \cdot \mathbf{n}_v \end{bmatrix} = \begin{bmatrix} \mathbf{r}_{uu} \cdot \mathbf{n} & \mathbf{r}_{uv} \cdot \mathbf{n} \\ \mathbf{r}_{vu} \cdot \mathbf{n} & \mathbf{r}_{vv} \cdot \mathbf{n} \end{bmatrix}. \tag{2.14}$$

(We apologize that pressure of notation has resulted in the use of M for both the surface and an entry in a matrix. There should be no possibility of confusion between these two!) Note that differentiating $\mathbf{r}_u \cdot \mathbf{n} = 0$ gives $\mathbf{r}_u \cdot \mathbf{n}_u + \mathbf{r}_{uu} \cdot \mathbf{n} = 0$ so that $\mathbf{r}_{uu} \cdot \mathbf{n} = -\mathbf{r}_u \cdot \mathbf{n}_u$. This and similar calculations show that the last two matrices in (2.14) are equal. This also shows the symmetry of the matrix II, since $\mathbf{r}_{uv} = \mathbf{r}_{vu}$.

Note that $-\mathrm{I}^{-1}\mathrm{II}$ itself is the 2×2 matrix of coefficients when $\mathbf{n}_u, \mathbf{n}_v$ are expressed as linear combinations of $\mathbf{r}_u, \mathbf{r}_v$:

$$\mathbf{n}_u = \alpha\mathbf{r}_u + \beta\mathbf{r}_v, \ \mathbf{n}_v = \gamma\mathbf{r}_u + \delta\mathbf{r}_v, \quad \begin{pmatrix} \alpha & \gamma \\ \beta & \delta \end{pmatrix} = -\mathrm{I}^{-1}\mathrm{II}.$$

In particular

$$\mathrm{II} \text{ is singular } (LN = M^2) \ \Leftrightarrow \ \mathbf{n}_u, \ \mathbf{n}_v \text{ are parallel.} \tag{2.15}$$

So far, II is just a matrix which depends on the particular parametrization of M, as well as on the point $\mathbf{p}$ of M under consideration. But we can turn II into a *bilinear form* which takes a pair of tangent vectors to M at $\mathbf{p}$ and produces a real number in such a way that the entries in the matrix II are produced by taking for tangent vectors the basis vectors $\mathbf{r}_u$ and $\mathbf{r}_v$. We now define $\mathrm{II}(\mathbf{a}, \mathbf{b})$ where $\mathbf{a}$ and $\mathbf{b}$ are tangent (column) vectors to M at the same point. To do this, we write $\mathbf{a}$ and $\mathbf{b}$ as linear combinations of $\mathbf{r}_u, \mathbf{r}_v$, say $\mathbf{a} = a_1\mathbf{r}_u + a_2\mathbf{r}_v$; $\mathbf{b} = b_1\mathbf{r}_u + b_2\mathbf{r}_v$. Then we define

$$\mathrm{II}(\mathbf{a}, \mathbf{b}) = (a_1, a_2)\mathrm{II}(b_1, b_2)^\top, \tag{2.16}$$

where II is the above matrix. Note that $\mathrm{II}(\mathbf{a}, \mathbf{b}) = \mathrm{II}(\mathbf{b}, \mathbf{a})$ since II is a symmetric matrix. Thus

$$\begin{aligned}
\mathrm{II}(\mathbf{r}_u, \mathbf{r}_u) &= (1, 0)\mathrm{II}(1, 0)^\top &&= L \\
\mathrm{II}(\mathbf{r}_u, \mathbf{r}_v) &= (1, 0)\mathrm{II}(0, 1)^\top &&= M \\
\mathrm{II}(\mathbf{r}_v, \mathbf{r}_u) &= (0, 1)\mathrm{II}(1, 0)^\top &&= M \\
\mathrm{II}(\mathbf{r}_v, \mathbf{r}_v) &= (0, 1)\mathrm{II}(0, 1)^\top &&= N.
\end{aligned} \tag{2.17}$$

The matrix equation (2.14) gives various ways of expressing the quantities L, M, N, for example $L = -\mathbf{r}_u \cdot \mathbf{n}_u = \mathbf{r}_{uu} \cdot \mathbf{n}$.

The 'second fundamental form' itself is the bilinear form on the tangent space associating to a pair of tangent vectors $\mathbf{a}, \mathbf{b}$ the number $\mathrm{II}(\mathbf{a}, \mathbf{b})$. As usual 'bilinear' means linear in each variable; for example, linearity in the first variable means $\mathrm{II}(\lambda\mathbf{a} + \mu\mathbf{b}, \mathbf{c}) = \lambda\mathrm{II}(\mathbf{a}, \mathbf{c}) + \mu\mathrm{II}(\mathbf{b}, \mathbf{c})$ for all real numbers λ, μ. Beware that we are using the same symbol II to denote both a bilinear form and a 2×2 matrix. The context will make it clear which one is intended at any moment.

Remark 2.8.1 Invariance of II(a,b)

The value of $\mathrm{II}(\mathbf{a}, \mathbf{b})$ is the same whatever parametrization of M we start from. It is of course possible to verify this directly, and we say something about how the matrix II changes when we change parametrization in Remark 2.8.10 below. But we can also interpret $\mathrm{II}(\mathbf{a}, \mathbf{a})$ geometrically as $||\mathbf{a}||^2$ times the curvature of the section of M by a plane containing $\mathbf{n}$ and $\mathbf{a}$ (see Definition 2.8.7 below), and then we can use the standard relation between a quadratic form and a symmetric bilinear form:

$$II(\mathbf{a} + \mathbf{b}, \mathbf{a} + \mathbf{b}) \;=\; II(\mathbf{a}, \mathbf{a}) + 2II(\mathbf{a}, \mathbf{b}) + II(\mathbf{b}, \mathbf{b}), \text{ so}$$

$$II(\mathbf{a}, \mathbf{b}) \;=\; \frac{1}{2} \left(II(\mathbf{a} + \mathbf{b}, \mathbf{a} + \mathbf{b}) - II(\mathbf{a}, \mathbf{a}) - II(\mathbf{b}, \mathbf{b}) \right)$$

to deduce that $II(\mathbf{a},\mathbf{b})$ also has a geometrical meaning and so is unchanged by local reparametrization of M. $\square$

The second fundamental form encodes the change in $\mathbf{n}$ which occurs when we move away from some point $\mathbf{p}$ in any direction on the surface. It is useful to have a formula for the dot product $\mathbf{a} \cdot \mathbf{n}'$ where $\mathbf{a}$ is any tangent vector at $\mathbf{p}$ and $\mathbf{n}'$ is measured in any other (or the same) tangent direction at $\mathbf{p}$. In fact, writing $\mathbf{a} = a_1\mathbf{r}_u + a_2\mathbf{r}_v$ as before we have

$$\mathbf{a} \cdot \mathbf{n}' \;=\; (a_1\mathbf{r}_u + a_2\mathbf{r}_v) \cdot (u'\mathbf{n}_u + v'\mathbf{n}_v)$$

$$=\; -(a_1 \; a_2) \begin{pmatrix} L & M \\ M & N \end{pmatrix} \begin{pmatrix} u' \\ v' \end{pmatrix}$$

$$=\; -II(\mathbf{a}, \mathbf{r}'),$$

the last using $\mathbf{r}' = u'\mathbf{r}_u + v'\mathbf{r}_v$, and the definition (2.16). Thus, for any curve $\mathbf{r}(t)$ on M through $\mathbf{p}$, and any tangent vector $\mathbf{a}$ at $\mathbf{p}$,

$$II(\mathbf{a}, \mathbf{r}') = -\mathbf{a} \cdot \mathbf{n}'. \tag{2.18}$$

Remember that, in (2.18), $\mathbf{n}$ is the unit normal, but $\mathbf{r}'$ need not be a unit vector. If say $\tilde{\mathbf{n}}$ is any nonzero normal field on M then the equation becomes

$$II(\mathbf{a}, \mathbf{r}') = -\frac{\mathbf{a} \cdot \tilde{\mathbf{n}}'}{||\tilde{\mathbf{n}}||},$$

where the denominator contains $\tilde{\mathbf{n}}$, not $\tilde{\mathbf{n}}'$! (Write $\tilde{\mathbf{n}} = \lambda\mathbf{n}$, where $\lambda = ||\tilde{\mathbf{n}}||$. This gives $\tilde{\mathbf{n}}' = \lambda'\mathbf{n} + \lambda\mathbf{n}'$, so that $\mathbf{a} \cdot \tilde{\mathbf{n}}' = \lambda\mathbf{a} \cdot \mathbf{n}'$, since $\mathbf{a}$ is tangent to M, making $\mathbf{a} \cdot \mathbf{n} = 0$.)

Definition 2.8.2 Conjugacy

The tangent directions $\mathbf{a}$ and $\mathbf{b}$ (equivalently, $\mathbf{b}$ and $\mathbf{a}$) at the same point $\mathbf{r}(u, v)$ are *conjugate* if $II(\mathbf{a}, \mathbf{b}) = 0$. (Note that $\mathbf{a}$ can be replaced by any nonzero multiple of $\mathbf{a}$ without affecting the definition, and similarly with $\mathbf{b}$.) Remember that to *evaluate* $II(\mathbf{a}, \mathbf{b})$ we express $\mathbf{a}$, $\mathbf{b}$ and the matrix for II in terms of a basis for the tangent plane at $\mathbf{r}(u, v)$ and use (2.16).

Taking a curve $\mathbf{r}(t)$ having $\mathbf{r}(t_0) = \mathbf{r}(u_0, v_0)$, say, and $\mathbf{r}'(t_0) = \mathbf{b}$, the conjugate direction $\mathbf{a}$ is therefore, by (2.18), *perpendicular to* $\mathbf{n}'(t_0)$ where $\mathbf{n}$ is the unit surface normal:

Property 2.8.3 Derivative of unit normal *The derivative of the unit normal in any direction is perpendicular to the conjugate to that direction.*

This is equivalent to saying that the conjugate to $\mathbf{r}'$ is parallel to $\mathbf{n}' \wedge \mathbf{n}$. Note that if $\tilde{\mathbf{n}}$ is any nonzero normal field (not necessarily unit), then say $\tilde{\mathbf{n}} = \lambda \mathbf{n}$ so $\tilde{\mathbf{n}}' = \lambda' \mathbf{n} + \lambda \mathbf{n}'$ and $\tilde{\mathbf{n}}' \wedge \tilde{\mathbf{n}} = \lambda^2 \mathbf{n}' \wedge \mathbf{n}$; so to find the conjugate direction we can use any normal field. Of course, if $\mathbf{n}' = \mathbf{0}$ then we have a degenerate situation where all directions are conjugate to $\mathbf{r}'$ (the point $\mathbf{r}$ is then parabolic and the direction $\mathbf{r}'$ asymptotic there; see Property 2.8.14 and Definition 2.8.11 below).

The following is immediate from Equation (2.17):

Property 2.8.4 *If the vectors $\mathbf{r}_u, \mathbf{r}_v$ are in conjugate directions, then the matrix of the second fundamental form is diagonal, that is, $M = 0$.*

For examples of conjugacy, see Example 2.8.16 below.

There is an alternative way of describing the way in which $\mathbf{n}$ changes in tangent directions at the point $\mathbf{p}$, based on (2.18).

Definition 2.8.5 Shape operator S

We write $S(\mathbf{b})$ for (minus) the derivative of $\mathbf{n}$ along the tangent vector $\mathbf{b}$ at $\mathbf{p}$. Thus $S(\mathbf{b})$ is also a tangent vector to M at $\mathbf{p}$, and by (2.18) we have

$$\mathbf{a} \cdot S(\mathbf{b}) = \mathrm{II}(\mathbf{a}, \mathbf{b}) \qquad (2.19)$$

for every tangent vector $\mathbf{a}$ at $\mathbf{r}$.

Note that $S(\mathbf{a}) \cdot \mathbf{b} = \mathbf{a} \cdot S(\mathbf{b})$ by the symmetry of II, and that $S(\mathbf{r}_u) \cdot \mathbf{r}_u = L$, $S(\mathbf{r}_u) \cdot \mathbf{r}_v = S(\mathbf{r}_v) \cdot \mathbf{r}_u = M$, $S(\mathbf{r}_v) \cdot \mathbf{r}_v = N$.
From the above, it follows that

the matrix of the linear map S is $\mathrm{I}^{-1}\mathrm{II}$.

This matrix is relative to the basis $\mathbf{r}_u, \mathbf{r}_v$ of tangent vectors to M at $\mathbf{r}$. Note that this matrix is not necessarily symmetric. It will be symmetric if I is a scalar matrix, that is, if $\mathbf{r}_u, \mathbf{r}_v$ are orthogonal vectors of the same length.

Remark 2.8.6 Weingarten map

Equation (2.13) defines a map between the tangent vector $\xi \mathbf{r}_u + \eta \mathbf{r}_v$ of the surface M and the vector $\mathbf{n}'$. We can regard $\mathbf{n}$ as a point of the *unit sphere S^2* consisting of unit vectors in 3-space—the map taking $\mathbf{r}$ to $\mathbf{n}$ is called the *Gauss map* of M, and in this context S^2 is referred to as the *Gauss* (or *Gaussian*) *sphere*. Since $\mathbf{n}'$

is orthogonal to **n**, we can think of **n**′ as a tangent vector to the Gaussian sphere. As such, (2.13) is known as the *Weingarten map*. It is the differential of the Gauss map. □

Definition 2.8.7 Sectional (or normal) curvature

Taking $\mathbf{a} = \mathbf{r}'$ in (2.18) the *sectional curvature* of M at $\mathbf{r}(u, v)$ in the direction **a** is (up to sign)

$$k = \frac{\mathrm{II}(\mathbf{a}, \mathbf{a})}{\mathrm{I}(\mathbf{a}, \mathbf{a})} = \frac{\mathrm{II}(\mathbf{a}, \mathbf{a})}{||\mathbf{a}||^2} = \frac{S(\mathbf{a}) \cdot \mathbf{a}}{||\mathbf{a}||^2} = -\frac{\mathbf{a} \cdot \mathbf{n}'}{||\mathbf{a}||^2}, \qquad (2.20)$$

where **n**′ is the derivative of the unit surface normal in the direction of the tangent vector **a**. Note that reversing the direction of **n** reverses the sign of k. In particular, if **a** is in the direction of the tangent vector $\mathbf{r}_u$ then the sectional curvature k is given by

$$k = L/E = \mathbf{r}_{uu} \cdot \mathbf{n}/\mathbf{r}_u \cdot \mathbf{r}_u \qquad (2.21)$$

since $\mathrm{II}(\mathbf{r}_u, \mathbf{r}_u) = L = \mathbf{r}_{uu} \cdot \mathbf{n}$ by (2.17) and (2.14). In general, if $\mathbf{a} = \xi\mathbf{r}_u + \eta\mathbf{r}_v$ then

$$k = \frac{\xi^2 L + 2\xi\eta M + \eta^2 N}{\xi^2 E + 2\xi\eta F + \eta^2 G}. \qquad (2.22)$$

In fact k is, up to sign, the curvature of the plane curve obtained by intersecting M with the plane containing **n** and **a**. See Figure 2.16. (Compare (Koenderink 1990, p. 197), and see §2.10 below.) The number k is also called the *normal curvature* of M in the direction **a** and is sometimes denoted by k_n.

For a non-unit normal **ñ**, we have

$$k = -\frac{\mathbf{a} \cdot \tilde{\mathbf{n}}'}{||\mathbf{a}||^2 ||\tilde{\mathbf{n}}||}. \qquad (2.23)$$

Let us use the first equality of (2.20) to locate the maxima and minima of the sectional curvature at a point. It is a standard result of linear algebra, called 'Rayleigh's principle' in (Strang 1988, p. 349), that the extrema of a ratio of quadratic forms

$$k = \frac{\mathrm{II}(\mathbf{a}, \mathbf{a})}{\mathrm{I}(\mathbf{a}, \mathbf{a})},$$

where the denominator is 'definite', that is never zero for $\mathbf{a} \neq \mathbf{0}$, are given by the values of the (necessarily real) relative eigenvalues:

$$\mathrm{II}\mathbf{a} = k\mathrm{I}\mathbf{a}.$$

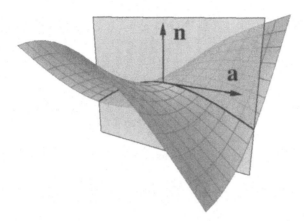

Fig. 2.16 Intersection of a surface with a normal plane, the tangent to the intersection curve being **a**.

Further, these extrema occur in the directions **a** given by the corresponding relative eigenvectors, which are the eigenvectors of $I^{-1}II$.[1] Applying this to the present case, we can make the following definition.

Definition 2.8.8 Principal directions and curvatures

The maximum and minimum values of k will occur for **a** in the direction of a vector which makes the vector $II\mathbf{a}$ parallel to $I\mathbf{a}$. These directions are eigenvectors of $I^{-1}II$, that is of the shape operator S. They are called *principal directions* at **r** and the corresponding curvatures k the *principal curvatures* κ_1, κ_2 at **r**. If $\kappa_1 = \kappa_2$ then every direction is principal and the point is called an *umbilic*. Otherwise there are two principal directions and they are perpendicular. Note that for this purpose **a** and $-\mathbf{a}$ count as the same 'principal direction'.

We can characterize principal directions by the way in which the normal changes in these directions. If **a**, which does not have to be a unit vector, is a principal direction at **r** then $S(\mathbf{a}) = \lambda\mathbf{a}$ for some scalar λ. Suppose $\mathbf{r}(t)$ is a curve through $\mathbf{r} = \mathbf{r}(t_0)$ say, with $\mathbf{r}'(t_0) = \mathbf{a}$, and that $\mathbf{n}(t)$ is the unit normal at $\mathbf{r}(t)$. Then $S(\mathbf{r}') \cdot \mathbf{b} = II(\mathbf{r}', \mathbf{b}) = -\mathbf{n}' \cdot \mathbf{b}$ for any tangent vector **b** at $\mathbf{r}(t_0)$, by (2.19), (2.18) and the symmetry of II. Thus $(\lambda\mathbf{r}' + \mathbf{n}') \cdot \mathbf{b} = 0$ for all tangent vectors **b**, which is only possible if $\mathbf{n}' = -\lambda\mathbf{r}'$.

---

[1] The principle is proved as follows. Using our notation for I and II, we have $k(E\xi^2 + 2F\xi\eta + G\eta^2) = L\xi^2 + 2M\xi\eta + N\eta^2$. Now a direct calculation shows that the extremum condition $k_\xi = k_\eta = 0$ for some $(\xi, \eta) \neq (0,0)$ is equivalent to $(II - kI)(\xi, \eta)^\top = 0$, provided I is definite. Note that the value of k is unaffected by multiplying (ξ, η) by a nonzero scalar, and taking this vector of unit length the extrema will exist since the function k is *bounded*.

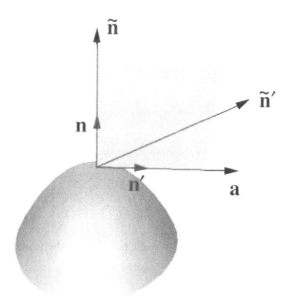

Fig. 2.17 Principal direction **a** at a point on a surface: **n′** (derivative of the unit normal **n** in the direction **a**) is parallel to **a**, and **ñ′** (derivative of an arbitrary normal in the direction **a**) is in the plane of **ñ** and **a**.

If **ñ** is a non-unit normal, **ñ** = λ**n** say, then **ñ′** = λ**n′** + λ′**n** so the extra component of **ñ′** as compared with **n′** is in the **n** direction, and we have the triple scalar product [**ñ′**, **ñ**, **a**] = 0, that is, the three vectors **ñ′**, **ñ**, **a** are coplanar. Hence:

Property 2.8.9 *Principal directions can be characterized by the property that they are those tangent directions* **a** *where the derivative of the unit surface normal* **n** *in the direction* **a** *is parallel to* **a**. *See Figure 2.17. In terms of conjugacy (Definition 2.8.2) this says that, for* **a** *to be principal, the conjugate of* **a** *is perpendicular to* **a** *(and the conjugate of* **a** *is also principal). For a non-unit normal field* **ñ** *we have* **ñ′**, **ñ**, **a** *are coplanar when* **a** *is principal.*

Remark 2.8.10 Change of basis

Since $S = \mathrm{I}^{-1}\mathrm{II}$ is not a symmetric matrix in general, it is not obvious that its eigenvectors and eigenvalues are *real*, though the interpretation of the eigenvalues as extreme sectional curvatures does indeed prove this! We note here the effect of *re-parametrization* on the matrices I, II and S. Thus consider a new parametrization of our surface patch, **s** = **r** ∘ φ where φ is a smooth invertible change of coordinates in the parameter plane (a 'diffeomorphism', possibly just locally defined). Let J be the (nonsingular) Jacobian matrix of ϕ (relative to standard bases in both parameter planes). Then calculation shows that the matrix of the first fundamental form obtained from the parametrization $\mathbf{s}$ is say I' where $I' = J^\top I J$. Now we can always choose J so that $I' = $ id. where id. here stands for the identity matrix. In fact the two columns of J can be thought of as two 'conjugate points' on the ellipse $Ex^2 + 2Fxy + Gy^2 = 1$ in the x, y-plane, that is the diameter through each point is parallel to the tangent line at the other.

Let us choose ϕ to be any *linear* map; this applies in particular if ϕ is chosen as above to make $I' = $ id. Let the matrix of ϕ be J. Then the matrix of II obtained from the parametrization $\mathbf{s}$ works out to be $J^\top II J$.

The matrix of S in the new parametrization is therefore

$$S' = (J^\top I J)^{-1} J^\top II J = J^{-1} S J.$$

This is the matrix of *the same* linear map but referred to the new basis given by $\mathbf{s}$. In particular if J is chosen to make $I' = $ id. then $S' = J^\top II J$, which is symmetric (and so has real eigenvalues). $\square$

Definition 2.8.11 Asymptotic directions

When the sectional curvature k is zero, we refer to the direction $\mathbf{a}$ as an *asymptotic* direction. (The directions $\mathbf{a}$ and $\lambda\mathbf{a}$ for any nonzero λ count as the same asymptotic direction.) Thus

$$\mathbf{a} \text{ asymptotic } \Leftrightarrow \text{II}(\mathbf{a}, \mathbf{a}) = 0 \Leftrightarrow S(\mathbf{a}) \cdot \mathbf{a} = 0.$$

This can also be expressed by saying that *asymptotic directions are self-conjugate*—compare Definition 2.8.2. If $\mathbf{r}(t)$ is a curve in the direction $\mathbf{a}$ through $\mathbf{r}$ then $\mathbf{n}'$ is *perpendicular* to $\mathbf{a}$ when $\mathbf{a}$ is asymptotic.

Property 2.8.12 *Asymptotic directions can be characterized by the property that they are those tangent directions $\mathbf{a}$ where the derivative of the unit normal vector $\mathbf{n}$ in the direction $\mathbf{a}$ is perpendicular to $\mathbf{a}$, or equally well directions $\mathbf{a}$ which are conjugate to themselves. For a non-unit normal field $\tilde{\mathbf{n}} = \lambda\mathbf{n}$ we have $\tilde{\mathbf{n}}' \cdot \mathbf{a} = \lambda\mathbf{n}' \cdot \mathbf{a}$ for any tangent vector $\mathbf{a}$, so we can also use a non-unit normal field to detect asymptotic directions.*

See §2.9 for a determination of the numbers of these asymptotic directions at different points of a surface.

We record here the definitions and standard formulae for Gauss curvature K and mean curvature H; see (O'Neill 1966 or 1997, Ch. V). Here, S is the shape operator.

$$K := \det[S] = \det \begin{bmatrix} L & M \\ M & N \end{bmatrix} \bigg/ \det \begin{bmatrix} E & F \\ F & G \end{bmatrix} = \frac{LN - M^2}{EG - F^2} \quad (2.24)$$

$$H := \frac{1}{2}\text{trace}[S] = \frac{1}{2}\text{trace} \left(\begin{bmatrix} E & F \\ F & G \end{bmatrix}^{-1} \begin{bmatrix} L & M \\ M & N \end{bmatrix} \right)$$

$$= \frac{EN + GL - 2FM}{2(EG - F^2)} \quad (2.25)$$

Thus from properties of eigenvalues,

$$K = \kappa_1 \kappa_2, \qquad H = \frac{(\kappa_1 + \kappa_2)}{2}.$$

The principal curvatures κ_1 and κ_2 are the roots of the quadratic equation

$$\kappa^2 - 2H\kappa + K = 0$$

with solution

$$\kappa_{1,2} = H \pm \sqrt{H^2 - K}.$$

Definition 2.8.13 Elliptic, parabolic, hyperbolic
A point of a surface is called

- *Elliptic* if $K > 0$ there, that is κ_1, κ_2 have the same signs;
- *Parabolic* if $K = 0$ there, that is $\kappa_1 = 0$ or $\kappa_2 = 0$;
- *Hyperbolic* if $K < 0$ there, that is κ_1, κ_2 have opposite signs.

Compare Figure 2.14. Note that $K = 0$ if and only if II is a singular matrix, which by (2.15) occurs if and only if $\mathbf{n}_u$ and $\mathbf{n}_v$ are parallel. Taking any curve $\mathbf{r}(t) = \mathbf{r}(u(t), v(t))$ on the surface through a given point $\mathbf{r}(t_0)$, the derivative of $\mathbf{n}$ in the direction $\mathbf{r}'(t_0) = \mathbf{r}_u u'(t_0) + \mathbf{r}_v v'(t_0)$ is $\mathbf{n}'(t_0) = \mathbf{n}_u u'(t_0) + \mathbf{n}_v v'(t_0)$, so when $\mathbf{n}_u$ and $\mathbf{n}_v$ are parallel all the vectors $\mathbf{n}'(t_0)$ are in the same direction. Furthermore the derivative of $\mathbf{n}$ in a suitable tangent direction will be *zero*: if $\mathbf{n}_u = \lambda \mathbf{n}_v$ for a real λ then choose $u'(t_0)$ and $v'(t_0)$ so that $v'(t_0) = -\lambda u'(t_0)$. Conversely if $\mathbf{n}' = \mathbf{0}$ in some direction then $\mathbf{n}_u$ and $\mathbf{n}_v$ must be parallel, and the point is parabolic. So parabolic points can be characterized in several ways:

Property 2.8.14 *A point $\mathbf{r}_0$ of a surface is parabolic if and only if any of the following hold:*

- *The Gauss curvature K is zero there;*
- *The matrix II is singular there;*

- *There is a nonzero tangent vector* **a** *such that* II(**a**, **b**) = 0 *for all tangent vectors* **b**;
- *The derivatives* $\mathbf{n}_u$ *and* $\mathbf{n}_v$ *are parallel;*
- *All derivatives* **n**′ *are parallel;*
- *Some derivative* **n**′ *is zero.*

If $\mathbf{n}_u$ *and* $\mathbf{n}_v$ *are both zero—so that* **n**′ = **0** *in every direction—then the point* $\mathbf{r}_0$ *is called* flat parabolic*: all sectional curvatures there are zero. Otherwise, the direction in which* **n**′ = **0** *is unique. All tangent directions at* $\mathbf{r}_0$ *are conjugate to this direction: if it is* **a** *then* II(**a**, **b**) = 0 *for all* **b**. *It is both the unique asymptotic direction and one of the two perpendicular principal directions (***n**′ *is both parallel and perpendicular to* **r**′ *at* $\mathbf{r}_0$; *see Definitions 2.8.8 and 2.8.11).*

Definition 2.8.15 Geodesic curvature

Suppose M is a surface and $\mathbf{p} = \mathbf{r}(t_0)$ is a point of M. Suppose as above we are given a curve C on M, parametrized as $\mathbf{r}(t)$ and passing through $\mathbf{p}$. The *geodesic curvature* g of C, as a curve lying on M, at $\mathbf{p}$ is given by

$$g = \frac{\mathbf{r}''(t_0)}{||\mathbf{r}'(t_0)||^2} \cdot \mathbf{v}, \tag{2.26}$$

where **v** is a unit vector in the direction $\mathbf{n}(t_0) \wedge \mathbf{r}'(t_0)$, that is, normal to the curve $\mathbf{r}(t)$ at $\mathbf{r}(t_0)$ and lying in the tangent plane to M there. Compare (Koenderink 1990, p. 197). Note that, unlike sectional (normal) curvature, this depends on the curve C, not just on the point $\mathbf{p}$ and the tangent to C at $\mathbf{p}$. For a curve lying in a plane surface M this is the 'usual' curvature of a curve. We postpone further discussion until Property 2.10.2 below.

Example 2.8.16 Conjugacy, principal and asymptotic directions

(i) **Sphere** Here all points on the sphere satisfy $\mathbf{r} = \rho\mathbf{n}$ where ρ is the radius of the sphere. So $\mathbf{r}' = \rho\mathbf{n}'$ for any curve on the sphere, that is, **n**′ is parallel to the tangent **r**′ to the curve. (In 'differential' form, $d\mathbf{r} = \rho d\mathbf{n}$.) Thus *conjugacy is the same as perpendicularity* for tangent vectors to the sphere. All directions are principal and there are no asymptotic directions.

(ii) **Circular cylinder** Let the axis of the cylinder M be in the direction of the unit vector **a** and the radius be ρ. Along the direction **a** on M the normal is *constant*: **n**′ = **0**. This is a degenerate case, where every direction is conjugate to the axis direction **a**, and every point is parabolic by Property 2.8.14. If $\mathbf{b} = \mathbf{r}'$ is a tangent direction to M at a point then the

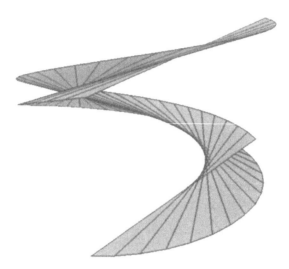

Fig. 2.18 The tangent developable surface of a space curve, with a cusp edge along the curve.

formula

$$\rho \mathbf{n}' = \mathbf{b} - (\mathbf{b} \cdot \mathbf{a})\mathbf{a}$$

works when $\mathbf{b}$ is parallel or perpendicular to $\mathbf{a}$. Therefore the formula, being linear in $\mathbf{b}$, is valid for any tangent direction as these directions form a basis for the tangent plane. It can be written in the 'differential' form

$$\rho d\mathbf{n} = d\mathbf{r} - (d\mathbf{r} \cdot \mathbf{a})\mathbf{a}.$$

Principal directions are along $\mathbf{a}$ and perpendicular to $\mathbf{a}$.

(iii) **Developable surface** A *generalized cylinder* consists of lines through the points of a space curve all parallel to a given direction, and a *generalized cone* consists of lines through the points of a space curve all passing through a fixed point in space. Along a particular one of the lines forming such a surface the tangent plane—assuming that it exists—is *constant*, so the surface normal $\mathbf{n}$ is constant and by Property 2.8.14 all points of such a surface are parabolic.

The same holds for the surface formed by the (infinite) tangent lines to a given space curve $\mathbf{r}$ whose curvature κ never vanishes—the so-called *tangent developable* of the space curve. This surface is parametrized $\mathbf{R}(t, u) = \mathbf{r}(t) + u\mathbf{T}(t)$ where $\mathbf{T}$ is the unit tangent to $\mathbf{r}$. Thus the tangent plane at $\mathbf{R}(u, t)$ is spanned by $\mathbf{R}_t = (\mathbf{T} + u\kappa\mathbf{N})\|\mathbf{r}'\|$ and $\mathbf{R}_u = \mathbf{T}$. This plane is the plane spanned by $\mathbf{T}(t)$ and $\mathbf{N}(t)$ (the osculating plane of $\mathbf{r}$ at $\mathbf{r}(t)$), independently

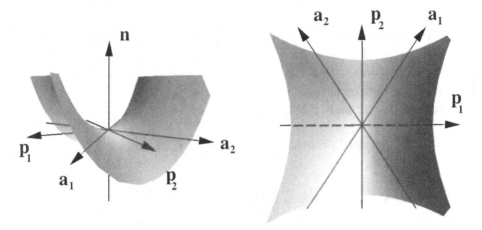

Fig. 2.19. Principal directions **p** and asymptotic directions **a** on a saddle surface.

of u, so long as $u \neq 0$. (Along $u = 0$ the vectors $\mathbf{R}_t$ and $\mathbf{R}_u$ are dependent and in fact the surface has a cusp edge there. See Figure 2.18.)

(iv) **Saddle surface** M with equation $z = xy$, parametrized $\mathbf{r}(x, y) = (x, y, xy)$. A (non-unit) normal vector is $\tilde{\mathbf{n}} = (-y, -x, 1)$ and if we consider the curve $\mathbf{r}(t) = (t, kt, kt^2)$ on M for a fixed k this passes through the origin in the direction $\mathbf{a} = (1, k, 0)$. Non-unit normals along the curve are $\tilde{\mathbf{n}}(t) = (-kt, -t, 1)$ and the conjugate direction to $\mathbf{a}$ is $\tilde{\mathbf{n}}'(0) \wedge \tilde{\mathbf{n}}(0) = (-1, k, 0)$. (See the note following Property 2.8.3.) Thus conjugacy at the origin amounts to reflexion in the x-axis, or equally well—since $\mathbf{a}$ and $-\mathbf{a}$ are not distinguished—the y-axis of the x, y-plane. The self-conjugate (asymptotic) directions are along the x-axis and along the y-axis and the principal directions are at $45°$ to these. Compare Property 2.10.1 below and see Figure 2.19.

2.9 Second fundamental form and curvatures: Monge form of surface

The surface is now represented as a graph $z = f(x, y)$, that is $\mathbf{r}(x, y) = (x, y, f(x, y))$, where u and v are here replaced by the more familiar x and y respectively. For the moment we allow f, f_x, f_y to be nonzero at $x = y = 0$. Then

$$\mathbf{r}_x = (1, 0, f_x) \qquad \mathbf{r}_y = (0, 1, f_y)$$
$$\mathbf{r}_{xx} = (0, 0, f_{xx}) \qquad \mathbf{r}_{yy} = (0, 0, f_{yy}) \qquad \mathbf{r}_{xy} = \mathbf{r}_{yx} = (0, 0, f_{xy})$$
$$\mathbf{n} = \frac{(-f_x, -f_y, 1)}{\sqrt{1 + f_x^2 + f_y^2}}.$$

The matrices of I and II become

$$\text{I}: \quad \begin{bmatrix} 1 + f_x^2 & f_x f_y \\ f_x f_y & 1 + f_y^2 \end{bmatrix}, \qquad \text{II}: \quad \frac{1}{\sqrt{1 + f_x^2 + f_y^2}} \begin{bmatrix} f_{xx} & f_{xy} \\ f_{xy} & f_{yy} \end{bmatrix}. \qquad (2.27)$$

The matrix of the shape operator is, as always, I^{-1}II.

Thus, from (2.24) and (2.25),

$$\text{Surface area} = \int \sqrt{1 + f_x^2 + f_y^2}\, du\, dv,$$

$$K = \frac{f_{xx} f_{yy} - f_{xy}^2}{(1 + f_x^2 + f_y^2)^2},$$

$$H = \frac{f_{xx} + f_{yy} + f_{xx} f_y^2 + f_{yy} f_x^2 - 2 f_x f_y f_{xy}}{2(1 + f_x^2 + f_y^2)^{3/2}}.$$

Since only the sign of K is necessary to distinguish the three basic types of surface points, we have the following.

Property 2.9.1 *Suppose M is given by $z = f(x, y)$ for some function f (that is, the surface is a graph). Then the surface is, at $\mathbf{r} = (x, y, f(x, y))$,*

- **elliptic** *if and only if $f_{xx} f_{yy} - f_{xy}^2 > 0$*
- **hyperbolic** *if and only if $f_{xx} f_{yy} - f_{xy}^2 < 0$*
- **parabolic** *if and only if $f_{xx} f_{yy} - f_{xy}^2 = 0$.*

This applies whether or not the tangent plane at $(x, y, f(x, y))$ is parallel to the plane $z = 0$.

Using Definition 2.8.11 the condition for a vector (u, v, w), at a point of M given by $(x_0, y_0, f(x_0, y_0))$, to be asymptotic is

$$f_{xx} u^2 + 2 f_{xy} uv + f_{yy} v^2 = 0, \qquad (2.28)$$
$$f_x u + f_y v = w$$

where the derivatives are evaluated at $x = x_0, y = y_0$ and the second condition just says that (u, v, w) is tangent to the surface: the tangent vector is $u\mathbf{r}_x + v\mathbf{r}_y$. The equation (2.28) is quadratic in u/v and has real roots if and only if $f_{xx} f_{yy} < f_{xy}^2$ at $x = x_0, y = y_0$.

Hence by Property 2.9.1

Property 2.9.2 *At an elliptic point there are no asymptotic directions; at a parabolic point there is one asymptotic direction; at a hyperbolic point there are two asymptotic directions.*

Finally let us note the condition for two tangent vectors

$$\mathbf{a} = a_1\mathbf{r}_x + a_2\mathbf{r}_y = (a_1, a_2, a_1 f_x + a_2 f_y), \quad \mathbf{b} = b_1\mathbf{r}_x + b_2\mathbf{r}_y = (b_1, b_2, b_1 f_x + b_2 f_y)$$

to be conjugate. According to Definition 2.8.2 and the formula for II in (2.27) the condition for conjugacy comes to

$$a_1 b_1 f_{xx} + (a_1 b_2 + a_2 b_1) f_{xy} + a_2 b_2 f_{yy} = 0.$$

Of course, the condition for self-conjugacy (asymptotic direction) is just a special case of this.

2.10 Special Monge form

When we take the surface to pass through the origin ($f(0,0) = 0$) and also to have a 'horizontal' tangent plane $z = 0$ there ($f_x(0,0) = f_y(0,0) = 0$), the surface near **O** takes the form

$$z = f(x, y) = \frac{1}{2}(ax^2 + 2bxy + cy^2) + \text{h.o.t.}, \qquad (2.29)$$

where 'h.o.t.' stands for 'higher order terms', that is cubic and higher terms. Note that $a = f_{xx}(0,0)$, $b = f_{xy}(0,0)$, $c = f_{yy}(0,0)$, so that $K = ac - b^2$ at the origin and the conditions for the surface M to have different types (§2.7) at the origin become
elliptic $b^2 < ac$;
hyperbolic $b^2 > ac$;
parabolic $b^2 = ac$.

The first fundamental form at (0,0) is now the identity, and the matrix of the second fundamental form II at the origin is

$$\begin{bmatrix} a & b \\ b & c \end{bmatrix}. \qquad (2.30)$$

Since the first fundamental form here is the identity, the shape operator S at the origin has matrix (2.30). The principal directions at the origin (Definition 2.8.8) are the (necessarily real) eigenvectors of the matrix (2.30). The principal curvatures at the origin are the (necessarily real) eigenvalues of this matrix.

A (non-unit) normal vector to M is

$$\tilde{\mathbf{n}} = (-ax - by + \cdots, \quad -bx - cy + \cdots, \quad 1), \qquad (2.31)$$

where each $\cdots$ represents terms of degree ≥ 2.

We make some calculations in this special Monge form to illustrate how useful it is. These often involve some further special choice of coordinate system.

1. Sectional curvature formula

Consider a surface M in the form (2.29) and consider a tangent vector $\mathbf{a}$ at the origin. We can rotate the surface about the z-axis until $\mathbf{a}$ becomes in the x-axis direction, say $\mathbf{a} = (1, 0, 0)$. Consider a curve in the x, y parameter plane whose tangent at $\mathbf{O}$ is along the x-axis, say $y = \lambda x^2 + \cdots$. Thus the normal $\tilde{\mathbf{n}}(x)$ along this curve is, using (2.31),

$$(-ax + \cdots, \quad -bx + \cdots, \quad 1),$$

since all terms coming from y give degree ≥ 2 in x. The derivative $\tilde{\mathbf{n}}'(0)$ (where $'$ means $\frac{d}{dx}$) is then $(-a, -b, 0)$. Thus the sectional curvature at the origin in the direction $\mathbf{a}$ is (compare (2.23))

$$-\frac{\mathbf{a} \cdot \tilde{\mathbf{n}}'}{||\tilde{\mathbf{n}}||} = a.$$

Note that a is the curvature of the section of M by the plane containing $\mathbf{a}$ and the normal $(0, 0, 1)$ at $\mathbf{O}$, since this curve is $z = \frac{1}{2}ax^2 + \cdots$ in the x, z-plane. This confirms the statement made in Definition 2.8.7, and indeed *proves in the general case* that the curvature of the normal plane section of M containing a tangent direction $\mathbf{a}$ is measured by (2.20); see also Figure 2.16.

Note that $\mathbf{a}$ is asymptotic at the origin if and only if $a = 0$.

2. Sectional curvatures in all directions

Consider a straight line in the x, y-plane given by $x = t\cos\theta, y = t\sin\theta$. Take the corresponding curve on the surface (2.29) to be the $\mathbf{r}$ of Definition 2.8.7 (equation (2.20)), so that $t_0 = 0$, $\mathbf{a} = (\cos\theta, \sin\theta, 0)$. Then using the normal vector (2.31) $\tilde{\mathbf{n}}'(0)$ comes to $(-a\cos\theta - b\sin\theta, -b\cos\theta - c\sin\theta, 0)$. Using the formula of (2.20), the sectional curvature k at the origin in the direction of $\mathbf{a}$ is

$$a\cos^2\theta + 2b\sin\theta\cos\theta + c\sin^2\theta. \tag{2.32}$$

3. Euler's formula

Rotating the surface about the z-axis to make $b = 0$ (compare §2.3) the principal directions at the origin become the directions $(1, 0, 0), (0, 1, 0)$ and the principal curvatures κ_1, κ_2 become a and c. Thus the Monge form is

$$z = \frac{1}{2}(\kappa_1 x^2 + \kappa_2 y^2) + \text{h.o.t.} \tag{2.33}$$

The sectional curvature in a direction $(\cos\theta, \sin\theta, 0)$ in the tangent plane at

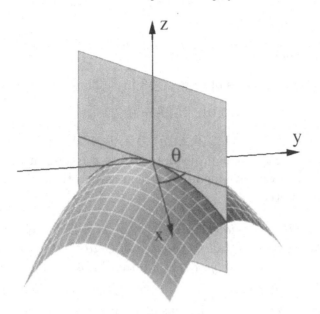

Fig. 2.20 Sectional curvature in a direction inclined at angle θ to a principal direction is given by Euler's formula (2.34).

the origin is (compare (2.32))

$$k(\theta) = \kappa_1 \cos^2 \theta + \kappa_2 \sin^2 \theta. \tag{2.34}$$

See Figure 2.20. This formula is due to L. Euler (1760). The asymptotic directions at the origin in (2.33) are, when $\kappa_1 \kappa_2 < 0$, given by $\tan^2 \theta = -\kappa_1/\kappa_2$. Notice that these have the x- and y-axes as their bisectors. Since we have made no assumptions about M, this is a general result:

Property 2.10.1 *At a hyperbolic point which is not an umbilic (i.e., for which $\kappa_1 \neq \kappa_2$), the principal directions are perpendicular and bisect the angles between the two asymptotic directions (Figure 2.19.)*

The condition for the origin to be a parabolic point when the surface is in the form (2.33) is simply $\kappa_1 = 0$ or $\kappa_2 = 0$, and the unique asymptotic direction is then $(1, 0, 0)$ or $(0, 1, 0)$ respectively.

4. Geodesic curvature

M is still as (2.29). Take a curve C on M through **O** and rotate M about the z-axis until the tangent to C is along the x-axis. Let the curve be given by

$$y = \lambda x^2 + \mu x^3 + \cdots.$$

Referring to Definition 2.8.15,

$$\mathbf{r}(x) = (x, \ \lambda x^2 + \cdots, \ \frac{1}{2}ax^2 + \cdots),$$

where each $\cdots$ stands for terms of degree ≥ 3 in x. Thus

$$\mathbf{r}'(0) = (1, 0, 0), \quad \mathbf{r}''(0) = (0, 2\lambda, a)$$

and the geodesic curvature at $\mathbf{O}$ is $(0, 2\lambda, a).(0, 1, 0) = 2\lambda$, which is precisely the curvature (up to sign) of the projection of C to the tangent plane, that is the x, y-plane. Since we have made no special assumptions about M, we have the general property:

Property 2.10.2 *The geodesic curvature g of a curve C on M through $\mathbf{r}_0$ is (up to sign) the curvature of the projection of C to the tangent plane to M at $\mathbf{r}_0$. In particular, $g = 0$ (a 'geodesic inflexion') if and only if this plane curve has an inflexion at $\mathbf{r}_0$.*

Note one other consequence of this calculation: the curvature κ of C as a space curve is given by (2.8), and in the present case, at $t = 0$, we have $\kappa^2 = a^2 + 4\lambda^2$. Since the sectional curvature k of M at the origin in the direction of the tangent to C is (up to sign) equal to a (see above), and the geodesic curvature of C at the origin is 2λ, we have the general result:

Property 2.10.3 *For a curve C on a surface M, and a point $\mathbf{p}$ of C, the sectional curvature k of M at $\mathbf{p}$ in the direction of the tangent to C, the geodesic curvature g of C at $\mathbf{p}$, and the curvature κ of C as a space curve at $\mathbf{p}$, are related by*

$$\kappa^2 = k^2 + g^2.$$

Example 2.10.4 Some quadrics

The sphere has been considered in Example 2.8.16(i).

Let a, b, c be > 0. Taking the ellipsoid $\frac{x^2}{a^2} + \frac{y^2}{b^2} + \frac{(z-c)^2}{c^2} = 1$, centred at $(0, 0, c)$ and with axes parallel to the coordinate axes, we have, close to (0,0,0),

$$z = c \left(1 - \left(1 - \frac{x^2}{a^2} - \frac{y^2}{b^2} \right)^{\frac{1}{2}} \right) = \frac{c}{2} \left(\frac{x^2}{a^2} + \frac{y^2}{b^2} \right) + \text{h.o.t.}$$

Thus the principal directions at (0,0,0) are along the x and y axes and the principal curvatures are c/a^2 and c/b^2.

The hyperboloid of one sheet $\frac{x^2}{a^2} - \frac{y^2}{b^2} + \frac{(z-c)^2}{c^2} = 1$ looks like a saddle surface near the origin (compare Figure 2.14, top right); the Monge form at the origin is

$$z = c\left(1 - \left(1 - \frac{x^2}{a^2} + \frac{y^2}{b^2}\right)^{\frac{1}{2}}\right) = \frac{c}{2}\left(\frac{x^2}{a^2} - \frac{y^2}{b^2}\right) + \text{h.o.t.}$$

so the principal directions at the origin are along the x and y axes, the principal curvatures are $c/a^2, -c/b^2$, and the asymptotic directions are given by $(\cos\theta, \sin\theta, 0)$ where $\tan\theta = \pm b/a$. $\square$

2.11 Second fundamental form: implicit form of surface

This is much harder, and we shall not have very much use for it, but we do record the following formulae for the Gauss curvature K and mean curvature H of a surface in implicit form $f(x,y,z) = 0$ which are given in (Berger and Gostiaux 1988, pp. 384, 392).

Let ∇f stand for the column vector $(f_x, f_y, f_z)^{\top}$ and A for the 3×3 matrix of second partial derivatives of f (the Hessian of f). Define a, b, c by the identity

$$\begin{vmatrix} A - \lambda \text{ id.} & \nabla f \\ (\nabla f)^{\top} & 0 \end{vmatrix} = a + b\lambda + c\lambda^2.$$

(Clearly there is no λ^3 term present because of the lower right-hand zero.) Then

$$K = \frac{a/c}{\|\nabla F\|^2},$$

$$H = -\frac{b/c}{2\|\nabla F\|}.$$

Example 2.11.1 Ellipsoid and hyperboloid

For the ellipsoid given by $\frac{x^2}{a^2} + \frac{y^2}{b^2} + \frac{z^2}{c^2} - 1 = 0$ the above formula gives $K = p^4/(a^2b^2c^2)$, where $p = 2/\|\nabla f\|$ is the (everywhere positive) distance from the origin to the tangent plane to the ellipsoid at (x,y,z).

For the hyperboloid of one sheet obtained by changing the sign of z^2/c^2 in the equation of the ellipsoid, the same calculation gives $K = -p^4/(a^2b^2c^2)$: the Gauss curvature is everywhere negative. $\square$

2.12 Special curves on a surface

The parabolic points on a surface M form a curve or set of curves called collectively the *parabolic curve* (or *parabolic set*) on M. For example, when M is given by $z = f(x,y)$ the parabolic curve is those points of M where $f_{xx}f_{yy} = f_{xy}^2$—see Property 2.9.1.

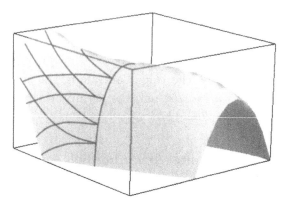

Fig. 2.21 Cusps on asymptotic curves along the parabolic curve ($K = 0$) on a surface. The asymptotic curves lie entirely in the hyperbolic region of the surface ($K < 0$), to the left of the central parabolic curve. The right hand portion of the surface is elliptic ($K > 0$) and contains no asymptotic curves. The cuspidal direction is the unique asymptotic direction at the cusp point; note that this is not tangential to the parabolic curve.

At every non-umbilic point of a surface M ($\kappa_1 \neq \kappa_2$) there are two principal directions, and these are perpendicular (Definition 2.8.8 and Property 2.10.1). The *principal curves* or *lines of curvature* on M are curves which are everywhere tangent to these principal directions. Thus the principal directions give two vector fields on M and principal curves are integral curves of these vector fields. At non-umbilic points there are two principal curves, but the vector fields have singularities at umbilics and principal curves end there. There is an extensive theory of principal curves; in particular the structure around umbilics has been investigated in detail—see for example (Sotomayor and Gutierrez 1982, Bruce and Fidal 1989, Porteous 1994, pp. 204–5, Bruce and Tari 1995, Gutierrez and Sotomayor 1998, Hallinan et al. 1999).

Likewise at every hyperbolic point there are two asymptotic directions (Definition 2.8.11 and Property 2.9.2), coalescing into one at parabolic points. The *asymptotic curves* are tangent to these asymptotic directions at each hyperbolic point. Thus there are two asymptotic curves through a hyperbolic point, and one through a parabolic point. The structure of asymptotic curves has also been studied in detail at special points of a surface. An asymptotic curve is in general nonsingular on M (free from cusps and other singularities), but where it meets the parabolic curve there is a cusp. See Figure 2.21. At more special points there is more complex behaviour; see for example (Banchoff et al. 1982, p. 43, Bruce and Tari 1995).

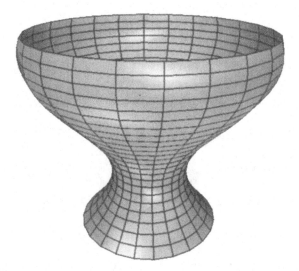

Fig. 2.22 Meridians and latitude circles on a surface of revolution are all principal curves.

Example 2.12.1 Surface of revolution

Consider a surface of revolution M swept out by rotating a plane curve C about an axis in its plane. Thus through any point $\mathbf{r}$ of M there is a 'meridian' curve $C_{\mathbf{r}}$—simply the curve obtained by rotating C to this particular position—and a 'latitude circle' which is a circle through $\mathbf{r}$ with its centre on the axis. The meridian and latitude circle are orthogonal. The unit normal $\mathbf{n}$ to M at any point $\mathbf{r}$ is, by the circular symmetry, in the plane containing $\mathbf{r}$ and the axis, normal to the meridian $C_{\mathbf{r}}$ through $\mathbf{r}$. Again, by symmetry, moving $\mathbf{r}$ along this meridian, the normal $\mathbf{n}$ has $\mathbf{n}'$ in the same plane as the meridian, that is along the tangent to the meridian $C_{\mathbf{r}}$. Thus meridians always point in a principal direction, by Property 2.8.9, so by definition the meridians are principal curves. Since the latitude circles are perpendicular to the meridians they too are principal curves. See Figure 2.22. The normals to M at points of a latitude circle all meet in one point on the axis. See Figure 2.23.

If the meridian $C_{\mathbf{r}}$ through $\mathbf{r}$ has an inflexion at $\mathbf{r}$, then the derivative of $\mathbf{n}$ along $C_{\mathbf{r}}$ will be zero at this point (the normal turns one way and then reverses, turning the other way). So $\mathbf{r}$ is parabolic, by Property 2.8.14, with unique asymptotic direction along the meridian $C_{\mathbf{r}}$.

There are other parabolic curves on M: if the tangent to C at $\mathbf{r}$ is perpendicular to the axis then there is a latitude circle through $\mathbf{r}$ at all of whose points M has the same tangent plane and the same normal vector. So $\mathbf{n}$ is

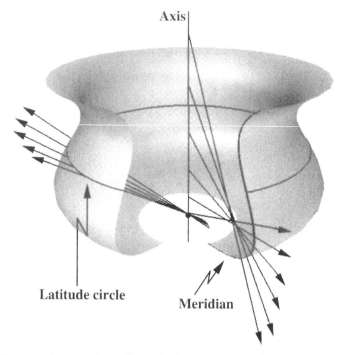

Fig. 2.23 Normals to a surface of revolution at points of a latitude circle all meet on the axis; normals at points of a meridian pass through the axis.

constant along this circle, and $\mathbf{n}' = \mathbf{0}$ in the direction of the circle, so all these points are parabolic, by Property 2.8.14, with the unique asymptotic direction along the latitude circle.

For example, when we construct a torus by rotating a circle about an axis in its plane, there are two such latitude circles, and placing the torus 'flat on the table' gives one of the two circles of parabolic points, where the torus is in contact with the table. See Figure 2.14 for the other circle of parabolic points. □

We give here a criterion for an asymptotic direction different from that in Definition 2.8.11, which leads naturally to the various 'degeneracies' which can occur.

2.13 Contact

Contact is most readily studied when the surface M is given by an equation $z = f(x, y)$.

Consider a line l through the point $\mathbf{r}_0 = (x_0, y_0, z_0)$, where $z_0 = f(x_0, y_0)$.

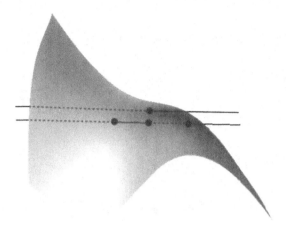

Fig. 2.24 A line in an asymptotic direction is perturbed to meet the surface in three nearby points.

Thus l is parametrized

$$(x_0, y_0, z_0) + \mu(u, v, w) = (x_0 + \mu u, y_0 + \mu v, z_0 + \mu w),$$

for a fixed nonzero vector (u, v, w) giving the *direction* of l, and $\mu \in \mathbf{R}$. This line intersects M where

$$z_0 + \mu w - f(x_0 + \mu u, y_0 + \mu v) = 0. \qquad (2.35)$$

Note that $\mu = 0$ corresponds to the point $\mathbf{r}_0$, so we can find the number of 'coincident points of intersection' which occur at $\mathbf{r}_0$ by finding the multiplicity of $\mu = 0$ as a solution of (2.35). The precise multiplicity is the whole number k such that the first $k - 1$ derivatives of the left side of (2.35) with respect to μ are zero at $\mu = 0$, but the kth derivative is nonzero. Compare (Bruce and Giblin 1992, p. 19). This amounts to saying that when l is perturbed slightly, it is possible to realize k, but no more, distinct intersection points. See Figure 2.24. But in practice some of these intersection points may have complex coordinates.) Note that an *odd* degree of contact implies that the line l passes through the surface while an *even* degree of contact means that it is tangent but stays locally on one side of the surface. See Figures 2.25 and 2.26.

The first two derivatives are

$$w - f_x u - f_y v, \quad -f_{xx} u^2 - 2f_{xy} uv - f_{yy} v^2,$$

where the derivatives of f are evaluated at $x = x_0, y = y_0$.

This gives the following conditions for k-point contact between M, given

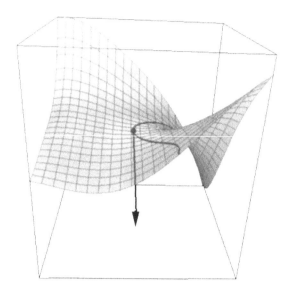

Fig. 2.25 A line in an asymptotic direction (3-point contact) pierces the surface. In fact the curve drawn is a 'contour generator' as defined in §3.1.

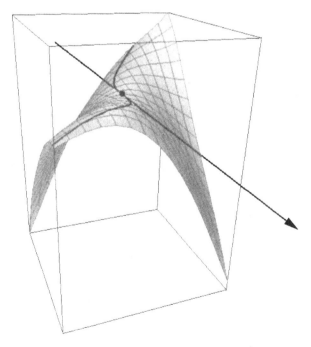

Fig. 2.26 A line with 4-point contact (asymptotic direction at a flecnode) does not pierce the surface. The curve on the surface here is a contour generator as defined in §3.1.

by $z = f(x, y)$, and the line l through $\mathbf{r}_0$ in the direction (u, v, w). All derivatives of f are evaluated at $x = x_0, y = y_0$.

(i) $k = 2$ (**simple contact**): $w = f_x u + f_y v$ and $f_{xx} u^2 + 2f_{xy} uv + f_{yy} v^2 \neq 0$.

(ii) $k \geq 3$ (**higher contact**): $w = f_x u + f_y v$ and $f_{xx} u^2 + 2f_{xy} uv + f_{yy} v^2 = 0$.

Of course, the first condition here (involving w) is exactly what we should expect: it says that the direction (u, v, w) is tangent to the surface (perpendicular to the normal $(-f_x, -f_y, 1)$). The second condition is precisely that for an asymptotic direction which we met before in (2.28).

Property 2.13.1 *Asymptotic directions at a point are the directions of straight lines having at least 3-point contact with the surface at that point.*

(iii) **Exactly 3-point contact** This requires that the conditions for $k \geq 3$ above are satisfied and also $u^3 f_{xxx} + 3u^2 v f_{xxy} + 3uv^2 f_{xyy} + v^3 f_{yyy} \neq 0$, the derivatives being evaluated at $x = x_0, y = y_0$. (Figure 2.25.)

(iv) **More than 3-point contact** This requires that the conditions for $k \geq 3$ above are satisfied and $u^3 f_{xxx} + 3u^2 v f_{xxy} + 3uv^2 f_{xyy} + v^3 f_{yyy} = 0$.

When a line has *more* than 3-point contact with M at $\mathbf{r}_0$ we say that $\mathbf{r}_0$ is a *flecnodal point* of M. This for the first time introduces the need for *third-order* derivatives of the surface. There is a curve FC on the non-elliptic part of M (Gauss curvature $K \leq 0$) called the *flecnodal curve*, which can be described in either of the following two ways, where it is assumed that $\mathbf{r}$ is not parabolic (otherwise the asymptotic curve is singular).

- $\mathbf{r} \in FC \Leftrightarrow$ a tangent line through $\mathbf{r}$ has 4-point contact (or more) with M at $\mathbf{r}$. (Figure 2.26 shows exactly 4-point contact.)
- $\mathbf{r} \in FC \Leftrightarrow$ an *asymptotic curve* through $\mathbf{r}$ has a geodesic inflexion there (see Property 2.10.2).

The equivalence of these two conditions can be established readily using the Monge form of the surface. This is sketched at the end of this section.

Drawing lines in the asymptotic directions at all points of FC generates a (ruled) surface in space called the *flecnodal scroll* ('scroll' means 'non-developable' in the context of ruled surfaces, that is surfaces made up entirely of straight lines).

Suppose that M is in the special Monge form of (2.29), with the point $\mathbf{r}_0$ under consideration being the origin and the tangent plane there being $z = 0$. Then, at $x = y = 0$, $f_{xx} = a$, $f_{xy} = b$, $f_{yy} = c$. It is often convenient to assume that the x-axis is in an asymptotic direction at the origin. Using the above conditions this simply says that $(u, v) = (1, 0)$ satisfies $au^2 + 2buv + cv^2 = 0$, so that $a = 0$. The condition for the origin to be a flecnodal point is then $f_{xxx}(0, 0) = 0$. $\square$

Example 2.13.2 Flecnodal curve on a surface of revolution

We take up the example of a surface of revolution given in Examples 2.2.5 and 2.12.1 to illustrate further the method of contact. To simplify things we assume that the curve α which is rotated about the x-axis is a graph: $\alpha(x) = (x, Y(x))$ for some function Y which is never zero. Thus consider the surface

$$\mathbf{r}(x, \theta) = (x, Y(x)\cos\theta, Y(x)\sin\theta).$$

The *equation* of the surface is $y^2 + z^2 = Y(x)^2$. We ask the question: writing Y_0 for $Y(0)$, when is $\mathbf{r}_0 = (0, Y_0, 0)$ a flecnodal point? Clearly, when this happens all points on the latitude circle through $\mathbf{r}_0$ will be flecnodal.

We consider a line $\mathbf{r}_0 + \mu(u, v, w)$ through $\mathbf{r}_0$ (so (u, v, w) is a fixed direction and μ is an arbitrary real number) and study its contact with the surface at $\mathbf{r}_0$. To do this we substitute the parametrization of the line into the equation of the surface:

$$(Y_0 + \mu v)^2 + \mu^2 w^2 = (Y(\mu u))^2.$$

To find the condition for some line to have 4-point contact, we differentiate with respect to μ three times and put $\mu = 0$: all these derivatives must then vanish. Leaving out factors of 2, the vanishing of these derivatives at $\mu = 0$ gives (Y and all derivatives are evaluated at $x = 0$):

$$
\begin{aligned}
Yv &= YY'u, \\
v^2 + w^2 &= (Y'^2 + YY'')u^2, \\
0 &= (3Y'Y'' + YY''')u^3.
\end{aligned}
$$

The first two specify the asymptotic directions since they say that there is at least 3-point contact. Thus the asymptotic directions are $(1, Y', \pm\sqrt{YY''})$, assuming that $YY'' > 0$. (A 'concave upwards' curve is needed to make a hyperbolic surface patch.) The third equation is a condition on the curve (note that u cannot be 0 from the second equation). In the special case when $Y' = 0$, that is when the tangent to the meridian curve is parallel to the axis of rotation, this says that $Y''' = 0$, which implies that the meridian curve has a *vertex*, that is the curvature is stationary. $\square$

Proof that the two flecnode conditions are equivalent Consider M set up as in (2.29), with $a = 0$, so that (1,0,0) is asymptotic. The asymptotic curve A through (0,0,0) in the direction of the x-axis is say $y = g(x)$, $z = f(x, g(x))$, where

$g'(0) = 0$; its projection to the tangent plane at $(0,0,0)$ is the plane curve $y = g(x)$. The tangent direction to A as a space curve (lying on M) is $(1, g', f_x + f_y g')$ where $'$ denotes differentiation with respect to x. The *line* l in this direction consists of points

$$(x, g, f(x, g)) + \lambda(1, g', f_x + f_y g'), \quad \lambda \in \mathbf{R}. \tag{2.36}$$

We need l to have 3-point contact with the surface at $\lambda = 0$ for all x (near to 0), as in (ii) above, so that all the tangents to A are in an asymptotic direction. To express the condition for this, we substitute the point (2.36) into the equation $z = f(x, y)$ of the surface. Putting in all the x variables, this gives

$$f(x, g(x)) + \lambda[f_x(x, g(x)) + f_y(x, g(x))g'(x)] = f(x + \lambda, g(x) + \lambda g'(x)).$$

To achieve 3-point contact, we need the first two derivatives of this equation with respect to λ to be zero at $\lambda = 0$. The first derivative gives

$$f_x(x, g(x)) + f_y(x, g(x))g'(x) = f_x(x + \lambda, g(x) + \lambda g'(x)) + f_y(x + \lambda, g(x) + \lambda g'(x))g'(x),$$

which is automatic at $\lambda = 0$. The second derivative, at $\lambda = 0$ and where all derivatives are at $(x, g(x))$, is

$$0 = f_{xx} + 2f_{xy}g' + f_{yy}g'^2.$$

This is therefore the differential equation to be satisfied by the asymptotic curve, and so holds for all (small) x. Differentiating this with respect to x and putting $x = 0$ we find, using $g'(0) = 0$,

$$f_{xxx} + 2f_{xy}g'' = 0.$$

Now $f_{xy} \neq 0$ at $x = y = 0$ by our assumption that the origin is not parabolic, so

$$g''(0) = 0 \text{ i.e. asymptotic curve has an inflexion}$$
$$\Leftrightarrow \quad f_{xxx}(0,0) = 0 \text{ i.e. the } x\text{-axis has 4-point contact (at least)}$$
$$\text{with } M \text{ at the origin.}$$

3

Views of Curves and Surfaces

We shall consider a smooth surface M, without any boundary rim, and project this either by parallel (orthogonal) or perspective (central) projection. For a curve or points in space, the image is a curve or points and we can use the whole image in our investigations. We say a little about the curve case in Example 3.6.7. The main difference in the surface case is that we concentrate our attention on those points of the surface which form the occluding contour in the image—the places in the image where the surface appears to end, because the visual ray is tangent to the surface.

3.1 Camera models: parallel (orthographic) projection

For orthogonal (or parallel or orthographic) projection in the direction $\mathbf{k}$ we can take an image plane through the origin $\mathbf{O}$, that is an image plane with equation $\mathbf{x} \cdot \mathbf{k} = 0$. Then $\mathbf{k}$ is called the *view direction* and the line through $\mathbf{r}$ in this direction is called the *visual ray*.

Let $\mathbf{r}$ be a point of M; then the corresponding point $\mathbf{p}$ of the image plane satisfies

$$\mathbf{r} = \mathbf{p} + \lambda \mathbf{k}, \tag{3.1}$$

where λ is the (signed) distance from the image plane to the point $\mathbf{r}$, provided $\mathbf{k}$ is unit. Note that, since $\mathbf{p}$ lies in the plane with equation $\mathbf{x} \cdot \mathbf{k} = 0$ we have $\mathbf{p} \cdot \mathbf{k} = 0$, and we can find $\mathbf{p}$ from $\mathbf{r}$ by

$$\mathbf{p} = \mathbf{r} - (\mathbf{r} \cdot \mathbf{k})\mathbf{k}. \tag{3.2}$$

Note also that $\mathbf{p}$ is the 'world coordinates' name for the image point; as yet no coordinate system in the image plane has been set up. Real cameras also include a scaling, s, so that $\mathbf{p} = s(\mathbf{r} - (\mathbf{r} \cdot \mathbf{k})\mathbf{k})$. Such imaging is known as *scaled orthographic* or *weak perspective*. This imaging model is a realistic one when the surface is distant from the camera compared to its relief, and the field of view is small.

We are particularly interested in the set of points $\mathbf{r}$ of M for which the visual ray is tangent to M at $\mathbf{r}$, or, equivalently, for which $\mathbf{k}$ is perpendicular to the normal at $\mathbf{r}$. These are the points where, viewed in the direction $\mathbf{k}$, the surface appears to fold, or to have a boundary or occluding contour.

The rays tangent to M at such points $\mathbf{r}$ form a 'cylinder' of tangent rays, and the curve along which this cylinder is tangent to M is the 'contour generator' Γ. The curve in which the cylinder meets the image plane is the 'apparent contour' γ. Note that both Γ and γ depend in an essential way on $\mathbf{k}$. The set Γ slips over the surface as $\mathbf{k}$ changes. For example, with M a sphere, Γ is the great circle orthogonal to $\mathbf{k}$. In this case, the contour generator Γ is a planar curve, but this is highly untypical.

Writing $\mathbf{n}$ for the normal, which here does not have to be a unit vector, the formal definitions are:

Definition 3.1.1 *The **contour generator** Γ on M is the set of points of M for which $\mathbf{n} \cdot \mathbf{k} = 0$. The corresponding **apparent contour** γ is the set of points $\mathbf{p}$ of the image plane forming the projection of Γ in the direction $\mathbf{k}$ to the image plane.*

See Figure 3.1.

The contour generator Γ is of course a curve in 3-space, and we can consider those points of Γ where its distance λ from the image plane is a maximum or minimum. These are the so-called *near and far points* of the contour generator. Note that from (3.1), parametrizing Γ by say s, we have $\lambda_s = \mathbf{r}_s \cdot \mathbf{k}$, so near and far points occur when the tangent to $\mathbf{r}_s$ to Γ is perpendicular to the view direction $\mathbf{k}$. See Figure 3.2. See also §3.5 below. (For the case that M is a sphere the distance l is actually *constant*.)

3.2 Perspective projection

The calculations and results here are very similar to those of §3.1 and the same methods of proof work here, with usually minor modifications. We give a number of examples below of these analogous lines of argument.

The setup is as in Figure 3.3, with a sphere of radius 1 centred at the optical centre $\mathbf{c}$, which is not allowed to be a point of M. The basic formula relating image point and surface point here is

$$\mathbf{r}(s) = \mathbf{c} + \lambda(s)\mathbf{p}(s), \tag{3.3}$$

where $\mathbf{p}(s)$ is the unit vector in the direction of the 'visual ray' from $\mathbf{c}$ to the

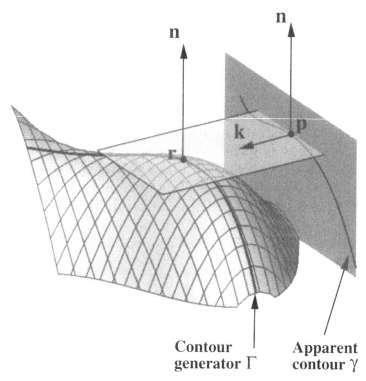

Fig. 3.1 Contour generator and apparent contour for parallel (orthographic) projection. The figure shows surface point **r**, image point **p** and surface normal **n** at **r**, which is also normal to the apparent contour at **p**.

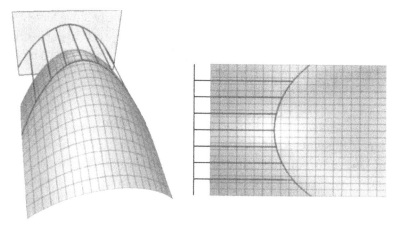

Fig. 3.2 Near and far points of a contour generator. Right: view from a point in the image plane, which therefore appears as a line at the left. In this example there is one near point.

Image sphere

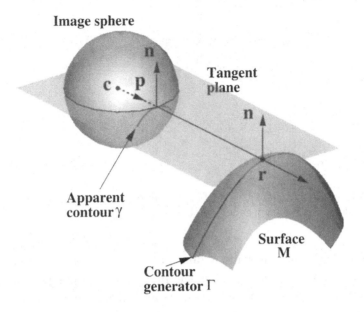

Tangent plane

n

Apparent contour γ

Surface M

Contour generator Γ

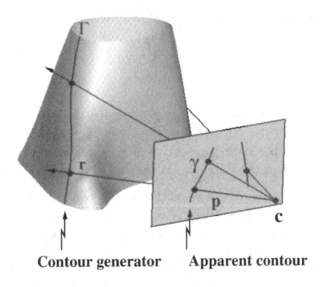

Contour generator   **Apparent contour**

Fig. 3.3 Contour generator and apparent contour for perspective projection. The upper figure shows surface point **r** in the foreground, camera centre **c** which is the centre of the image *sphere*, visual ray in the direction **p** from **c** to **r**, and surface normal **n**, which is parallel to a normal to the apparent contour. The lower figure shows a surface in the background, with an image *plane*, so that the vector from **c** in the direction **p** meets the image plane in a point of the apparent contour γ.

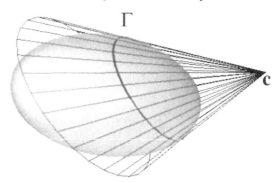

Fig. 3.4 Cone of rays tangent to a surface through the camera centre **c**, tangent to the surface along the contour generator Γ.

surface point **r**(s), and s is some regular parameter on the apparent contour (formal definitions are below). Thus the image point is **c** + **p**(s). Note that $\lambda(s)$ is the distance from **c** to **r**(s); the distance from image point to surface point is $\lambda(s) - 1$. The distance $\lambda(s)$ is always taken as *positive*.

Dropping the variable s from the notation, we can solve for **p** in terms of **r** and **c**:

$$\mathbf{p} = \frac{\mathbf{r} - \mathbf{c}}{\| \mathbf{r} - \mathbf{c} \|}, \tag{3.4}$$

since $\lambda > 0$.

Remark Note that the vector **p** for perspective projection, being along the visual ray, plays the same role as the vector **k** for parallel projection. Likewise the vector **p** + **c** for perspective projection, being the image point as a world point, plays the same role as the vector **p** for parallel projection.

In Chapter 4, we need also to allow the camera coordinates to be rotated with respect to **p**, that is we have **p** = R**q** where R is a rotation matrix. (See (Cipolla and Blake 1992), where **p**, **q** appear as **Q**, $\tilde{\mathbf{Q}}$.)

Definition 3.2.1 *The* **contour generator** *Γ is the set of points* **r** $\in M$ *for which* $(\mathbf{r} - \mathbf{c}) \cdot \mathbf{n} = 0$, **n** *being a unit normal to M at* **r**, *or indeed any nonzero normal. The* **apparent contour** *γ is the image of Γ in the image sphere, and is taken to be the set of* **p** *(rather than* **c**+**p***) for which* **r**, *given by (3.3), lies in Γ.*

Thus $γ$, being a set of points **p**, is contained in a unit sphere centred at the origin. The world points in the moving image sphere are the corresponding points **c** + **p**. For a given **c**, we can consider the cone of rays through **c** which are tangent to M. See Figure 3.4. The curve on M along which this cone is tangent to M is the contour generator and the curve where the cone meets the image sphere is the apparent contour. We can also intersect the cone with an image *plane*. For the most part we use the image sphere for convenience of calculation, but when M is a quadric surface the apparent contour in a *plane* has the attractive property of being a conic (degree 2 curve); see Example 3.6.6.

As in the case of orthogonal projection, the contour generator is a space curve, and we can consider the points of Γ whose distance from the (fixed point) $\mathbf{c}$ is extremal, the *near and far points* of Γ. By (3.3), using say s as parameter on Γ, we have $\mathbf{r}_s = \lambda_s \mathbf{p} + \lambda \mathbf{p}_s$ so that $\lambda_s = \mathbf{r}_s \cdot \mathbf{p}$ (note that as $\mathbf{p}$ is a unit vector, $\mathbf{p}_s$ is perpendicular to $\mathbf{p}$). Thus near and far points, which are characterized by $\lambda_s = 0$, are also characterized by the tangent to Γ being perpendicular to the visual ray direction $\mathbf{p}$. See also §3.6, following Property 3.6.1.

3.3 Opaque vs. semi-transparent surfaces

The above definitions are framed for the case of a 'semi-transparent surface' where light rays penetrate any number of layers before arriving at the image plane or optical centre.

A light ray proceeding from a point $\mathbf{r}$ of an *opaque* surface M will only reach the image plane or optical centre $\mathbf{c}$ if there are no other points of M in the way. We then take a point $\mathbf{p}$ to be on the apparent contour γ provided the condition of Definition 3.1.1 (resp. 3.2.1) holds and the ray from $\mathbf{p}$ to $\mathbf{r}$ (resp. the ray from $\mathbf{c}$ to $\mathbf{r}$) meets M for the first time at a tangency point. See Figure 3.5.

From time to time we shall state what effect the change from semi-transparent to opaque makes to our discussion.

3.4 Static properties of contour generators and apparent contours

In this section we shall study *individual* contour generators and apparent contours. (In Chapter 4 we study the 'dynamic' case where the view direction $\mathbf{k}$ or the centre of projection $\mathbf{c}$ is moving.) To determine whether a point $\mathbf{r}$ of M is on a contour generator we need only know the tangent plane to M at $\mathbf{r}$, that is 'first-order information' about M. To determine the *tangent* to the contour generator we need to know 'second-order information', namely the conjugacy relation on M. Although we do not go into this here, in order to find say the curvature and torsion of the contour generator as a space

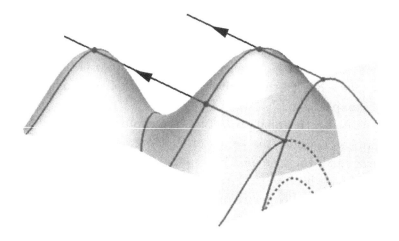

Fig. 3.5 Opaque versus semi-transparent surfaces. The dashed line in the image plane is the part of the apparent contour which is not present when the surface is opaque.

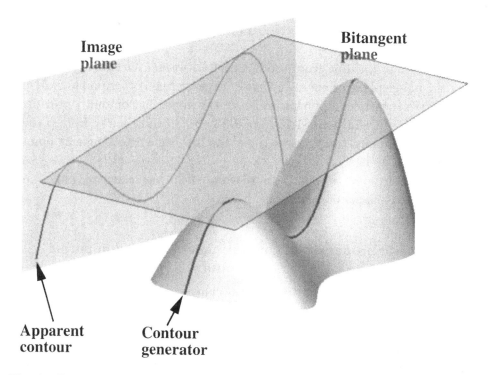

Fig. 3.6 Bitangent plane to a surface gives bitangent line to an apparent contour. This figure could apply either to orthogonal or to perspective projection.

curve we should need still higher order information about M. In fact it is more useful to relate the curvature of the apparent contour with the Gauss curvature of M.

Bearing in mind that the apparent contour γ is obtained by projecting the contour generator Γ along the visual rays we can expect special features on γ when this projection is along a tangent to Γ: projecting a Γ along a tangent gives a *cusp* on the projected curve γ. See Figure 3.7 and §4.9. If the visual ray is tangent to Γ with higher order—at an inflexion point of Γ—then we can expect a degenerate cusp on γ. It is more useful to frame these conditions in terms of the contact of the visual ray with M itself, and this is what we do. For the precise definition of contact see §2.13.

The tangent plane to M projects to the tangent line to the apparent contour; see Properties 3.5.1 and 3.6.1 for precise statements and also Figures 3.1 and 3.3. Thus if there is a *bitangent* plane to M containing the view direction (resp. through the optical centre) then the apparent contour will have a *bitangent line* (resp. *bitangent great circle* in the image sphere or bitangent line in an image plane). See Figure 3.6.

We give several methods of proof for the properties below, starting in §3.7.

3.5 Properties: orthogonal projection

Property 3.5.1 *(i) Assume that Γ is a smooth curve on M. Then the tangent to Γ at $\mathbf{r}$ is conjugate to the view direction $\mathbf{k}$ (Definition 2.8.2).*
(ii) The apparent contour normal at $\mathbf{p}$ is parallel to the surface normal $\mathbf{n}$ at $\mathbf{r}$ when the apparent contour is smooth. See Figure 3.1. When s is a regular parameter on the apparent contour, so that $\mathbf{p}_s$ is along the tangent to γ, $\mathbf{n}$ is parallel to $\mathbf{k} \wedge \mathbf{p}_s$. In the more special case when the apparent contour has an ordinary cusp[1] the 'cusp normal'—the limit of normals to the apparent contour at nearby regular points—is parallel to the surface normal. The tangent plane to M at $\mathbf{r}$ meets the image plane in the tangent line to γ at $\mathbf{p}$.

Note that the conjugacy property implies that, for near and far points of Γ (§3.1), the tangent to Γ, being both perpendicular to and conjugate to $\mathbf{k}$, is in a principal direction for M at $\mathbf{r}$, by Property 2.8.9.

Property 3.5.2 *(i) The apparent contour γ is smooth at $\mathbf{p}$ except when the view direction $\mathbf{k}$ is asymptotic at the corresponding point $\mathbf{r}$ of Γ. The*

---

[1] 'ordinary' here means that in a suitable coordinate system the cusp 'looks like' $y^2 = x^3$. The precise definition is that $\gamma' = 0$ and γ', γ'' are linearly independent at the cusp point.

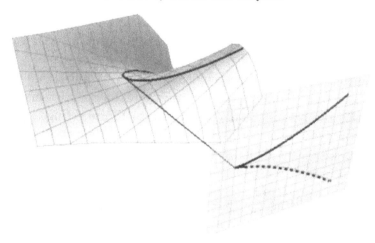

Fig. 3.7 Cusp on an apparent contour where the visual ray is along an asymptotic direction.

apparent contour has an ordinary cusp (for an opaque surface a contour ending) when the line through **r** *in the view direction* **k** *is asymptotic and in fact has exactly 3-point contact with* M *at* **r**. *(See §2.13 for a precise definition.) See Figure 3.7.*

(ii) The contour generator Γ *is smooth at* **r** *unless the point* **r** *is parabolic on* M *and* **k** *is asymptotic at* **r**. *See Figure 3.8, although this is actually drawn for perspective projection. This is called a 'beaks' point (*Γ *has a crossing); see also (Koenderink 1990, p. 458), and §4.7 below.*

Note that a singular contour generator, usually an isolated point ('lips') or a crossing of branches('beaks'), is a much less likely event than a singular apparent contour (usually a cusp).

Property 3.5.3 Koenderink's formula for Gauss curvature *Assume that the apparent contour is smooth at* **p**. *Let* κ^p *be the curvature of the apparent contour at* **p** *and* κ^t *be the sectional curvature of* M *at* **r** *in the direction of the tangent vector* **k** *(Definition 2.8.7). The curvature* κ^t *is also known as the 'transverse' curvature: hence the superscript t. Then the Gauss curvature* K *of* M *at* **r** *is given by* $K = \kappa^p \kappa^t$. *In particular an inflexion of the apparent contour (*$\kappa^p = 0$*) always indicates a parabolic point of* M *(*$K = 0$*). See below for a note on orientations.*

In addition, the sectional curvature κ^s *of* M *in the direction of the contour generator is given by* $\kappa^s = \kappa^p \sin^2 \theta$, *where* θ *is the angle between the view direction* **k** *and the contour generator.*

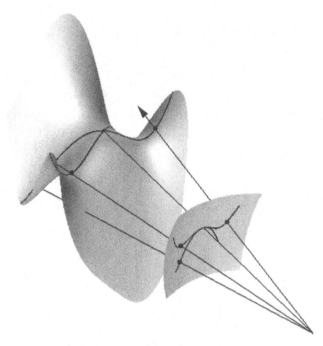

Fig. 3.8 Crossing on a contour generator and two tangential branches on the apparent contour at a 'beaks' point.

Notes on Property 3.5.3

1. At singular points of the apparent contour the formula has the form $K = \infty \times 0$: a cusp has infinite curvature and the sectional curvature of M in an asymptotic direction (see Property 3.5.2(i)) is zero. See Definition 2.8.11. This situation is studied in (Giblin and Soares 1988, Fletcher and Giblin 1996, Cipolla et al. 1997).

2. The Gauss curvature of M is independent of orientations, so we should say what orientations are taken for the apparent contour and the transverse section. There are a number of ways of doing this and here is one of them.

Suppose we are given an oriented curve C which lies in a plane, the plane being in 3-space. We cannot give the curvature of C a sign until we have oriented the *plane*. This is done by choosing two orthogonal axis directions in the plane, and naming them in a particular order, say $\mathbf{a}, \mathbf{b}$. (This is equivalent to giving an oriented normal to the plane, which would be along $\mathbf{a} \wedge \mathbf{b}$. Reversing the order then reverses the normal direction to $\mathbf{b} \wedge \mathbf{a}$.) 'Looking down' on the plane so that the rotation through 90° which sends $\mathbf{a}$ to $\mathbf{b}$ is anticlockwise, then the normal to C is 90° anticlockwise from the

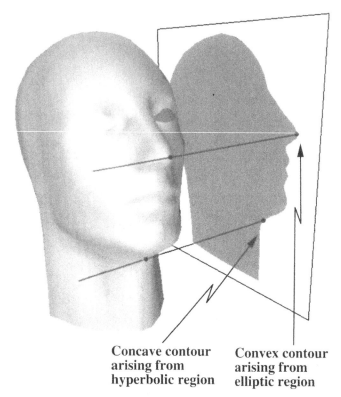

Concave contour   Convex contour
arising from   arising from
hyperbolic region   elliptic region

Fig. 3.9 Concave apparent contours from a hyperbolic region (negative K) and convex ones from an elliptic region (positive K).

tangent (remember C is oriented, so the tangent has a definite direction) and curvature is defined as in (2.9).

In the present instance, given a normal $\mathbf{n}$ to the surface, we can choose the tangent $\mathbf{T}$ to the apparent contour to be such that $\mathbf{T}, \mathbf{n}, \mathbf{k}$ is right-handed. Then we orient the 'transverse' plane (the plane of $\mathbf{k}$ and $\mathbf{n}$) by giving $\mathbf{k}, \mathbf{n}$ as the axes, and we orient the image plane by giving $\mathbf{T}, \mathbf{n}$ as the axes. Orient the transverse curve itself by declaring that the unit tangent is $\mathbf{k}$, and orient the apparent contour by $\mathbf{T}$. With these orientations, the curvatures κ^p, κ^t give the correct sign for K. Reversing the surface normal $\mathbf{n}$ leaves K unchanged and changes the signs of both κ^p and κ^t.

In practice the important thing is that, as illustrated in Figure 3.9, convex apparent contours give positive K and concave ones give negative K.

The contour generator under *orthogonal projection* consists of those surface points $\mathbf{r}$ where the normal is perpendicular to the view direction $\mathbf{k}$. Note that for a *closed smooth* surface there is a normal in every possible direction, so that *any two contour generators are bound to meet*. For if the view directions are k_1, k_2 then there will always be a point of M where the normal is parallel to $k_1 \wedge k_2$.

In the language of Remark 2.8.6, the unit normal, thought of simply as a vector, i.e. as a point of the Gauss sphere, is constrained to lie on a certain great circle, namely that perpendicular to k. In other words, the contour generator can be thought of as the preimage under the Gauss map of the great circle on the Gauss sphere perpendicular to the direction k.

Example 3.5.4 Sphere and cylinder

For a sphere, Γ is the great circle orthogonal to k, and this ties in with Example 2.8.16(i). The apparent contour is also a circle. For a circular cylinder, Γ is two straight diametrically opposite generators of the cylinder, and *any* direction k is conjugate to the direction along a generator (Example 2.8.16(ii)). Here, γ is two parallel lines. $\square$

We now illustrate Property 3.5.2.

Example 3.5.5 (i) Cusped apparent contour, (ii) singular contour generator

(i) Let the surface have equation $z = xy + y^2 + x^3$ and let $k = (1, 0, 0)$. Then a non-unit normal at (x, y, z) is

$$\tilde{n} = (-\partial z/\partial x, -\partial z/\partial y, 1) = (-y - 3x^2, -x - 2y, 1),$$

and the contour generator is given by $\tilde{n} \cdot k = 0$, i.e. $\partial z/\partial x = 0$, which gives $y = -3x^2$, so that $z = -2x^3 + 9x^4$. This is a curve Γ in space, parametrized by x, whose tangent at O points along k. The projection γ to the y, z-plane is the set of points $(-3x^2, -2x^3 + 9x^4)$, which has a cusp at O. Compare Figure 3.7.

(ii) Let the surface have equation $z = y^2 + x^3 + x^2 y$ and let $k = (1, 0, 0)$. Then the contour generator Γ is given by $\partial z/\partial x = 0$, i.e. $x(3x + 2y) = 0$, which is the singular curve made up of the two lines $x = 0$, $y = -3x/2$ in parameter space. These 'lift' to two curves on M, the first to the set of points $(0, y, y^2)$ and the second to the set of points $(x, -3x/2, 9x^2/4 - x^3/2)$. Thus Γ consists of these two curves, which cross at O, making Γ singular. This is a 'beaks' point; compare Figure 3.8.

Similarly $z = y^2 + x^3 + xy^2$ (and the same k) gives Γ as $3x^2 + y^2 = 0$, which is singular because it has an isolated point at O. (This is a 'lips' point.)$\square$

Note that the simplistic example $f(x, y) = y^2 + x^3$, which, for $k = (1, 0, 0)$, gives Γ as $x = 0$, disguises the truth by being non-generic: Γ is really given by $x^2 = 0$, which has two *coincident* branches at **O**.

3.6 Properties: perspective projection

The properties here are essentially identical with those in the orthogonal projection case, but we proceed to give details. Proofs start in §3.9.

Property 3.6.1 *(i) If the contour generator Γ is smooth at **r** then its tangent is conjugate to the visual ray **r** − **c**.*
*(ii) When γ is smooth, the apparent contour normal is parallel to the surface normal **n** (Figure 3.3). With regular parameter s on γ, the normal **n** is parallel to $\mathbf{p} \wedge \mathbf{p}_s$. When γ has an ordinary cusp, the cuspidal normal is parallel to the surface normal. The tangent plane to M at **r** meets the image sphere in a great circle which is tangent to the apparent contour at the corresponding point $\mathbf{c} + \mathbf{p}$.*

Note that the conjugacy property implies that near and far points on the contour generator (see §3.2) have the tangent to Γ both conjugate and perpendicular to the visual ray direction **p**. Hence for these points, the tangent to Γ is a principal direction on the surface (Property 2.8.9).

Property 3.6.2 *(i) The apparent contour γ is smooth at **p** except when the visual ray **r** − **c** is asymptotic at the corresponding point **r**. See Figure 3.10. The apparent contour has an ordinary cusp (for an opaque surface a contour ending) when the line through **r** in the visual ray direction has exactly 3-point contact (see §2.13) with M at **r**.*
*(ii) The contour generator Γ is smooth at **r** unless the point **r** is parabolic on M and the visual ray **r** − **c** is asymptotic at **r**. See Figure 3.8, where Γ has a crossing ('beaks'); it can also have an isolated point ('lips'). See also Figures 4.11 and 4.12.*

Property 3.6.3 Koenderink's formula for Gauss curvature *In the perspective projection case, the geodesic curvature κ^p of the apparent contour at **p** in the image sphere (Definition 2.8.15), the 'transverse' sectional curvature κ^t of M in the visual ray direction **p** (i.e., in the direction **r** − **c**), and the Gauss curvature K of M at **r** are related by $K = \kappa^p \kappa^t / \lambda$ where λ is the distance from **c** to **r**. See also (Koenderink 1990, p. 197). Note that an inflexion on the apparent contour ($\kappa^p = 0$) always gives a parabolic point on the surface ($K = 0$).*

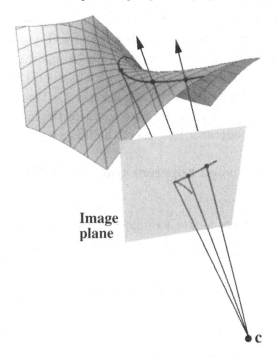

**Image
plane**

c

Fig. 3.10 Cusp on an apparent contour when the visual ray is along an asymptotic direction: perspective projection case. The lower section of the apparent contour is the part not present when the surface is opaque.

In addition, the sectional curvature κ^s of M in the direction of the contour generator is given by $\kappa^s = \kappa^p \sin^2 \theta / \lambda$, where θ is the angle between the visual ray $\mathbf{p}$ and the contour generator.

The same remarks as before apply to the sign of K in Property 3.6.3. Again the important thing is that concave contours give $K < 0$ and convex ones give $K > 0$. See Figure 3.9.

Example 3.6.4 $M =$ Sphere and cylinder

Here, the contour generator is a circle, where the circular cone of rays through $\mathbf{c}$ touches M. The tangent to this contour generator is perpendicular to the visual ray, and, as remarked above in Example 2.8.16, perpendicularity is the same as conjugacy on the sphere. The apparent contour in the image sphere is also a circle, and the normal to this circle in the tangent plane to the image sphere is clearly parallel to the normal to M. Note that for perspective projection, two contour generators need not meet, as is made clear by this example of the sphere: moving $\mathbf{c}$ directly towards the centre

of the sphere will result in non-intersecting contour generators—they are
parallels of latitude when $\mathbf{c}$ is directly above the north pole.

For a circular cylinder, the contour generator is again two straight generator lines (with the cylinder as $x^2 + z^2 = 1$ and $\mathbf{c} = (a, 0, 0)$ the contour
generators are given by $x = \frac{1}{a}, z = \pm\frac{\sqrt{a^2-1}}{a}$ for $a > 1$). The apparent contour
is two half great circles on the image sphere, where the half-planes spanned
by $\mathbf{c}$ and the contour generator lines meet the image sphere. $\square$

Example 3.6.5 (i) Cusped apparent contour, (ii) Singular contour generator

We take the same surfaces as in Example 3.5.5, and $\mathbf{c} = (k, 0, 0)$.
(i) The contour generator has equation $(\mathbf{r} - \mathbf{c}) \cdot \tilde{\mathbf{n}} = 0$, that is (compare
(2.2))

$$(x - k, y, z) \cdot (-y - 3x^2, -x - 2y, 1) = 0, \text{ where } z = xy + y^2 + y^3,$$

which comes to

$$ky + 3kx^2 - xy - y^2 - 2x^3 = 0.$$

As a power series in x, this has a unique solution

$$y = -3x^2 - \frac{1}{k}x^3 + \cdots.$$

Instead of projecting to the sphere, we can examine the apparent contour
by projecting Γ from the same point $(k, 0, 0)$ to the plane $x = k - 1$, which is
tangent to the sphere at $(k - 1, 0, 0)$. See Figure 3.10. So consider a general
point

$$\lambda(x, y, z) + (1 - \lambda)(k, 0, 0)$$

on the line from the surface point (x, y, z) to the camera centre $(k, 0, 0)$,
and impose the condition that the first coordinate is $k - 1$. This gives $\lambda = 1/(k - x)$. Thus we are using the map

$$(x, y, z) \rightarrow \left(\frac{y}{k - x}, \frac{z}{k - x}\right)$$

to project Γ to the image plane. Expanding

$$\frac{1}{k - x} = \frac{1}{k}\left(1 + \frac{x}{k} + \frac{x^2}{k^2} + \cdots\right),$$

and substituting for y and z, the result is the curve

$$\frac{1}{k}(-3x^2 + \cdots, -2x^3 + \cdots),$$

which has an ordinary cusp at $x = 0$, because of the powers 2,3.

(ii) Here, Γ is those surface points (x, y, z) satisfying

$$3kx^2 + 2kxy - y^2 - 2x^3 - 2x^2y = 0.$$

The lowest terms here are $3kx^2 + 2kxy - y^2$ which gives an isolated point at $x = y = 0$ if there are no real linear factors, that is if $k^2 + 3k < 0$, which is equivalent to $-3 < k < 0$. If $k > 0$ or $k < -3$ then there are two real linear factors, which means that Γ has two branches crossing at the origin. Figure 3.8 illustrates the latter case. See also Figures 4.11 and 4.12. $\square$

Example 3.6.6 Quadric surfaces

In Example 2.4.1 we showed that the contour generator of a quadric surface M defined by $\mathbf{X}^\top \mathbf{Q} \mathbf{X} = 0$, with camera centre $\mathbf{c}$, represented by the 4-vector $\mathbf{C}$, is the intersection of M with the plane $\mathbf{X}^\top \mathbf{Q} \mathbf{C} = 0$. In fact it is easy to describe the cone of rays through $\mathbf{c}$ tangent to M by essentially the same argument as was used in Example 2.4.1. Thus take any point $\mathbf{x}$ represented by the 4-vector $\mathbf{X}$; the line joining it to $\mathbf{c}$ has points represented by 4-vectors $\lambda \mathbf{C} + (1 - \lambda)\mathbf{X}$. This line meets M for values of λ given by the quadratic equation

$$(\lambda \mathbf{C}^\top + (1 - \lambda)\mathbf{X}^\top)\mathbf{Q}(\lambda \mathbf{C} + (1 - \lambda)\mathbf{X}) = 0.$$

The line is tangent to M provided the quadratic has equal roots, and the condition for this, writing the quadratic as say $a\lambda^2 + 2b\lambda + c = 0$, is $b^2 = ac$. Using $\mathbf{Q} = \mathbf{Q}^\top$ and $\mathbf{X}^\top \mathbf{Q} \mathbf{C} = \mathbf{C}^\top \mathbf{Q} \mathbf{X}$ (this is a 1×1 matrix, hence equal to its transpose!), some manipulation gives

$$(\mathbf{X}^\top \mathbf{Q} \mathbf{C})^2 - (\mathbf{C}^\top \mathbf{Q} \mathbf{C})(\mathbf{X}^\top \mathbf{Q} \mathbf{X}) = 0.$$

Since $\mathbf{C}^\top \mathbf{Q} \mathbf{C}$ is also a scalar, we can write this equation as $\mathbf{X}^\top \mathbf{S} \mathbf{X} = 0$ where

$$\mathbf{S} = \mathbf{Q} \mathbf{C}(\mathbf{Q} \mathbf{C})^\top - (\mathbf{C}^\top \mathbf{Q} \mathbf{C})\mathbf{Q}.$$

Thus $\mathbf{S}$ is the (singular) matrix of the quadric cone with vertex $\mathbf{c}$ and consisting of lines through $\mathbf{c}$ tangent to M.

As an example, take $\mathbf{c}$ at the origin, so that $\mathbf{C} = (0, 0, 0, 1)^\top$. Then a short calculation shows that, in the notation of Example 2.4.1,

$$\mathbf{S} = \begin{bmatrix} \mathbf{qq}^\top - Q_{44}\mathbf{Q}_3 & \mathbf{0} \\ \mathbf{0} & 0 \end{bmatrix}.$$

The tangent cone then has equation

$$0 = \mathbf{qq}^\top - \mathbf{x}^\top (Q_{44}\mathbf{Q}_3)\mathbf{x} = (\mathbf{q} \cdot \mathbf{x})^2 - Q_{44}\mathbf{x}^\top \mathbf{Q}_3.$$

If the image plane is say $z = f$ then the apparent contour in this plane is the intersection of the cone of tangent rays with the plane, namely the points $\mathbf{x} = (x, y, f)^\top$ where

$$\mathbf{x}^\top (\mathbf{qq}^\top - Q_{44}\mathbf{Q}_3)\mathbf{x} = 0.$$

Continuing the sphere example in Example 2.4.1, writing $\mathbf{x} = (x, y, z)^\top$ the tangent cone has equation

$$b^2 z^2 - (b^2 - a^2)(x, y, z) \begin{bmatrix} 1 & 0 & 0 \\ 0 & 1 & 0 \\ 0 & 0 & 1 \end{bmatrix} \begin{bmatrix} x \\ y \\ z \end{bmatrix} = 0.$$

If the image plane is at $z = 1$, then the apparent contour is the conic (obviously a circle in this example) $x^2 + y^2 = a^2/(b^2 - a^2)$. $\square$

Example 3.6.7 Projections of curves

Suppose that Γ is a smooth curve in 3-space with non-vanishing curvature κ, projected to a sphere of radius 1 centred at $\mathbf{c}$, the 'image sphere'. Let s be a regular parameter on Γ and let $\mathbf{r}(s)$ be a parametrization, with the projection described by (compare (3.3))

$$\mathbf{r}(s) = \mathbf{c} + \lambda(s)\mathbf{p}(s). \tag{3.5}$$

The curve Γ plays the role of the 'contour generator' and the image curve γ, whose world coordinates are the points $\mathbf{c} + \mathbf{p}$, plays the role of the 'apparent contour' in this situation, although of course we have the great simplification here that Γ is the entire world object being studied. Differentiating (3.5) with respect to s we obtain

$$\mathbf{r}_s = \lambda_s \mathbf{p} + \lambda \mathbf{p}_s, \tag{3.6}$$

where it will be assumed that the depth λ is always > 0. Note that $\mathbf{r}_s$ is tangent to Γ and $\mathbf{p}_s$ is tangent to γ. In particular, $\mathbf{p}_s = \mathbf{0}$ if and only if $\mathbf{r}_s - \lambda_s \mathbf{p} = 0$, i.e., $\mathbf{r}_s$ is in the direction of the visual ray $\mathbf{p}$. This simply says that γ is smooth unless we are projecting along a tangent line to Γ. See

Figure 2.12, where the projection 'to the left' is along a tangent line. Let us assume that $\mathbf{p}_s$ is not zero. Then $\mathbf{p}_s$ is in the direction of the tangent to γ, so that defining

$$\mathbf{n}^p = \mathbf{p} \wedge \frac{\mathbf{p}_s}{||\mathbf{p}_s||}.$$

$\mathbf{n}^p$ is a unit vector tangent to the image sphere and in the direction normal to γ. From (3.6), the tangent $\mathbf{r}_s$ to Γ is perpendicular to $\mathbf{n}^p$, so that $\mathbf{n}^p$ is a unit normal vector to the curve Γ. Of course, if Γ lies on some surface M, there is no guarantee that $\mathbf{n}^p$ will be the normal to M.

It is natural to ask for the connexion between the curvature κ^p of the image curve and the geometry of Γ in relation to the visual ray from $\mathbf{c}$ to $\mathbf{r}$. Since the image curve lies in a sphere we use geodesic curvature—see Definition 2.8.15. Thus

$$\kappa^p = \frac{\mathbf{p}_{ss} \cdot \mathbf{n}^p}{||\mathbf{p}_s||^2}. \tag{3.7}$$

Let us write $\mathbf{T}$, $\mathbf{N}$, $\mathbf{B}$, κ for the unit tangent, principal normal, binormal and curvature of Γ (§2.6). Thus

$$\mathbf{r}_s = ||\mathbf{r}_s||\mathbf{T}, \text{ and, differentiating, } \mathbf{r}_{ss} = \frac{\mathbf{r}_s \cdot \mathbf{r}_{ss}}{||\mathbf{r}_s||}\mathbf{T} + ||\mathbf{r}_s||^2\kappa\mathbf{N}. \tag{3.8}$$

Here we use the fact that for any vector $\mathbf{v}(t)$ we have $\mathbf{v} \cdot \mathbf{v} = ||\mathbf{v}||^2$, so that $||\mathbf{v}||' = \mathbf{v} \cdot \mathbf{v}'/||\mathbf{v}||$, and the formula $\mathbf{T}' = \kappa\mathbf{N}||\mathbf{r}_s||$; compare §2.6. In particular

$$\mathbf{r}_{ss} \cdot \mathbf{n}^p = ||\mathbf{r}_s||^2\kappa\mathbf{N} \cdot \mathbf{n}^p. \tag{3.9}$$

Differentiating (3.6) and taking the scalar product with $\mathbf{n}^p$ we get

$$\mathbf{r}_{ss} \cdot \mathbf{n}^p = \lambda\mathbf{p}_{ss} \cdot \mathbf{n}^p,$$

and combining the last two equations we can substitute for $\mathbf{p}_{ss} \cdot \mathbf{n}^p$ in (3.7):

$$\kappa^p = \frac{\kappa\mathbf{N} \cdot \mathbf{n}^p}{\lambda}\frac{||\mathbf{r}_s||^2}{||\mathbf{p}_s||^2}. \tag{3.10}$$

We can also obtain an equation for the second fraction in this equation, as follows. Since $\mathbf{p}$ and $\mathbf{p}_s$ are perpendicular ($\mathbf{p}$ being a unit vector), (3.6) gives $\mathbf{r}_s \cdot \mathbf{p} = \lambda_s$ and

$$||\mathbf{r}_s||^2 = (\mathbf{r}_s \cdot \mathbf{p})^2 + \lambda^2||\mathbf{p}_s||^2, \text{ so } 1 = (\mathbf{p} \cdot \mathbf{T})^2 + \lambda^2\frac{||\mathbf{p}_s||^2}{||\mathbf{r}_s||^2}, \tag{3.11}$$

since $\mathbf{T} = \mathbf{r}_s/||\mathbf{r}_s||$. Using this in (3.10) we get

$$\kappa^p = \frac{\lambda\kappa\mathbf{N} \cdot \mathbf{n}^p}{1 - (\mathbf{p} \cdot \mathbf{T})^2}. \tag{3.12}$$

We can eliminate $\mathbf{n}^p$ from this equation by introducing the binormal $\mathbf{B}$. In fact, using the definition of $\mathbf{n}^p$,

$$
\begin{aligned}
\mathbf{N} \cdot \mathbf{n}^p &= \left[\mathbf{N}, \mathbf{p}, \frac{\mathbf{p}_s}{\|\mathbf{p}_s\|} \right] \\
&= \left[\mathbf{N}, \mathbf{p}, \frac{\mathbf{r}_s}{\lambda\|\mathbf{p}_s\|} \right] \text{ from (3.6)} \\
&= \left[\mathbf{N}, \mathbf{p}, \frac{\mathbf{T}}{\sqrt{1 - (\mathbf{p} \cdot \mathbf{T})^2}} \right] \text{ from(3.11)} \\
&= \frac{\mathbf{p} \cdot \mathbf{B}}{\sqrt{1 - (\mathbf{p} \cdot \mathbf{T})^2}}.
\end{aligned}
$$

$$
\text{Hence } \quad \kappa^p = \frac{\lambda \kappa \mathbf{p} \cdot \mathbf{B}}{(1 - (\mathbf{p} \cdot \mathbf{T})^2)^{3/2}},
$$

from (3.12). Note that if $\mathbf{p} \cdot \mathbf{T} = 1$ then the curve tangent $\mathbf{T}$ is along the visual ray $\mathbf{p}$ and we get a cusp, which comes out of the last equation as $\kappa^p = \infty$. On the other hand, if $\mathbf{p} \cdot \mathbf{T} \neq 1$ and $\mathbf{p} \cdot \mathbf{B} = 0$ then $\kappa^p = 0$. That is, projecting along any direction in the osculating plane except the tangent direction gives an inflexion on the apparent contour (Cipolla and Zisserman 1992). □

3.7 Methods of proof: Monge–Taylor proofs

There are several techniques for proving or discovering results about apparent contours, contour generators etc., just as, in Chapter 2, there were several ways of studying surfaces. We give three approaches, proving some results in several different ways to illustrate the usefulness of each approach.

'Monge–Taylor' is the name we give to proofs which involve taking our surface M in the special Monge form—see §2.10:

$$
z = f(x, y) = \frac{1}{2} \left(ax^2 + 2bxy + cy^2 \right) + \text{h.o.t.} \tag{3.13}
$$

Here, the tangent plane to M at the origin $\mathbf{O}$ is the x, y-plane. Since apparent contours have a great deal to do with tangent planes, it is convenient to have one of these in a standard position.

3.8 Monge–Taylor proofs: orthogonal projection

Let us project M, given by (3.13), to the y, z-plane, that is taking $\mathbf{k} = (1, 0, 0)$. The condition for the normal at $\mathbf{r} = (x, y, f(x, y))$ to be perpendicular to $\mathbf{k}$ is $(-f_x, -f_y, 1).(1, 0, 0) = 0$, i.e., $f_x = 0$. Thus the equations of Γ

have the form

$$ax + by + \text{h.o.t.} = 0, \qquad z = f(x, y). \tag{3.14}$$

Proofs of Properties 3.5.1(ii) and 3.5.2 From the above, Γ will certainly be *smooth*, provided a or b is nonzero. Since $a = b = 0$ is precisely the condition for the origin to be a parabolic point with $\mathbf{k} = (1, 0, 0)$ asymptotic there (see §2.10), this proves Property 3.5.1(ii). In fact, Γ will be (locally) parametrized by x if $b \neq 0$ and by y if $a \neq 0$.

Let us suppose $a \neq 0$, so that (3.14) becomes $x = -(b/a)y + \cdots$, where $\cdots$ here represents higher powers of y. The projection γ to the y, z-plane is then

$$z = f(-(b/a)y + \cdots, y) = \frac{ac - b^2}{2a} y^2 + \text{h.o.t.}, \tag{3.15}$$

which is a smooth curve. Since z starts with degree 2 terms, this curve is tangent to the y-axis in the y, z-plane, so that its normal is in the direction $(0, 0, 1)$ in space. *Thus the apparent contour normal is parallel to the surface normal at the corresponding point.* Also $\mathbf{k} = (1, 0, 0)$ and the tangent to the apparent contour is parallel to $(0, 1, 0)$ so the wedge product of these is along $(0, 0, 1)$ which is indeed the surface normal at the origin. The tangent plane to M at $(0,0,0)$ meets the image plane $x = 0$ in the tangent to the apparent contour, namely the y-axis. (That was a lot a work for a simple result, but now the next part comes almost for free.)

On the other hand, if $a = 0$ but $b \neq 0$, then the first equation of (3.14) takes the form $y = Ax^2 + \cdots$, writing y as a function of x this time. Thus the set γ is given by

$$\{(y, z) = (y, f(x, y)) : y = Ax^2 + \cdots\} = \{(Ax^2 + \cdots, Abx^3 + \cdots)\}$$

where A is nonzero provided there is a nonzero coefficient of x^3 in f. (This says that the x-axis, which is in an asymptotic direction at $\mathbf{O}$ (see Property 3.5.2), should have 3-point *and not higher* contact with M at $\mathbf{O}$. See §2.13 and §4.7.) Thus γ is definitely a singular curve, indeed an ordinary cusp when $A \neq 0$ (assuming as above that $b \neq 0$). Notice that the cuspidal tangent is $(1, 0)$ in the y, z-plane, so the 'cuspidal normal' is in the direction $(0, 0, 1)$ in space. *The cuspidal normal is parallel to the surface normal.*

Property 3.5.2 now follows because $a = 0$ is precisely the condition for $\mathbf{k} = (1, 0, 0)$ to be asymptotic at $\mathbf{O}$. □

Note that at a parabolic point there is precisely one asymptotic direction (see §2.9) unless the point is a flat parabolic point, $a = b = c = 0$, in which case all directions are asymptotic. (This is in a sense a particularly degenerate case since the apparent contour from *all directions* in the tangent plane is singular, and we shall not cover it here.) Figure 3.8 shows one of the local pictures—actually for perspective projection—of Γ at $\mathbf{O}$ when $\mathbf{k}$ is asymptotic and $\mathbf{O}$ is parabolic but not flat: two transverse smooth curves. The other possibility is that $\mathbf{O}$ is an isolated point (this is easily derived by use of the Morse Lemma; see for example (Bruce and Giblin 1992, §4.35)). Both are illustrated in Figures 4.11 and 4.12. See also Example 3.5.5(ii).

Proof of Property 3.5.1(i) Using the setup above, with M in Monge form (3.13), choose the x-axis so that $\mathbf{k} = (1,0,0)$. Let us work in the tangent plane $z = 0$ at the origin, using the natural basis $(1,0,0), (0,1,0)$. Relative to this basis, $\mathbf{k}$ has coordinates $(1,0)$. We need the coordinates of the tangent to Γ at the origin. Suppose $a \neq 0$; then Γ is, as above, given by $x = -(b/a)y + \cdots$, $z = f(x,y)$ so that the tangent at the origin is parallel to $(-b/a, 1, 0)$, or equally well to $(-b, a, 0)$. A similar argument applies if $b \neq 0$. In either case, expressed as a linear combination of the basis $(1,0,0), (0,1,0)$ in the tangent plane, the tangent to Γ has coordinates $(-b, a)$. Clearly, the vectors $(1,0)$ (from $\mathbf{k}$) and $(-b, a)$ (from the tangent to Γ) satisfy $(1,0)\mathrm{II}(-b, a)^{\top} = 0$, using the matrix for II given in (2.30), so that conjugacy follows from Definition 2.8.2. $\square$

Proof of Property 3.5.3 Taking the same setup as before, and using (3.15), the curvature κ^p of the apparent contour is $(ac - b^2)/a$. The plane curve of intersection of M and the plane $y = 0$ is the curve $z = \frac{1}{2}ax^2 + \text{h.o.t.}$ with curvature $\kappa^t = a$, while the Gauss curvature K of M at the origin is $ac - b^2$ (§2.10). The result follows. (The sign is checked as follows: $\kappa^t > 0$ amounts to $a > 0$, which says that in order to have the fold on the left of the apparent contour it must be oriented with increasing y. This makes κ^p have the value above, which has the same sign as K.)

For the last part, we can use the formula (2.22) to find the sectional curvature κ^s of M in the direction $(-b, a)$ of the contour generator. Thus, in (2.22) we have $\xi = -b, \eta = a, L = a, M = b, N = c, E = 1, F = 0, G = 1$ and we find $\kappa^s = a(ac - b^2)/(a^2 + b^2)$. Since $\sin^2 \theta = a^2/(a^2 + b^2)$ and $\kappa^p = (ac - b^2)/a$ as above, the result now follows. $\square$.

3.9 Monge–Taylor proofs: perspective projection

With M as in (3.13) we can without loss of generality take $\mathbf{c} = (\lambda, 0, 0)$ for some $\lambda > 0$, since we want $\mathbf{c}$ to be in the tangent plane at the origin and can rotate axes so that it lies on the x-axis. Then Γ has equation

$$(x - \lambda, y, f) \cdot (-f_x, -f_y, 1) = 0,$$
$$(x - \lambda)f_x + yf_y - f = 0. \tag{3.16}$$

Most perspective projection proofs are straightforward analogues of the correponding orthogonal projection proofs. We give the arguments for Properties 3.6.2 and 3.6.3 below.

Proof of Property 3.6.2 We ask when Γ and γ are smooth. The equation of the contour generator is, from (3.16),

$$\lambda(ax + by) + \text{h.o.t.} = 0,$$

and we require a or b to be nonzero for this to be smooth. When $a = b = 0$, the origin is parabolic and $(1,0,0)$ asymptotic there (§2.10).

Assuming now that Γ is smooth, the tangent to Γ is along $(-b, a, 0)$ and this is in the direction $(1,0,0)$ towards $\mathbf{c}$ if and only if $a = 0$. Thus γ is smooth is and only if $a \neq 0$, which is the same as saying that $(1,0,0)$ is not asymptotic. $\square$

Proof of Property 3.6.3 K and κ^t have the same values as in the proof of Property 3.5.3. The calculation of κ^p is complicated by the fact that the apparent contour lies in a sphere; however we can use the general fact that the geodesic curvature of a curve on a surface at $\mathbf{p}$ equals the (ordinary) curvature of the orthogonal projection of that curve to the tangent plane at $\mathbf{p}$ (Property 2.10.2). This allows us to project the apparent contour from the sphere to the plane $x = \lambda - 1$ tangent to the image sphere at $\mathbf{p}$. Nevertheless the calculation is messy; we find that the projected apparent contour takes the form

$$\frac{1}{\lambda}\left(y + \text{h.o.t.}, \quad \frac{y^2}{2a}(ac - b^2) + \text{h.o.t.}\right).$$

Thus a local parametrization of the apparent contour is

$$\left(v, \frac{\lambda(ac - b^2)}{2a}v^2 + \text{h.o.t}\right),$$

so that $\kappa^p = \lambda(ac - b^2)/a$, which gives the required result.

For the last part, the proof is very similar to the orthogonal projection case. The formulae for κ^s and $\sin\theta$ in terms of a, b, c are the same as before, and κ^p has, as above, acquired a factor of λ. This gives the result. $\square$

3.10 Vector proofs: orthogonal projection

Proof of Property 3.5.1 Assume the contour generator and apparent contour are smooth, with regular parameter s, say, on the latter, so that (3.1) reads $\mathbf{r}(s) = \mathbf{p}(s) + \lambda(s)\mathbf{k}$. Differentiating with respect to s gives

$$\mathbf{r}_s = \mathbf{p}_s + \lambda_s\mathbf{k}, \quad \text{so} \quad 0 = \mathbf{r}_s \cdot \mathbf{n} = \mathbf{p}_s \cdot \mathbf{n},$$

using $\mathbf{n}$ for the unit surface normal, which is perpendicular to $\mathbf{k}$ for all s by definition of contour generator. Hence the (never zero) tangent $\mathbf{p}_s$ to the apparent contour is perpendicular to the surface normal $\mathbf{n}$. The *normal* to the apparent contour is then parallel to $\mathbf{k} \wedge \mathbf{p}_s$, that is parallel to $\mathbf{n}$.

Also, from (3.1), $(\mathbf{r} - \mathbf{p}) \cdot \mathbf{n} = 0$ and differentiating with respect to s now gives $(\mathbf{r} - \mathbf{p}) \cdot \mathbf{n}_s = 0$. But this says precisely that the 'visual ray' $\mathbf{r} - \mathbf{p}$ is along the conjugate to the tangent to the s-parameter curve, i.e. to the contour generator (see Property 2.8.3).

The property for an apparent contour with a cusp follows by taking limits at nonsingular points of the apparent contour. $\square$

Proof of Property 3.5.3 We note a useful formula, which follows from (3.2). Let s be a parameter on the apparent contour, assumed smooth. Then, differentiating (3.2) with respect to s:

$$\mathbf{p}_s = \mathbf{r}_s - \lambda_s \cdot \mathbf{k} = \mathbf{r}_s - (\mathbf{r}_s \cdot \mathbf{k})\mathbf{k}, \tag{3.17}$$

the second equality coming by dotting the first one with $\mathbf{k}$ to find λ_s.

We assume that Γ and γ are smooth. We can then take M locally parametrized as $\mathbf{r}(u, s)$, in such a way that Γ is the curve $\mathbf{r}(u_0, s)$ for constant u_0, with tangent $\mathbf{r}_s$. Since $\mathbf{k}$ will not be tangent to Γ (γ is smooth) we can take $\mathbf{r}_u$ parallel to $\mathbf{k}$ along Γ. Because $\mathbf{r}_u$ and $\mathbf{r}_s$ are then conjugate (Property 3.5.1) we have, in the notation of §2.8, $M = 0$. (This is one of the rare occasions where M as in the second fundamental form clashes with M as a surface!) Sometimes in Chapter 4, where we consider moving apparent contours, the parameter u here appears as time t.

The curvatures occurring in the statement of the Property are (see §2.8 for the notation)

$$\kappa^t = -\frac{\mathbf{n}_u \cdot \mathbf{r}_u}{||\mathbf{r}_u||^2} = \frac{\mathbf{n} \cdot \mathbf{r}_{uu}}{||\mathbf{r}_u||^2} = \frac{L}{E}, \quad \kappa^p = \frac{\mathbf{p}_{ss} \cdot \mathbf{n}}{||\mathbf{p}_s||^2}. \tag{3.18}$$

Differentiating (3.1) twice with respect to s gives $\mathbf{p}_{ss} \cdot \mathbf{n} = \mathbf{r}_{ss} \cdot \mathbf{n} = N$. Finally from (3.17)

$$||\mathbf{p}_s||^2 = ||\mathbf{r}_s||^2 - (\mathbf{r}_s \cdot \mathbf{k})^2 = ||\mathbf{r}_s||^2 - \left(\mathbf{r}_s \cdot \frac{\mathbf{r}_u}{||\mathbf{r}_u||}\right)^2 = G - \frac{F^2}{E}.$$

Putting these together and using the formula (2.24) for K in §2.8 gives the result.

For the last part,

$$\cos^2 \theta = \frac{(\mathbf{r}_s \cdot \mathbf{k})^2}{||\mathbf{r}_s||^2} = \frac{\lambda_s^2}{||\mathbf{p}_s||^2 + \lambda_s^2},$$

since θ is the angle between $\mathbf{r}_s$ and $\mathbf{k}$. Hence

$$\kappa^s = \frac{\mathbf{r}_{ss} \cdot \mathbf{n}}{||\mathbf{r}_s||^2} = \frac{\kappa^p ||\mathbf{p}_s||^2}{||\mathbf{p}_s||^2 + \lambda_s^2} = \kappa^p \sin^2 \theta. \quad \square$$

3.11 Vector proofs: perspective projection

Proof of Property 3.6.1 Assume that Γ and γ are smooth, and use a regular parameter s on γ to make (3.3) into $\mathbf{r}(s) = \mathbf{c} + \lambda(s)\mathbf{p}(s)$. Differentiating with respect to s gives

$$\mathbf{r}_s = \lambda_s \mathbf{p} + \lambda \mathbf{p}_s, \quad \text{so that} \quad \mathbf{r}_s \cdot \mathbf{n} = \lambda \mathbf{p}_s \cdot \mathbf{n},$$

where $\mathbf{n}$ is the (unit) surface normal which for all s is perpendicular to $\mathbf{p}$ by definition of apparent contour. Thus the (never zero) tangent $\mathbf{p}_s$ to the apparent contour is perpendicular to the surface normal $\mathbf{n}$. Since $\mathbf{p}$ is a unit vector, $\mathbf{p}_s$ is also perpendicular to $\mathbf{p}$, so the surface normal $\mathbf{n}$ is parallel to $\mathbf{p} \wedge \mathbf{p}_s$, that is $\mathbf{n}$ is parallel to the *normal* to the apparent contour.

Further, from (3.3),

$$(\mathbf{r} - \mathbf{c}) \cdot \mathbf{n} = 0, \quad \text{so} \quad \mathbf{r}_s \cdot \mathbf{n} + (\mathbf{r} - \mathbf{c}) \cdot \mathbf{n}_s = 0.$$

But the first term is zero since $\mathbf{r}_s$ is tangent to M. The equation then says precisely that $\mathbf{r} - \mathbf{c}$ is conjugate to the tangent to Γ (Property 2.8.3). $\square$

Proof of Property 3.6.3 The analogue of (3.17) is

$$\lambda \mathbf{p}_s = \mathbf{r}_s - \lambda_s \cdot \mathbf{p} = \mathbf{r}_s - (\mathbf{r}_s \cdot \mathbf{p})\mathbf{p}. \tag{3.19}$$

We can set up a local parametrization of M as in the proof of Property 3.5.3. The analogues of (3.18) are identical here except that now $\mathbf{p}_{ss} \cdot \mathbf{n} = \mathbf{r}_{ss} \cdot \mathbf{n}/\lambda$. Also, from (3.19) we find $\lambda^2 ||\mathbf{p}_s||^2 = G - (F^2/E)$ by the same reasoning as before. Putting these formulae together gives the required result.

The proof of the formula for κ^s is very similar to the orthogonal case. Now,

$$\cos^2 \theta = \frac{(\mathbf{r}_s \cdot \mathbf{p})^2}{||\mathbf{r}_s||^2} = \frac{\lambda_s^2}{\lambda_s^2 + \lambda^2 ||\mathbf{p}_s||^2},$$

so that

$$\kappa^s = \frac{\lambda \kappa^p ||\mathbf{p}_s||^2}{||\mathbf{r}_s||^2} = \frac{\kappa^p \sin^2 \theta}{\lambda}. \quad \Box$$

3.12 Methods of proof: pure geometric proofs

These are not so useful for proving quantitative results such as Properties 3.5.3 and 3.6.3 but there are parts of Properties 3.5.1, 3.5.2 and their counterparts Properties 3.6.1, 3.6.2 which become more intuitive with pure geometrical reasoning. We proceed to give some examples.

Proof of Properties 3.5.1, 3.6.1 This uses the idea of 'hinges' of an envelope of planes, as in (Koenderink 1990). Given a smooth curve Δ on a surface M, we can consider the envelope of tangent planes to M at points of Δ. This is a ruled surface and the 'hinge' (that is, ruling) is, at each point of Δ, conjugate to the tangent to Δ. See (Koenderink 1990, p. 205).

Applying this to Γ, assuming it is smooth, the ruled surface is, for orthogonal projection, just a cylinder with generators (rulings) along $\mathbf{k}$, tangent to M along Γ. For perspective projection it is a cone with rulings along the visual rays $\mathbf{r} - \mathbf{c}$ tangent to M along Γ (Figure 3.4). In each case (i) of the Property is then immediate.

For (ii) we can see that the tangent plane π to M at $\mathbf{r} \in \Gamma$ intersects the image plane (orthogonal projection) orthogonally in a line and intersects the image sphere (perspective projection) orthogonally in a great circle. This line or circle is tangent to γ at $\mathbf{p}$. Furthermore the normal to π at $\mathbf{p}$ will lie in the image plane or the tangent plane to the image sphere because of orthogonality. Hence it will be parallel to the normal to γ at $\mathbf{p}$. $\Box$.

Proof of Properties 3.5.2(i) and 3.6.2(i) We consider Γ as a space curve (assumed smooth) on M. A singular apparent contour γ occurs just when Γ is being projected along a tangent line, which occurs (by Property 3.5.1(i) or 3.6.1(i)) when $\mathbf{k}$ or $\mathbf{r} - \mathbf{c}$ is conjugate to *itself*, i.e. when it is asymptotic. $\Box$

4

Dynamic Analysis of Apparent Contours

In this chapter we shall show how information from the apparent contours of a surface M for *more than one* camera centre can be combined. One crucial problem besets this kind of analysis: as the camera centre moves, so the contour generator 'slips over the surface', so that the apparent contours are not projections of a single space curve into the image but each one is a projection of a different space curve. See Figure 4.1.

In view of the fact that the contour generator slips over the surface it is perhaps surprising that anything can be deduced from apparent contours of surfaces. But the following geometrical argument suggests otherwise. We suppose perspective projection and a continuous motion of the camera centre **c**. Each camera centre gives rise to a cone of rays tangent to M; see §3.1, §3.2 and Figure 3.4. Thus, as the camera centre moves, we have a moving cone which is tangent to M. In fact M can be viewed as the *envelope* of these cones, that is, as a surface which is uniquely determined by being tangent to all of them. So knowledge of the path of **c** and of the apparent contour for each time should in fact lead to exact knowledge of M, or at least of the region of M where the various cones are tangent. It was this basic intuition which led to the reconstruction of surfaces from apparent contours, for the case of orthogonal projection and a special motion, in (Giblin and Weiss 1987). Later, a more direct approach was found in (Cipolla and Blake 1990 and 1992) and it is this approach which we follow below. We nevertheless describe the envelope construction in some more detail in §4.2.1.

When contour generators intersect on M, so that one or more points of M *do* contribute to two different apparent contours, there is sometimes additional information to be obtained. This observation appears in a special case in (Rieger 1986) and was later extended to more general situations by several authors; see §4.8 and Chapter 6 for details.

For the present we shall assume that the apparent contours over time t

79

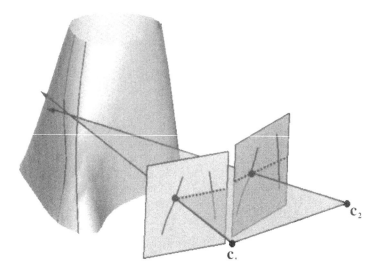

Fig. 4.1 The contour generator slips over the surface as the camera centre moves. Two camera centres c_1, c_2 and their corresponding contour generators are shown along with an 'epipolar plane' spanned by two visual rays and the baseline. See §4.4 below.

are parametrized by $\mathbf{p}(s, t)$, and that the resulting parametrization $\mathbf{r}(s, t)$ of our surface is regular, that is, the vectors $\mathbf{r}_s = \frac{\partial \mathbf{r}}{\partial s}$ and $\mathbf{r}_t = \frac{\partial \mathbf{r}}{\partial t}$ are always independent. We consider the exceptions to this in §4.6.

4.1 Orthogonal projection

We cover this case fairly briefly since the main interest lies with the more realistic case of perspective projection. As in §3.10 we use the equation $\mathbf{r} = \mathbf{p} + \lambda \mathbf{k}$ (which appeared as (3.1)). We now assume that $\mathbf{p}$ is a function of two variables s (a regular parameter along each apparent contour) and t, which we think of as time. Thus $\mathbf{p}_s$ is tangent to the apparent contour for a given t. We have, writing in the variables,

$$\mathbf{r}(s, t) = \mathbf{p}(s, t) + \lambda(s, t)\mathbf{k}(t).$$

Differentiating with respect to t and using the surface normal $\mathbf{n}$ (which is parallel to $\mathbf{k} \wedge \mathbf{p}_s$; see Property 3.5.1(ii)) gives

$$\mathbf{r}_t = \mathbf{p}_t + \lambda_t \mathbf{k} + \lambda \mathbf{k}_t, \quad \text{so} \quad 0 = \mathbf{r}_t \cdot \mathbf{n} = \mathbf{p}_t \cdot \mathbf{n} + \lambda \mathbf{k}_t \cdot \mathbf{n}.$$

From this we deduce the *distance formula* or *depth formula*

$$\lambda = -\frac{\mathbf{p}_t \cdot \mathbf{n}}{\mathbf{k}_t \cdot \mathbf{n}}, \tag{4.1}$$

which tells us the depth $\lambda(s,t)$ from the image point $\mathbf{p}(s,t)$ to the surface point $\mathbf{r}(s,t)$, in the direction $\mathbf{k}(t)$:

$$\mathbf{r} = \mathbf{p} - \frac{\mathbf{p}_t \cdot \mathbf{n}}{\mathbf{k}_t \cdot \mathbf{n}}\mathbf{k}. \tag{4.2}$$

Notes on these formulae

1. We have not specified the nature of the parameter s on apparent contours: the formulae above are independent of this choice, for the following reason. If $s = S(u,t)$ say, for a new parameter u, and if $\mathbf{P}(u,t) = \mathbf{p}(S(u,t),t)$, then by the chain rule, $\mathbf{P}_t = \mathbf{p}_s S_t + \mathbf{p}_t$, and the first term on the right-hand side, which is along the tangent to the apparent contour, disappears when we take the scalar product with the normal $\mathbf{n}$. Thus $\mathbf{P}_t \cdot \mathbf{n} = \mathbf{p}_t \cdot \mathbf{n}$. Of course, the view direction $\mathbf{k}$ is a function of time t *only*, so that is completely unaffected by reparametrization of the apparent contours.

There is a particular parametrization which is related to the motion itself, called the *epipolar parametrization*. This was first introduced in (Blake and Cipolla 1990). We shall make particular use of this in the perspective case, but we say something about the orthogonal projection case in §4.2 below.

2. Assume that λ is never zero or infinite—that is, assume the image plane never meets the surface and the surface is bounded. Then we have

$$\mathbf{p}_t \cdot \mathbf{n} = 0 \text{ if and only if } \mathbf{k}_t \cdot \mathbf{n} = 0.$$

When these happen, the depth formula becomes indeterminate. We follow this up in some detail in the case of perspective projection in §4.8.

3. Note that in order to recover M using the depth formula we need to know the *world* coordinates of the apparent contour points $\mathbf{p}$, that is we need to know not only the position of the apparent contour in the image plane coordinate system, but also the relationship of this to world coordinates.

4. If the image plane is moved parallel to itself through a distance a then the apparent contour is, as a curve in the image plane, unchanged under orthogonal projection. The effect of this is to replace $\mathbf{p}$ by $\mathbf{p} + a\mathbf{k}$ and hence $\mathbf{p}_t$ by $\mathbf{p}_t + a\mathbf{k}_t + a_t\mathbf{k}$. As $\mathbf{k} \cdot \mathbf{n} = 0$ the depth formula (4.1) now has $-a$ on the right side, so that λ is decreased by a, as we would expect.

It is clear that the parametrization (4.2) can be used to determine the surface M, in particular the Gauss curvature of M, using the formula (2.24). In (Giblin and Weiss 1987), a special coordinate system was set up in the image plane which was rotating about a fixed axis.

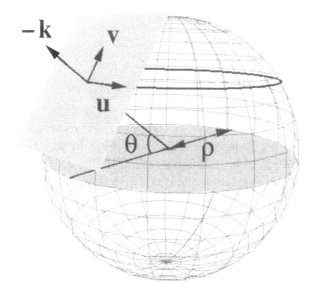

Fig. 4.2 Circular motion and orthogonal projection: the image plane is carried round the axis of rotation, remaining tangent to the sphere of radius ρ at a point with latitude θ.

Example 4.1.1 Circular motion: orthographic projection

We briefly describe an example which is simple enough for most of the calculations to be carried out explicitly. Consider a sphere of radius ρ and a parallel of latitude with angle θ to the horizontal (Figure 4.2). Take a viewplane tangent to the sphere at the point with longitude ϕ, that is, at the point

$$\mathbf{o}(t) = (\rho\cos\theta\cos\phi, \rho\cos\theta\sin\phi, \rho\sin\theta).$$

We take $\theta = $ constant, $\phi = \omega t$, that is the viewplane rotates round the vertical axis with constant angular speed ω. The viewplane does not pass through the origin, but this does not affect calculations materially. (To make it pass through the origin, replace $\mathbf{p}$ by $\mathbf{p} + \rho\mathbf{k}$.) All the view directions

$$\mathbf{k}(t) = (-\cos\theta\cos\phi, -\cos\theta\sin\phi, -\sin\theta), \quad \phi = \omega t$$

'fixate' on the origin of world coordinates, and the 'origin' $\mathbf{o}(t)$ of the viewplane at time t is $-\rho\mathbf{k}(t)$. This is exactly equivalent to an object moving on a rotating turntable with a camera fixating on a point of the axis of rotation.

We take axes in the viewplane, one of which is along the unit tangent vector $\mathbf{u}$ to the parallel of latitude, and the other of which is along the unit vector $\mathbf{v} = \mathbf{u} \wedge \mathbf{k}$:

$$\mathbf{u} = (-\sin\phi, \cos\phi, 0), \quad \mathbf{v} = (-\sin\theta\cos\phi, -\sin\theta\sin\phi, \cos\theta).$$

Thus

$$\mathbf{u}_t = \omega\sin\theta\mathbf{v} + \omega\cos\theta\mathbf{k}, \quad \mathbf{v}_t = -\omega\sin\theta\mathbf{u}, \quad \mathbf{k}_t = -\omega\cos\theta\mathbf{u}.$$

The apparent contours will be expressed as curves

$$\mathbf{p}(s,t) = -\rho\mathbf{k}(t) + a(s,t)\mathbf{u}(t) + b(s,t)\mathbf{v}(t),$$

for functions $a(s,t), b(s,t)$ which give the coordinates of apparent contour points in the viewplane. For simplicity in what follows let us take $b(s,t) = s$ for all s, t: this means that the apparent contours are expressed as graphs $b = b(a,t)$ where the 'b-axis' is along $\mathbf{v}$ and the 'a-axis' is along $\mathbf{u}$. The case where this is *not* possible is when the apparent contour is parallel to the vector $\mathbf{u}$, which happens when $\mathbf{k}_t \cdot \mathbf{n} = 0$, the so-called 'frontier points'. We discuss these in detail in the perspective projection case in §4.8 below.

The (non-unit) normal vector $\tilde{\mathbf{n}}$ then works out as $\tilde{\mathbf{n}} = \mathbf{u} - a_s\mathbf{v}$, and the depth λ as

$$\lambda = \rho + \frac{a_t - \omega\sin\theta(s + aa_s)}{\omega\cos\theta}.$$

The reconstructed surface point is

$$\mathbf{r}(s,t) = \mathbf{p} + \lambda\mathbf{k} = a\mathbf{u} + s\mathbf{v} + \frac{a_t - \omega\sin\theta(s + aa_s)}{\omega\cos\theta}\mathbf{k}.$$

Expressing everything in terms of the moving triad $\mathbf{u}, \mathbf{v}, \mathbf{k}$, it is possible to write down $\mathbf{r}_s, \mathbf{r}_t, \mathbf{r}_{ss}, \mathbf{r}_{st}, \mathbf{r}_{tt}$ explicitly and so calculate the second fundamental form of the surface M relative to the basis $\mathbf{r}_s, \mathbf{r}_t$ of the tangent plane.

Naturally these formulae are rather complicated; for a simplification let us put $\theta = 0$: this is the 'planar motion' originally considered in (Giblin and Weiss 1987). Then, in the notation of (2.5) and (2.14), the variables now being s and t,

$$E = \frac{\omega^2 + \omega^2 a_s^2 + a_{st}^2}{\omega^2}, \quad F = \frac{a_{st}(a\omega^2 + a_{tt})}{\omega^2}, \quad G = \frac{\omega^4 a^2 + 2\omega^2 aa_{tt} + a_{tt}^2}{\omega^2},$$

$$L = \frac{a_{ss}}{\sqrt{1 + a_s^2}}, \quad M = 0, \quad N = -\frac{a_{tt}a\omega^2}{\sqrt{1 + a_s^2}}.$$

From these it follows that the Gauss curvature K is given by

$$K = \frac{\omega^2 a_{ss}}{(\omega^2 a + a_{tt})(1 + a_s^2)^2},$$

a formula equivalent to that in (Giblin and Weiss 1987). □

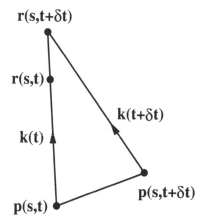

Fig. 4.3 Epipolar matching in the orthogonal projection case. Two surface points $\mathbf{r}(s,t), \mathbf{r}(s, t+\delta t)$, are shown and, for small δt, the visual ray through the first also passes through the second. The plane of the diagram is the epipolar plane.

4.2 Epipolar parametrization: orthogonal case

We shall make particular use of the epipolar parametrization in the case of perspective projection—see §4.4. It is the analogue for continuous motion of the epipolar constraint in stereo vision (described briefly in Chapter 5).

The epipolar parametrization assumes that the vector $\mathbf{r}_t$ (tangent to the curve $s = constant$ on M) is always in the view direction $\mathbf{k}$.

The vectors $\mathbf{r}_s$ (tangent to the contour generator) and $\mathbf{r}_t$ are then always *conjugate,* by Property 3.5.1(i). Successive apparent contours are 'matched' by associating points $\mathbf{p}(s,t)$ and $\mathbf{p}(s, t+\delta t)$, and these are such that the resulting vector $\mathbf{r}_t$ is along the view direction $\mathbf{k}$.

The geometrical significance of this is that the point $\mathbf{r}(s, t+\delta t)$ lies (in the limit as $\delta t \to 0$) both on the visual ray through $\mathbf{p}(s,t)$ in direction $\mathbf{k}(t)$ and on the visual ray through $\mathbf{p}(s, t+\delta t)$ in direction $\mathbf{k}(t+\delta t)$. Thus the points $\mathbf{p}(s,t), \mathbf{p}(s, t+\delta t), \mathbf{r}(s,t), \mathbf{r}(s, t+\delta t)$ are all in a plane: the *epipolar plane*. See Figure 4.3. We give a fuller discussion of the epipolar parametrization in the perspective case, §4.4.

Using

$$\mathbf{r} = \mathbf{p} + \lambda\mathbf{k}, \quad 0 = \mathbf{r}_t \wedge \mathbf{k} = \mathbf{p}_t \wedge \mathbf{k} + \lambda\mathbf{k}_t \wedge \mathbf{k},$$

we obtain

$$(\mathbf{p}_t \wedge \mathbf{k}) \wedge \mathbf{k} = \lambda\mathbf{k}_t.$$

Now taking all the image planes through the origin, so that $\mathbf{p} \cdot \mathbf{k} = 0$, we have $\mathbf{p}_t \cdot \mathbf{k} = -\mathbf{p} \cdot \mathbf{k}_t$ and the last equation then gives

$$\mathbf{p}_t = -\mathbf{k}(\mathbf{p} \cdot \mathbf{k}_t) - \lambda \mathbf{k}_t.$$

This is the 'epipolar matching' of apparent contours, in the case where all image planes pass through the origin.

Remark 4.2.1 Connexion with the envelope construction

The reconstruction of surfaces from apparent contours described above is really a reconstruction of *tangent planes* of surfaces rather than *points*. For the tangent plane to M is recovered directly from the apparent contour as the plane spanned by the tangent line $\mathbf{p}_s$ to the apparent contour and the visual ray in direction $\mathbf{k}$ starting at $\mathbf{p}$. Thus the recovery of points is best seen as a consequence of the recovery of tangent planes (a recovery of the 'dual' of M).

We can regard this recovery of M by its tangent planes as a two-stage process. First we fix t and consider a single apparent contour γ. For each tangent line to γ at $\mathbf{p}$ we obtain a tangent plane to M as the span of this tangent line and the line through $\mathbf{p}$ in direction $\mathbf{k}$ (which is now fixed). These planes are all tangent to a *cylinder* whose base is γ and whose straight line generators are all in the direction $\mathbf{k}$. The second stage is to allow t to vary, so that these cylinders move in space to envelop the surface M.

A parametrization of the cylinder is (for fixed t)

$$\mathbf{R}(s, u, t) = \mathbf{p}(s, t) + u\mathbf{k}(t).$$

The rule for forming envelopes of a family of surfaces which are parametrized is this: The envelope points corresponding to a particular t (the 'characteristic points') are given by the condition that

$\mathbf{R}_t = \mathbf{p}_t + u\mathbf{k}_t$ is a linear combination of $\mathbf{R}_s = \mathbf{p}_s$ and $\mathbf{R}_u = \mathbf{k}$.

Thus defining $\tilde{\mathbf{n}} = \mathbf{p}_s \wedge \mathbf{k}$ we find that $(\mathbf{p}_t + u\mathbf{k}_t) \cdot \tilde{\mathbf{n}} = 0$, giving for u the same value as λ in (4.1): the envelope point along the ray from $\mathbf{p}(s, t)$ parallel to $\mathbf{k}$ is the point previously constructed as belonging to M.

Thus the 'envelope of cylinders' construction gives the same points as the depth formula (4.1).

4.3 Perspective projection

We now derive the formulae for the case of perspective projection with a calibrated camera and rotated coordinates. (In Chapters 5 and 6 we also consider the uncalibrated case.) We start with (3.3), which related the points of a single apparent contour with the points of the corresponding contour generator. This equation now holds for each value of t, so that it becomes

$$\mathbf{r}(s, t) = \mathbf{c}(t) + \lambda(s, t)\mathbf{p}(s, t). \tag{4.3}$$

Dropping the variables s, t from the notation,

$$\mathbf{r}_s = \lambda_s \mathbf{p} + \lambda \mathbf{p}_s, \quad \mathbf{r}_t = \mathbf{c}_t + \lambda_t \mathbf{p} + \lambda \mathbf{p}_t. \tag{4.4}$$

Recall from Property 3.6.1 that the unit normal $\mathbf{n}$ to M is parallel to the vector $\mathbf{p} \wedge \mathbf{p}_s$, this vector being nonzero provided the apparent contours are nonsingular, so that $\mathbf{p}_s$ is nonzero.

We therefore have

$$0 = \mathbf{r}_t \cdot \mathbf{n} = (\mathbf{c}_t + \lambda_t \mathbf{p} + \lambda \mathbf{p}_t) \cdot \mathbf{n} = \mathbf{c}_t \cdot \mathbf{n} + \lambda \mathbf{p}_t \cdot \mathbf{n}.$$

This implies that (assuming λ is never zero or infinite) $\mathbf{c}_t \cdot \mathbf{n} = 0$ if and only if $\mathbf{p}_t \cdot \mathbf{n} = 0$, and when neither is zero the depth λ is given by

$$\lambda = -\frac{\mathbf{c}_t \cdot \mathbf{n}}{\mathbf{p}_t \cdot \mathbf{n}}, \quad \text{so} \quad \mathbf{r} = \mathbf{c} - \frac{\mathbf{c}_t \cdot \mathbf{n}}{\mathbf{p}_t \cdot \mathbf{n}} \mathbf{p}. \tag{4.5}$$

Thus the surface points $\mathbf{r}(s, t)$ are determined by the apparent contours $\mathbf{p}(s, t)$ and the camera centres $\mathbf{c}(t)$, at any rate away from 'frontier' points where $\mathbf{c}_t \cdot \mathbf{n} = 0$ and assuming that the apparent contours are nonsingular. (We discuss these exceptional cases in §4.6 and §4.8.)

Note that the apparent contours lie in the various image spheres, centred at $\mathbf{c}(t)$, and to use (4.5) we need the coordinates of the vectors $\mathbf{p}(s, t)$ joining $\mathbf{c}(t)$ to the apparent contour points in some fixed world coordinate system. In practice the camera, which we think of as a unit sphere centred at $\mathbf{c}(t)$, will have its own coordinate system which is rotated with respect to the world coordinates. We express this by saying

$$\mathbf{p}(s, t) = R(t)\mathbf{q}(s, t), \tag{4.6}$$

where R is a rotation. When we use '$\mathbf{q}$ coordinates' we are assuming that the camera model is a *calibrated camera*, that is the relationship between internal $\mathbf{q}$ coordinates and world $\mathbf{p}$ coordinates is known. In Chapter 6 we discuss, in a special case, the recovery of camera *motion* from apparent contours.

If R is actually constant then we say that the camera is undergoing *pure translation*. If in addition the path of the camera is a straight line then we describe this as *linear motion* of the camera. Both these situations will arise in Chapters 5 and 6.

We pause here to consider the exact meaning of (4.6). Let $\mathbf{e}_1, \mathbf{e}_2, \mathbf{e}_3$ be the world coordinates basis in 3-space, which we take to be an orthonormal triad, that is all $\mathbf{e}_i$ are unit vectors and mutually orthogonal. Let $\mathbf{p} = p_1 \mathbf{e}_1 + p_2 \mathbf{e}_2 + p_3 \mathbf{e}_3$ be a point in 3-space. We want to write down the point $\mathbf{p}$ but relative to a rotated coordinate frame, namely the vectors $R\mathbf{e}_1, R\mathbf{e}_2, R\mathbf{e}_3$

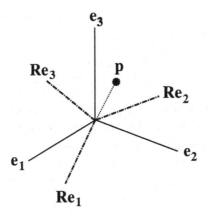

Fig. 4.4 World coordinates and a coordinate system obtained from them by a rotation R.

where R is a rotation of 3-space. See Figure 4.4. Let the coordinates of $\mathbf{p}$ relative to this rotated coordinate system be q_1, q_2, q_3. Thus

$$\mathbf{p} = q_1 R\mathbf{e}_1 + q_2 R\mathbf{e}_2 + q_3 R\mathbf{e}_3 = R(q_1\mathbf{e}_1 + q_2\mathbf{e}_2 + q_3\mathbf{e}_3).$$

Thus, defining

$$\mathbf{q} = q_1\mathbf{e}_1 + q_2\mathbf{e}_2 + q_3\mathbf{e}_3,$$

we have $\mathbf{p} = R\mathbf{q}$. Hence:

the coordinates q_1, q_2, q_3 are those of the world point $\mathbf{p}$ relative to the rotated coordinate system $R\mathbf{e}_1, R\mathbf{e}_2, R\mathbf{e}_3$, and they are related to the coordinates p_1, p_2, p_3 of $\mathbf{p}$ relative to the world coordinate system $\mathbf{e}_1, \mathbf{e}_2, \mathbf{e}_3$ by

$$\begin{bmatrix} p_1 \\ p_2 \\ p_3 \end{bmatrix} = \begin{bmatrix} \text{Matrix of rotation} \\ R \text{ relative to} \\ \text{world coordinates} \end{bmatrix} \begin{bmatrix} q_1 \\ q_2 \\ q_3 \end{bmatrix}. \tag{4.7}$$

Example 4.3.1 Circular motion: perspective projection

As a simple example of the foregoing, consider the case of a camera centre $\mathbf{c}(t)$ rotating at constant angular speed ω around the z-axis in world coordinates, at a 'latitude' θ (Figure 4.5), so that

$$\mathbf{c}(t) = \rho(\cos\theta\cos\omega t, \cos\theta\sin\omega t, \sin\theta).$$

(Compare Example 4.1.1.) We take the camera coordinate axes to be, at $t = 0$, $R_0\mathbf{e}_1, R_0\mathbf{e}_2, R_0\mathbf{e}_3$ where $\mathbf{e}_1 = (1,0,0)$ etc. and R_0 is some initial rotation, for example a rotation about the $\mathbf{e}_2$ axis through θ to make the rotated $\mathbf{e}_1$ axis pass through the origin. Thereafter the camera axes rotate rigidly with the camera, that is

$$R(t) = S(t)R_0,$$

where $S(t)$ is rotation about the z-axis through ωt.

This situation is essentially the same as keeping the *camera* fixed and rotating the *surface* about an axis. In fact when we implement circular motion in Chapter 6 we do use a fixed camera.

Let A be the matrix of R_0 relative to world coordinates. Then the matrix of R^{-1} relative to world coordinates is

$$A^{-1}S(t)^{-1} = A^{-1} \begin{bmatrix} \cos\omega t & \sin\omega t & 0 \\ -\sin\omega t & \cos\omega t & 0 \\ 0 & 0 & 1 \end{bmatrix},$$

and from (4.7) we obtain the 'q-coordinates' of a vector by multiplying the 'p-coordinates' by this matrix. For example, if $R_0 = $ identity and $\mathbf{p}$ is the tangent vector to the circle of latitude along which $\mathbf{c}$ moves, namely

$$\mathbf{p} = (-\sin\omega t, \cos\omega t, 0),$$

then this point has 'q-coordinates' $(0, 1, 0)$, which (an obvious fact) is constant in the moving coordinate frame. $\square$

We return now to the general case. Differentiating (4.6) with respect to t gives (omitting the variables now)[1]

$$\mathbf{p}_t = R\mathbf{q}_t + \Omega \wedge R\mathbf{q}, \tag{4.8}$$

where Ω is a vector whose direction is that of the instantaneous axis of rotation for R at time t and whose magnitude is the angular speed of R. Sometimes we assume that, for $t = 0$, we have $R(0) = $ identity; then at $t = 0$ the above equation reads $\mathbf{p}_t = \mathbf{q}_t + \Omega \wedge \mathbf{q}$.

Example 4.3.2 Case of constant rotation about z-axis

As a simple example, let $R(t)$ be rotation about the z-axis through an angle ωt where ω is a constant. The matrix for this rotation, relative to standard coordinates in $\mathbf{R}^3$, is

$$\begin{bmatrix} \cos\omega t & -\sin\omega t & 0 \\ \sin\omega t & \cos\omega t & 0 \\ 0 & 0 & 1 \end{bmatrix}.$$

---

[1] This is a standard result of kinematics, and is proved in books on mechanics, e.g. under the heading 'infinitesimal rotations'. The calculation in Example 4.3.2 essentially covers the general case.

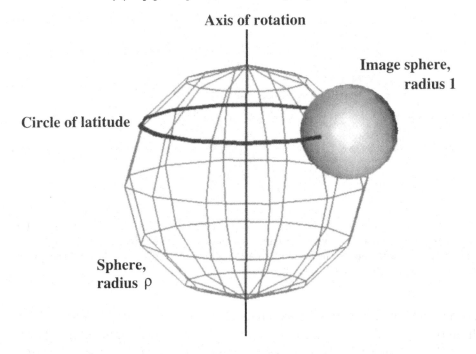

Axis of rotation

Image sphere, radius 1

Circle of latitude

Sphere, radius ρ

Fig. 4.5 Circular motion, the perspective case. Here the camera centre moves on a circle of latitude of a sphere radius ρ, carrying with it an image sphere with a $\mathbf{q}$ coordinate system which rotates around the (vertical) axis.

Thus writing $\mathbf{q} = (q_1, q_2, q_3)$,

$$R\mathbf{q} = \begin{bmatrix} q_1 \cos \omega t - q_2 \sin \omega t \\ q_1 \sin \omega t + q_2 \cos \omega t \\ q_3 \end{bmatrix}.$$

By direct differentiation,

$$\frac{d}{dt} R\mathbf{q} = R\frac{d}{dt}\mathbf{q} + \omega \begin{bmatrix} -q_1 \sin \omega t - q_2 \cos \omega t \\ q_1 \cos \omega t - q_2 \sin \omega t \\ 0 \end{bmatrix}$$

$$= R\frac{d}{dt}\mathbf{q} + (0, 0, \omega)^\top \wedge R\mathbf{q},$$

so that here $\Omega = (0, 0, \omega)^\top$. □

4.4 Epipolar parametrization: perspective case

The epipolar parametrization is a special parametrization of contour generators and apparent contours which leads to simplified formulae for recon-

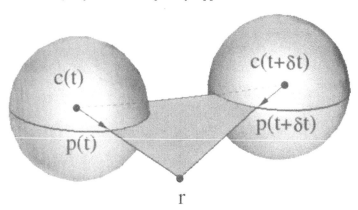

Fig. 4.6 Viewing a single point $\mathbf{r}$ from two positions $\mathbf{c}(t)$ and $\mathbf{c}(t+\delta t)$, the epipolar plane spans the base line between camera centres and the visual ray through $\mathbf{c}(t)$ and $\mathbf{r}$. This plane meets the second image sphere in a great circle and the point $\mathbf{c}(t+\delta t) + \mathbf{p}(t+\delta t)$ must lie on this circle.

struction. The idea comes from stereo vision. If we look at the *same* point $\mathbf{r}$ from two viewpoints $\mathbf{c}(t)$ and $\mathbf{c}(t+\delta t)$ then the plane containing $\mathbf{c}(t), \mathbf{c}(t+\delta t)$ and $\mathbf{r}$ is an *epipolar plane*. If we know only $\mathbf{c}(t), \mathbf{c}(t+\delta t)$ and the image $\mathbf{p}(t)$ of $\mathbf{r}$ in the first view, then we still know the epipolar plane, since $\mathbf{c}(t), \mathbf{r}$ and $\mathbf{c}(t) + \mathbf{p}(t)$ are in a straight line, and we also know that the image of $\mathbf{r}$ in the second view must be on the great circle where the epipolar plane meets the image sphere centred at $\mathbf{c}(t+\delta t)$. See Figure 4.6.

There is no exact analogy of this in the context of contour generators and apparent contours, since we do not any longer see the same point of a contour generator in two successive views—unless the contour generators meet on the surface, a case we look at in §4.8. But there is a very suggestive analogy, as follows.

In Figure 4.7, top, we show a sequence of visual rays from camera centres

$$\mathbf{c}(t - \delta t), \mathbf{c}(t), \mathbf{c}(t + \delta t),$$

each of which is *nearly* tangent to the surface, i.e., meets the surface in two *nearby* points. Each visual ray determines the next: join the next camera centre to the second point of intersection of the current ray with the surface. Any two consecutive visual rays, for example those through $\mathbf{c}(t)$ and $\mathbf{c}(t+\delta t)$, are then coplanar (since they intersect). The plane containing these two rays is analogous to the epipolar plane in the point case above.

As the visual rays become more nearly tangent to the surface, they become tangent to a curve on the surface which is called an *epipolar curve*. The tangents to the epipolar curve are thus always along visual rays. This is

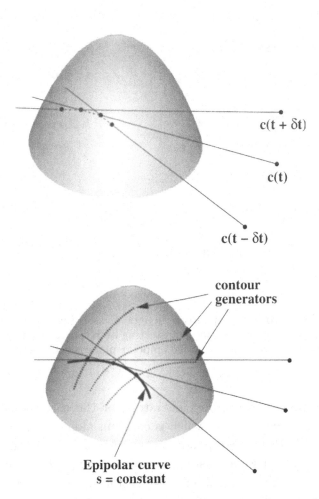

Fig. 4.7 Top: several visual rays almost tangent to the surface, with each ray determining the next. Bottom: what happens when the visual rays become tangent to the surface. They are tangent to a curve on the surface called the epipolar curve. This crosses the contour generators on the surface. Epipolar curves and contour generators generally provide a coordinate grid on the surface.

illustrated in Figure 4.7, bottom. Epipolar curves are studied in detail in (Giblin and Weiss 1995). The *epipolar planes* in this 'continuous' situation are spanned by a visual ray and the base line joining two 'infinitely close' camera centres, that is by a visual ray and the tangent line $c_t(t)$ to the path of centres. Thus

The normal to the epipolar plane is $c_t \wedge p$.

If c_t is parallel to p, that is, if the camera motion is instantaneously towards the surface point r, then *the epipolar plane is indeterminate.*

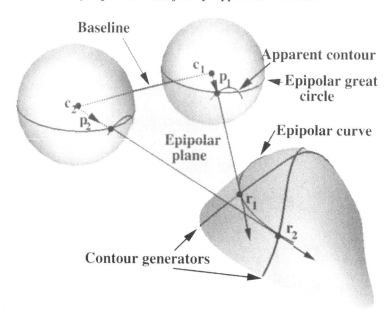

Fig. 4.8 A surface, two image spheres (thought of as being very close together) and the corresponding epipolar plane, intersecting each sphere in an 'epipolar great circle'. When image *planes* are used, the epipolar plane meets each of these in an epipolar *line*.

When we parametrize contour generators, or the corresponding apparent contours, by a parameter s which is constant along the epipolar curves in the surface (or their corresponding images in the image sphere or image plane) we say that we are using the *epipolar parametrization*. Thus the surface is parametrized $\mathbf{r}(s,t)$ where $t = $ constant gives the contour generators, and $s = $ constant gives the epipolar curves. The apparent contours are parametrized $\mathbf{p}(s,t)$, where each apparent contour is given by $t = $ constant. We then have

For the epipolar parametrization $\mathbf{r}_t(s,t)$ is parallel to $\mathbf{p}(s,t)$ (4.9)

for all values of s,t.

Figure 4.8 is another illustration of this situation. The baseline here is drawn as finite, but we are to imagine that the two image spheres are very close together, the two visual rays being tangent to an epipolar curve and spanning an epipolar plane. This plane meets each sphere in an 'epipolar great circle'. The points $\mathbf{p}_1, \mathbf{p}_2$ where the visual rays meet this circle are points of apparent contours in 'epipolar correspondence', and will have the same s parameter value when the epipolar parametrization is used. The same goes for the corresponding surface points $\mathbf{r}_1, \mathbf{r}_2$.

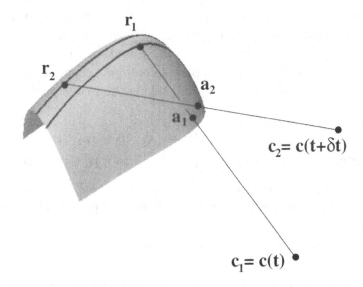

Fig. 4.9 Two visual rays have their closest points at $\mathbf{a}_1, \mathbf{a}_2$, which may not be near the corresponding surface points. However, for the epipolar parametrization the closest points do approach the surface point $\mathbf{r}_1$ as $\delta t \to 0$.

Remark 4.4.1 Geometry of the visual rays

1. Suppose we take two visual rays, from centres $\mathbf{c}_1 = \mathbf{c}(t)$ and $\mathbf{c}_2 = \mathbf{c}(t + \delta t)$ to two points $\mathbf{r}_1, \mathbf{r}_2$ of the corresponding contour generators. These visual rays, being straight lines in 3-space, will not in general intersect, but there will be points $\mathbf{a}_1, \mathbf{a}_2$ say on the two rays where they come as close together as possible. See Figure 4.9. (Thus $\mathbf{a}_1, \mathbf{a}_2$ are the feet of the common perpendicular to the two rays.) When $\delta t \to 0$ the point $\mathbf{a}_1$ on the first visual ray will approach some limiting position, which *may not be the surface point* $\mathbf{r}_1$. But there are two cases where $\mathbf{a}_1$ does approach $\mathbf{r}_1$. One of these is when the vector joining $\mathbf{r}_1$ and $\mathbf{r}_2$ approaches the direction of the visual ray from $\mathbf{c}(t)$ to $\mathbf{r}_1$. This will happen automatically when the rays come from an epipolar parametrization $\mathbf{p}(s, t), \mathbf{r}(s, t)$ and have the same value of s, for that says precisely that $\mathbf{r}_t$ is parallel to the visual ray. (The other case is that of a 'normal parametrization' where $\mathbf{p}_t$ is parallel to $\mathbf{n}$.) For details, see (Giblin and Weiss 1995).

2. Taking the epipolar parametrization, the family of visual rays tangent to an epipolar curve on M, that is the family of rays joining $\mathbf{c}(t)$ to $\mathbf{r}(s, t)$ for a fixed s, forms a *developable surface*, in fact the envelope of the epipolar planes. For a general parametrization $\mathbf{r}(s, t)$, the rays joining $\mathbf{c}(t)$ to $\mathbf{r}(s, t)$ for a fixed s form a developable surface provided $\mathbf{p}, \mathbf{p}_t$ and $\mathbf{c}_t$ are coplanar for all s, t, and the surface is the envelope of these planes. So we are saying that a sufficient condition for this to happen is that $\mathbf{r}_t$ is always parallel to $\mathbf{p}$.

Notice that, in order for (4.9) to be possible, it is crucial that $\mathbf{p}$ is *not* along the direction $\mathbf{r}_s$, that is not along the tangent to the contour generator. For otherwise we should have $\mathbf{r}_s$ and $\mathbf{r}_t$ parallel, which is not allowed for a parametrization of a surface (compare §2.2). This and other degeneracies of the epipolar parametrization are discussed below, starting in §4.6.

When the epipolar parametrization (4.9) is used, many of the formulae for deriving surface geometry from apparent contours become much simpler. Differentiating (4.3) with respect to t and taking the wedge product with $\mathbf{p}$ we get

$$0 = \mathbf{c}_t \wedge \mathbf{p} + \lambda \mathbf{p}_t \wedge \mathbf{p},$$

so $\mathbf{p}(\mathbf{c}_t \cdot \mathbf{p}) - \mathbf{c}_t = (\mathbf{c}_t \wedge \mathbf{p}) \wedge \mathbf{p} = -\lambda(\mathbf{p}_t \wedge \mathbf{p}) \wedge \mathbf{p} = \lambda \mathbf{p}_t.$

This tells us that $\mathbf{c}_t, \mathbf{p}$ and $\mathbf{p}_t$ are coplanar—their plane is the epipolar plane—and gives an explicit formula for $\mathbf{p}_t$ in terms of $\mathbf{p}$, the camera velocity $\mathbf{c}_t$, and λ, namely

$$\mathbf{p}_t = \frac{(\mathbf{c}_t \wedge \mathbf{p}) \wedge \mathbf{p}}{\lambda}. \tag{4.10}$$

Note that the same calculation for the image motion of a point $\mathbf{r}$ which is *fixed* in world coordinates shows that the image velocity is given by the same formula. Thus image velocity does not depend on surface characteristics.

In 'rotated' coordinates $\mathbf{p} = R\mathbf{q}$, using (4.8), (4.10) and the fact that $R(\mathbf{a} \wedge \mathbf{b}) = R(\mathbf{a}) \wedge R(\mathbf{b})$ for vectors $\mathbf{a}, \mathbf{b}$ and rotation R, we get

$$(R^{-1}\mathbf{c}_t \wedge \mathbf{q}) \wedge \mathbf{q} = \lambda(\mathbf{q}_t + R^{-1}\Omega \wedge \mathbf{q}),$$

$$\text{so that } \mathbf{q}_t = \frac{(R^{-1}\mathbf{c}_t \wedge \mathbf{q}) \wedge \mathbf{q}}{\lambda} - R^{-1}\Omega \wedge \mathbf{q}.$$

When we take $R =$ identity at $t = 0$ then the occurrences of R^{-1} can be suppressed in this formula at $t = 0$. As above, this $\mathbf{q}_t$ is also the image velocity of a point which is fixed in world coordinates.

4.5 Surface curvatures using the epipolar parametrization

We show briefly how formulae for surface characteristics become simpler when the epipolar parametrization is used. See also (Cipolla 1991 and 1995, Cipolla and Blake 1992).

Since $\mathbf{r}_t$ is parallel to $\mathbf{p}$, and $\mathbf{p}$ is a unit vector, we have

$$\mathbf{r}_t = (\mathbf{r}_t \cdot \mathbf{p})\mathbf{p} = (\mathbf{c}_t \cdot \mathbf{p} + \lambda_t)\mathbf{p},$$

using (4.4). Differentiating again, we can find $\mathbf{r}_{tt}$; in particular since $\mathbf{p} \cdot \mathbf{n} = 0$ we have

$$\mathbf{r}_{tt} \cdot \mathbf{n} = (\mathbf{c}_t \cdot \mathbf{p} + \lambda_t)(\mathbf{p}_t \cdot \mathbf{n}).$$

We can apply the standard formula (2.21) (replacing u there by t) to derive the *transverse curvature* κ^t, that is the sectional curvature of M in the direction of the visual ray $\mathbf{p}$:

$$\kappa^t = \frac{\mathbf{r}_{tt} \cdot \mathbf{n}}{\mathbf{r}_t \cdot \mathbf{r}_t} = \frac{\mathbf{p}_t \cdot \mathbf{n}}{\mathbf{c}_t \cdot \mathbf{p} + \lambda_t} = -\frac{\mathbf{c}_t \cdot \mathbf{n}}{\lambda(\mathbf{c}_t \cdot \mathbf{p} + \lambda_t)},$$

the last equality following from the depth formula (4.5).

The curvature κ^s of M in the direction of the contour generator Γ does not depend on dynamic considerations, and the formula was proved in Chapter 3 (Properties 3.5.3 for orthogonal projection and 3.6.3 for perspective projection). In the latter case we have

$$\kappa^s = \frac{\kappa^p \sin^2 \theta}{\lambda},$$

where θ is the angle between the visual ray and the contour generator. The formula for $\cos^2 \theta$ in the proof (§3.11) of Property 3.6.3 implies that

$$\tan \theta = \pm \frac{\lambda \|\mathbf{p}_s\|}{\lambda_s}.$$

We can obtain the Gauss curvature of M as follows. The directions $\mathbf{r}_s, \mathbf{r}_t$ are conjugate for the epipolar parametrization (Property 3.6.1 and (4.9)), so that the matrix of the second fundamental form relative to these vectors is diagonal (Property 2.8.4). Indeed if we take *unit* vectors in the two directions as our basis then the matrices of I and II become

$$\mathrm{I}: \begin{bmatrix} 1 & \cos\theta \\ \cos\theta & 1 \end{bmatrix} \qquad \mathrm{II}: \begin{bmatrix} \kappa^s & 0 \\ 0 & \kappa^t \end{bmatrix}$$

Thus the Gauss curvature K is given by (2.24)

$$K = \frac{\kappa^s \kappa^t}{\sin^2 \theta}. \tag{4.11}$$

Note that in order to calculate K we shall need to calculate *second* partial derivatives of $\mathbf{p}$ with respect to space s and time t.

4.6 Degeneracies of the epipolar parametrization

It was noted in §4.4 that it is not always possible to set up the epipolar parametrization $\mathbf{r}(s, t)$ of M. There are various ways in which failure can occur:

(i) *The vector $\mathbf{r}_s$ can be parallel to $\mathbf{p}$*, in which case we cannot require that $\mathbf{r}_t$ is also parallel to $\mathbf{p}$ since for a valid parametrization $\mathbf{r}(s, t)$ we must have $\mathbf{r}_s, \mathbf{r}_t$ independent. This is the case of a *cusp on the apparent contour*, or, more degenerately, a 'swallowtail'. Cusps on apparent contours—or contour endings, as they are for opaque surfaces—are stable phenomena: they persist under observer movement. We have already met them in Examples 3.5.5(i), 3.6.5(i); see Figures 3.7 and 3.10. See also Properties 3.5.2(i) and 3.6.2(i). We analyse the *movement* of cusps in §4.9. The swallowtail phenomenon is described in §4.7.

(ii) The contour generators can be smooth curves but fail to form part of a coordinate grid at all on M. This is what happens along the *frontier*; see §4.8.

(iii) The contour generators can be *singular curves* on M. This happens at a 'lips' or 'beaks' point; see §4.7 and recall Properties 3.5.2(ii), 3.6.2, and Examples 3.5.5(ii), 3.6.5(ii).

(iv) We note that another degeneracy of a slightly different kind occurs if we are in fact viewing a *space curve* rather than a surface. In that case we have $\mathbf{r}_s$ parallel to $\mathbf{r}_t$ for all s and t.

4.7 Visual events: swallowtail, lips and beaks

The condition for a cusp on an apparent contour at $\mathbf{p}$ is that the visual ray should be asymptotic at the corresponding surface point $\mathbf{r}$ (Property 3.5.2(i) for orthogonal projection and Property 3.6.2(i) for perspective projection). This means that the visual ray has 3-point contact with the surface at $\mathbf{r}$; compare §2.13. It can happen as the camera centre moves in space that the contact of the visual ray at a point of the contour generator can increase from 3 to 4. This happens when the ray is in an asymptotic direction at a *flecnodal* point of M (Property 2.13.1). The flecnodal rays form a ruled surface, the flecnodal scroll (again, see §2.13), and when the camera centre crosses this ruled surface there will be a visual ray with 4-point contact with M. What happens on the apparent contour during the transit through the flecnodal scroll is called a *swallowtail transition* and is illustrated in Figure 4.10.

The other visual events which occur as the camera centre moves along a trajectory in space are the 'lips' and 'beaks' events already mentioned in Properties 3.5.2(ii) and 3.6.2(ii). When one of these happens, the contour generator itself becomes singular—a pair of crossing curves for a beaks and an isolated point for a lips. The asymptotic lines at all the parabolic points of M form a surface in space (sometimes called the *cylinder axis developable*),

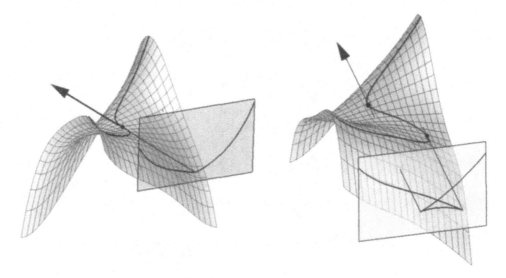

Fig. 4.10 A swallowtail transition on apparent contours, which occurs when the camera centre crosses the flecnodal scroll, i.e. where there is a visual ray with 4-point contact with M. The moment of crossing is shown in the left-hand figure and a nearby position of the camera centre, where the swallowtail has 'opened out' into two cusps and a crossing, in the right-hand figure.

and as the camera centre crosses this surface there is a lips or beaks transition on the apparent contours.

These are illustrated in Figures 4.11 and 4.12.

4.8 Frontiers (epipolar tangencies)

It can happen that the contour generators do not form part of a coordinate grid on M no matter how they are parametrized. In that case we cannot 'use t and another parameter' to parametrize the surface M. To see how this occurs, it is best to 'step back' and to suppose that we have a surface M which is parametrized, at any rate locally, by two parameters u, v: the surface is given by $\mathbf{r}(u, v)$. We are also given the curve of camera centres $\mathbf{c}(t)$ which produces contour generators $\Gamma(t)$, corresponding to the various time instants. Using the normal $\mathbf{n}(u, v)$ the condition for $\mathbf{r}(u, v)$ to be on $\Gamma(t)$ is

$$(\mathbf{r}(u, v) - \mathbf{c}(t)) \cdot \mathbf{n}(u, v) = 0. \tag{4.12}$$

This is one equation in three unknowns u, v, t. We want to know the following.

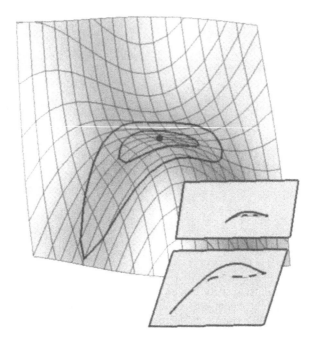

Fig. 4.11 A lips transition on apparent contours, when the camera centre crosses the cylinder axis developable. Two contour generators are shown, from different camera centres, and the corresponding apparent contours are drawn in image planes. Dashed parts are invisible for an opaque surface. The dot on the surface is a third, singular contour generator. The corresponding apparent contour (not shown) is also a dot, and further movement of the camera centre causes the apparent contour to vanish.

Question. When is it possible to use t and say u as local coordinates on M? That is, when can we effect an allowable change of coordinates in the parameter plane of M from (u, v) to (u, t)?

This is of course a purely mathematical question, and the purely mathematical answer, using the implicit function theorem, is:

Answer. Provided the partial derivatives of the left-hand side of (4.12) with respect to v and t are *both* nonzero.

We follow up this answer before giving a more geometrical way of thinking of the question. See (Giblin and Weiss 1995, p. 43) for a proof of the correctness of the answer.

The partial derivatives in question (or rather in answer) are

$$\frac{\partial}{\partial v}: \mathbf{r}_v \cdot \mathbf{n} + (\mathbf{r} - \mathbf{c}) \cdot \mathbf{n}_v = (\mathbf{r} - \mathbf{c}) \cdot \mathbf{n}_v; \quad \frac{\partial}{\partial t}: -\mathbf{c}_t \cdot \mathbf{n}.$$

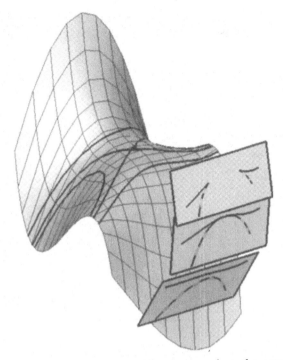

Fig. 4.12 A beaks transition on apparent contours, when the camera centre crosses the cylinder axis developable. Three contour generators are shown, one of them singular (a crossing), and the corresponding apparent contours in three image planes. Dashed parts are invisible for an opaque surface.

We use here the fact that $\mathbf{r}_v$ is tangent to M and hence perpendicular to $\mathbf{n}$. Now $\mathbf{n}_v$ is the derivative of the unit surface normal along the direction of $\mathbf{r}_v$, that is in the direction of the curve $u = $ constant on the surface M. We know that $\mathbf{n}_v$ is perpendicular to the conjugate to the tangent vector $\mathbf{r}_v$ (Property 2.8.3(i)). So $(\mathbf{r} - \mathbf{c}) \cdot \mathbf{n}_v = 0$ if and only if $\mathbf{r} - \mathbf{c}$ and $\mathbf{r}_v$ are conjugate directions. But the visual ray $\mathbf{r} - \mathbf{c}$ is conjugate to the tangent to the contour generator (Property 3.6.1) so the partial derivative above with respect to v is nonzero if and only if $\mathbf{r}_v$ (in the direction $u = $ constant) is not tangent to the contour generator (in the direction $t = $ constant). It is hardly surprising that this is required for u, t to be local coordinates on M since coordinate curves cannot be tangent to one another. Notice that we have assumed that the contour generator is smooth (and so has a tangent). Thus we must avoid the lips/beaks situation described in §4.7.

We concentrate on the other condition, $\mathbf{c}_t \cdot \mathbf{n} \neq 0$. It says that the direction of travel of the camera centre is not in the tangent plane to M at the corresponding surface point $\mathbf{r}$. In terms of the definition of epipolar plane in

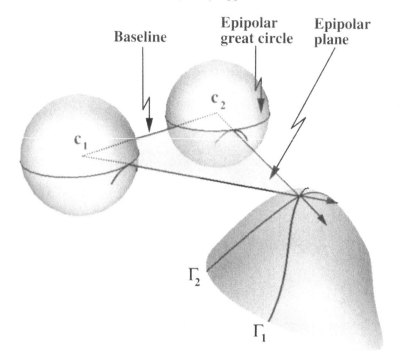

Fig. 4.13 An epipolar tangency with camera centres separated by a finite distance. The epipolar tangency of the text is the limiting case, which corresponds with c_1 and c_2 tending to coincidence. The intersection of Γ_1 and Γ_2 then becomes an envelope point of the contour generators.

§4.4 (plane spanned by c_t and the visual ray $r - c$) the condition is simply that the epipolar plane at time t corresponding to the surface point r is not the tangent plane to M at r. (This assumes that the epipolar plane is *defined*, i.e. that c_t is not parallel to $r - c$.) Thus:

to use t as one local parameter on M we must avoid the epipolar tangencies given by $c_t \cdot n = 0$.

Figure 4.13 shows an epipolar tangency where the camera centres are separated by a finite distance. The epipolar tangency signalled by $c_t \cdot n = 0$ is the limiting case of this as the centres c_1, c_2 tend to coincidence.

There are several other ways of looking at the condition $c_t \cdot n = 0$. One is to treat (4.12) as the equation of a surface in u, v, t-space. As such, it is called the *spatio-temporal surface $\widetilde{M}$*: geometrically $\widetilde{M}$ is obtained by taking the contour generators as curves in the (u, v) parameter space of M and 'spreading them out' in the t-direction. See Figures 4.14 and 4.16. The

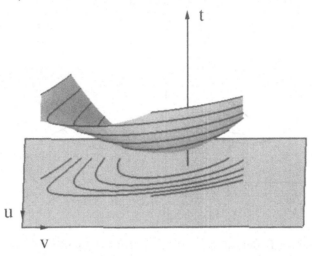

Fig. 4.14 The plane at the bottom is the u, v-parameter plane for a surface M. On this are drawn some contour generators as they appear in the parameter plane. Above is the spatio-temporal surface $\widetilde{M}$, formed by raising the contour generator for time t to a height t.

condition $\mathbf{c}_t \cdot \mathbf{n} = 0$ then becomes simply the condition for the tangent plane to $\widetilde{M}$ to be 'vertical', that is in the t-direction.[1]

Yet another way of interpreting the condition $\mathbf{c}_t \cdot \mathbf{n} = 0$ is to consider the family of curves on M given by the contour generators $\Gamma(t)$. Working in the (u, v) parameter space, the equation (4.12) gives us this family, one curve for each t. To obtain the picture in M itself we then need to carry each curve in parameter space to M by means of the parametrization $\mathbf{r}$. We can form the *envelope* of the family in u, v-space by solving (4.12) simultaneously with the derivative with respect to t:

$$0 = \frac{\partial}{\partial t}(\mathbf{r} - \mathbf{c}) \cdot \mathbf{n} = -\mathbf{c}_t \cdot \mathbf{n}.$$

(This is the general procedure for forming envelopes; see for example (Bruce and Giblin 1992, Ch. 4).) Taking the curves onto M by means of $\mathbf{r}$ means that the $\mathbf{c}_t \cdot \mathbf{n} = 0$ points are just those on the *envelope of contour generators*. See Figures 4.15 and 4.16. It is clear that when contour generators form an envelope in this way they cannot be used as one system of coordinate curves on M, for they cannot form part of a 'grid' on M.

Following this general discussion, we proceed to summarize the various

---

[1] Thus the $\mathbf{c}_t \cdot \mathbf{n} = 0$ curve, which arises in the study of apparent contours, is also closely connected with the apparent contour of the surface $\widetilde{M}$ under orthogonal projection to the u, v-plane.

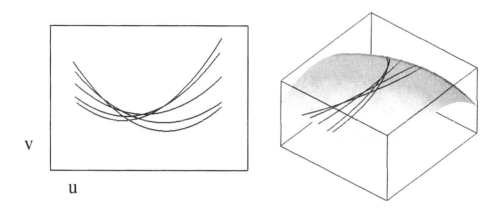

Fig. 4.15 Envelope of contour generators (left) in the parameter plane of M and (right) on M itself. The frontier points on M are envelope points where two 'very nearby' contour generators meet.

interpretations of frontier points. The proof that they are all equivalent is given at the end of this section.

Suppose that we use the coordinate system which is unrotated with respect to world coordinates. Suppose that a smooth surface M with local parametrization $\mathbf{r}(u, v)$, and a camera motion $\mathbf{c}(t)$, give a family of smooth contour generators on M and a family of smooth apparent contours in the image sphere.

Let $\mathbf{p}(s, t)$ be a parametrization of the apparent contours, that is s is a regular parameter on each apparent contour $t = $ constant. The corresponding surface point $\mathbf{r}$ to $\mathbf{p}(s, t)$ will have parameters $u = U(s, t)$, $v = V(s, t)$ say. It is important to note that $(s, t) \rightarrow (u, v)$ may not be a valid change of parameters on M: as above, at frontier points, t is not a valid parameter on M. To emphasize this, we write $\mathbf{R}(s, t) = \mathbf{r}(U(s, t), V(s, t))$, recognizing that $\mathbf{R}$ will not be a local parametrization near the frontier. For a suitable depth function λ, we have

$$\mathbf{R}(s, t) := \mathbf{r}(U(s, t), V(s, t)) = \mathbf{c}(t) + \lambda(s, t)\mathbf{p}(s, t). \qquad (4.13)$$

As usual, we use $\mathbf{n}$ for the unit surface normal parallel to $\mathbf{p} \wedge \mathbf{p}_s$ (strictly, $\mathbf{n}(s, t) = \mathbf{n}(U(s, t), V(s, t))$).

Property 4.8.1 *The following are equivalent, and when any of them occur we say that the point $\mathbf{r}(s, t)$ of M is a frontier point.*

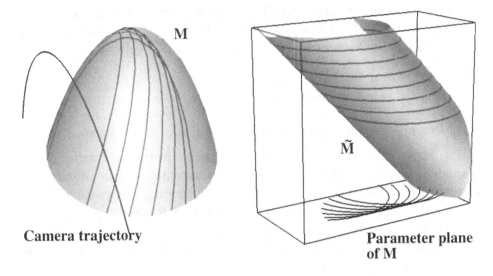

Camera trajectory

**Parameter plane
of M**

Fig. 4.16 Left: a camera trajectory and contour generators forming an envelope
on the surface M. Right: the spatio-temporal surface $\widetilde{M}$ with the horizontal curves
corresponding to the same contour generators, and their projection to the parameter
plane of M, forming an envelope there. The envelope points in the parameter plane
are under the 'fold curve' of $\widetilde{M}$, which consists of points of $\widetilde{M}$ where the tangent
plane is vertical.

(i) $\mathbf{r}(s,t)$ *is an envelope point of the contour generators on* M: $\mathbf{R}_s$ *is
parallel to* $\mathbf{R}_t$ *there;*

(ii) $\mathbf{c}_t \cdot \mathbf{n} = 0$ *at* (s,t);

(iii) $\mathbf{p}_t \cdot \mathbf{n} = 0$ *at* (s,t);

(iv) $\mathbf{p}(s,t)$ *is an envelope point of the apparent contours:* $\mathbf{p}_s$ *is parallel to*
$\mathbf{p}_t$. *Note that this assumes* unrotated *coordinates.*

(v) *Provided* $\mathbf{c}_t$ *is not parallel to* $\mathbf{p}$, *the epipolar plane spanned by* $\mathbf{c}_t$ *and
the visual ray is tangent to the surface at* $\mathbf{r}$. *(The excluded case occurs
when camera motion is directly towards the surface point.)*

(vi) *The projection from the spatio-temporal surface* $\widetilde{M}$ *down to* M *is
'folded', that is the tangent plane to* $\widetilde{M}$ *contains the* t *direction.*

Notes on the above Property
1. At frontier points, the depth formula (4.5) becomes *indeterminate*, since
the numerator and denominator are both zero. It is still possible (in principle!) to determine the depth by taking limits or, what amounts to the same

thing, by using higher derivatives. Thus the equation $\mathbf{c}_t \cdot \mathbf{n} + \lambda \mathbf{p}_t \cdot \mathbf{n} = 0$ can be differentiated with respect to s or t and the resulting equation solved for λ. For example, differentiating with respect to s, and using $\mathbf{p}_t \cdot \mathbf{n} = 0$, we obtain

$$\mathbf{c}_t \cdot \mathbf{n}_s + \lambda (\mathbf{p}_{st} \cdot \mathbf{n} + \mathbf{p}_t \cdot \mathbf{n}_s) = 0,$$

which can be solved for λ provided the coefficient of λ is nonzero.

2. The above Property says that the only visible feature of frontier points is that, *in unrotated coordinates*, the apparent contours form an envelope. In *rotated coordinates* $\mathbf{q}$, the apparent contours form an envelope at image points corresponding to the frontier if the rotation R is *constant*, but not in general otherwise. This is exactly what makes frontier points hard to detect. In Chapter 6 we give an iterative approach which appears to work well for detecting frontier points in the image, when the camera motion is circular.

There is discussion in (Fletcher 1996) of what happens if we are simply given a family of curves $\mathbf{p}(s, t)$ in the image sphere forming an envelope, and a camera motion $\mathbf{c}(t)$, and use the depth formula to construct a surface. It turns out that the surface may actually be singular, and the curves $\mathbf{p}(s, t)$ may fail to be the complete apparent contours of this surface. We have excluded all such cases by our assumptions prior to stating the above result.

If we use rotated coordinates as in §4.3 then from (4.8) the condition $\mathbf{p}_t \cdot \mathbf{n} = 0$ becomes

$$R(\mathbf{q}_t) \cdot \mathbf{n} + [\Omega, R\mathbf{q}, \mathbf{n}] = 0.$$

If we use the convention that at $t = 0$ we have $R = $ identity then the R can be omitted from this equation at $t = 0$. Alternatively, if we measure $\mathbf{n}$ in the rotated coordinate frame too, calling the result $\mathbf{N} = R^{-1}\mathbf{n}$, then, for a vector $\Psi = R^{-1}\Omega$, we have

$$\mathbf{q}_t \cdot \mathbf{N} = -[\Psi, \mathbf{q}, \mathbf{N}] \tag{4.14}$$

for any time t.

Proof of Property 4.8.1 Differentiating (4.13) with respect to t gives

$$\mathbf{r}_u U_t + \mathbf{r}_v V_t = \mathbf{R}_t = \mathbf{c}_t + \lambda_t \mathbf{p} + \lambda \mathbf{p}_t.$$

Now taking the scalar product with $\mathbf{n}$, which is perpendicular to the tangent vector $\mathbf{R}_t$, gives

$$0 = \mathbf{c}_t \cdot \mathbf{n} + \lambda \mathbf{p}_t \cdot \mathbf{n},$$

exactly as in the usual depth formula (4.5). It follows that

$$\mathbf{c}_t \cdot \mathbf{n} = 0 \Leftrightarrow \mathbf{p}_t \cdot \mathbf{n} = 0 \Leftrightarrow \mathbf{p}_t \text{ is parallel to } \mathbf{p}_s,$$

the last equivalence being because $\mathbf{p}_t$ is perpendicular to $\mathbf{p}$, and hence perpendicular to $\mathbf{n} = \mathbf{p} \wedge \mathbf{p}_s$ if and only if it is parallel to $\mathbf{p}_s$. Note that we are excluding $\mathbf{p}_s = 0$ since the apparent contours are assumed to be smooth.

Next, the above formula for $\mathbf{R}_t$ can be rewritten

$$\mathrm{II}(\mathbf{R} - \mathbf{c}, \mathbf{R}_t) = \mathrm{II}(\lambda \mathbf{p}, \mathbf{R}_t) = -\lambda \mathbf{p} \cdot \mathbf{n}_t = \lambda \mathbf{p}_t \cdot \mathbf{n} = -\mathbf{c}_t \cdot \mathbf{n},$$

using (2.18) and $\mathbf{p} \cdot \mathbf{n} = 0$. Hence $\mathbf{R} - \mathbf{c}$ is conjugate to $\mathbf{R}_t$ if and only if $\mathbf{c}_t \cdot \mathbf{n} = 0$ (Definition 2.8.2). Note that $\mathbf{R} - \mathbf{c}$ is always conjugate to $\mathbf{R}_s$ (differentiate (4.13) with respect to s, or recall Property 3.6.1).

It is clear, then, that if $\mathbf{R}_t$ is parallel to $\mathbf{R}_s$ then $\mathbf{c}_t \cdot \mathbf{n} = 0$. Conversely, if $\mathbf{c}_t \cdot \mathbf{n} = 0$, then $\mathbf{R}_s$ and $\mathbf{R}_t$ are *both* conjugate to the visual ray $\mathbf{R} - \mathbf{c}$. This can only happen if the vectors $\mathbf{R}_s$ and $\mathbf{R}_t$ are parallel, or if the surface point is parabolic, with $\mathbf{R} - \mathbf{c}$ along the asymptotic direction there—in which case all tangent vectors are conjugate to this one (Property 2.8.14). But we have excluded this by assuming that apparent contours and contour generators are smooth.

This establishes the equivalence of the first four conditions of the Property above; the other two follow from the previous discussion. □

4.9 Following cusps

In this section we give a brief account of how formulae for Gauss and mean curvature of a surface, measured from apparent contours, are simplified if we can follow cusps in the apparent contours. For full details, see (Cipolla et al. 1997, Fletcher 1996). In principle cusps are visible features of apparent contours, although they appear only as contour endings in the more realistic case of opaque surfaces (see Figure 3.7), and are difficult to localize. The cusps trace out a curve in the image, and on the surface M there will be a *cusp generator curve* C. For each point $\mathbf{r}$ of C there will be a camera position where the visual ray from the camera centre to $\mathbf{r}$ is along an asymptotic direction at $\mathbf{r}$, thereby causing a cusp to appear at the image of $\mathbf{r}$ (Property 3.6.2).

We assume here that cameras are calibrated and the motion known, so that we may work with the '$\mathbf{p}$ coordinates' of §4.3, and we can convert to '$\mathbf{q}$ coordinates' using (4.6).

4.10 Formulae for K and H by following cusps

When a family of apparent contours is parametrized as $\mathbf{p}(s, t)$ the cusp points will be given by the condition that the velocity $\mathbf{p}_s$ becomes zero. We shall take for granted here that in general the cusp generator curve C on M is *smooth* and parametrized by t, and the same applies to the *cusp locus*—the image of C in the image sphere. Detailed conditions for these assumptions to hold are in (Cipolla et al. 1997), where our coordinate s appears as u.

Thus there is a function $s = S(t)$ say such that C is the curve of points $\mathbf{r}(S(t), t)$ and the cusps themselves in the image sphere lie along the cusp locus $\mathbf{p}(S(t), t)$:

$$\mathbf{p}_s(S(t), t) = 0 \quad \text{for all } t. \tag{4.15}$$

Indeed we can customize our coordinate system so that the cusp locus is $s = 0$, but none of the main results below depends on this assumption and we shall not use it.

For a nonsingular apparent contour the tangent is along the vector $\mathbf{p}_s$, but when there is a cusp this is zero so we need a new vector for the tangent. We have (Cipolla et al. 1997):

Property 4.10.1 *At an ordinary cusp point the vector $\mathbf{p}_{ss}$ is nonzero and along the cuspidal tangent.*

From Property 4.10.1 we have

$$\mathbf{p} \cdot \mathbf{n} = 0, \quad \mathbf{p}_s = 0, \quad \mathbf{p}_{ss} \cdot \mathbf{p} = 0, \quad \mathbf{p}_{ss} \cdot \mathbf{n} = 0 \tag{4.16}$$

at cusp points. Differentiating (4.15) with respect to t and using (4.16) we get (using $'$ for $\frac{d}{dt}$)

$$\mathbf{p}_{ss}S' + \mathbf{p}_{st} = 0, \text{ so } \mathbf{p}_{st} \cdot \mathbf{n} = 0 \text{ at cusp points.}$$

The velocity of the cusp along its trajectory in the image sphere is

$$\frac{d}{dt}\mathbf{p}(S(t), t) = \mathbf{p}_s S' + \mathbf{p}_t = \mathbf{p}_t \text{ at cusp points,} \tag{4.17}$$

while the acceleration in the normal direction is

$$\left(\frac{d}{dt}(\mathbf{p}_s S' + \mathbf{p}_t)\right) \cdot \mathbf{n} = (\mathbf{p}_{ss}S'^2 + \mathbf{p}_{st}S' + \mathbf{p}_s S'' + \mathbf{p}_{tt}) \cdot \mathbf{n} = \mathbf{p}_{tt} \cdot \mathbf{n} \quad (4.18)$$

at cusp points.

In order to calculate the Gauss curvature and mean curvature of M using the formulae (2.24) and (2.25) we need to calculate derivatives of $\mathbf{r}$, where this is connected to $\mathbf{p}$ by the usual equation $\mathbf{r} = \mathbf{c} + \lambda\mathbf{p}$ of perspective projection (4.3). Thus, using the notation of (2.5) and (2.14) we have

$$
\begin{aligned}
E &= \mathbf{r}_s \cdot \mathbf{r}_s = \lambda_s^2, \\
F &= \mathbf{r}_s \cdot \mathbf{r}_t = \lambda_s(\mathbf{p} \cdot \mathbf{c}_t + \lambda_t), \\
G &= \mathbf{r}_t \cdot \mathbf{r}_t = (\mathbf{c}_t + \lambda_t\mathbf{p} + \lambda\mathbf{p}_t)^2.
\end{aligned}
$$

Hence the expression occurring in the denominators of K, H is

$$EG - F^2 = \lambda_s^2((\mathbf{c}_t + \lambda \mathbf{p}_t)^2 - (\mathbf{p} \cdot \mathbf{c}_t)^2).$$ (4.19)

Also

$$\begin{aligned} L = \mathbf{r}_{ss} \cdot \mathbf{n} &= \lambda \mathbf{p}_{ss} \cdot \mathbf{n} = 0, \\ M = \mathbf{r}_{st} \cdot \mathbf{n} &= \lambda_s \mathbf{p}_t \cdot \mathbf{n}, \\ N = \mathbf{r}_{tt} \cdot \mathbf{n} &= (\mathbf{c}_{tt} + 2\lambda_t \mathbf{p}_t + \lambda \mathbf{p}_{tt}) \cdot \mathbf{n} \end{aligned}$$

It is noteworthy that when using the formulae (2.24) and (2.25) for K and H, the occurrences of λ_t and λ_s all disappear. After using (4.5) to substitute for λ in (4.19), we want to simplify the new denominator

$$((\mathbf{p}_t \cdot \mathbf{n})\mathbf{c}_t - (\mathbf{c}_t \cdot \mathbf{n})\mathbf{p}_t)^2 - (\mathbf{p} \cdot \mathbf{c}_t \, \mathbf{p}_t \cdot \mathbf{n})^2.$$ (4.20)

This equals

$$[\mathbf{p}, \mathbf{c}_t, \mathbf{p}_t]^2.$$ (4.21)

Now we can write down the formulae for K, H which result from the formulae (2.24) and (2.25), using the above values of E, F, G, L, M, N and (4.21). We shall assume $\mathbf{p}_t \cdot \mathbf{n}$ and $\mathbf{c}_t \cdot \mathbf{n}$ are nonzero, which says that we are not working at a 'frontier' point as well as a cusp point. See §4.6. A short calculation shows the following.

$$K = \frac{-(\mathbf{p}_t \cdot \mathbf{n})^4}{[\mathbf{p}, \mathbf{c}_t, \mathbf{p}_t]^2}.$$ (4.22)

$$H = \frac{\mathbf{p}_t \cdot \mathbf{n}(\mathbf{c}_{tt} \cdot \mathbf{n} \, \mathbf{p}_t \cdot \mathbf{n} - \mathbf{c}_t \cdot \mathbf{n} \, \mathbf{p}_{tt} \cdot \mathbf{n} - 2\mathbf{p} \cdot \mathbf{c}_t (\mathbf{p}_t \cdot \mathbf{n})^2)}{2[\mathbf{p}, \mathbf{c}_t, \mathbf{p}_t]^2}.$$ (4.23)

Notes on the formulae
1. Recall that the standard formula for K (see (Cipolla and Blake 1992, §4.3) and §4.5 above) depends on second temporal derivatives of camera position and image, and also on the curvature of the image. It is therefore a striking feature of the above formula for K that it lacks *second* derivatives. Using the special geometry of cusp points, we have obtained a formula for Gauss curvature which depends on the first derivatives of the motion only.

2. The denominator of the expressions for K and H cannot be zero so long as the cusp is not moving instantaneously in the epipolar plane.

3. The normal $\mathbf{n}$ in the above formulae is assumed to be in the direction of $\mathbf{r}_u \wedge \mathbf{r}_t$. It is not immediately clear that this direction can be found from the image. However, it is shown in (Cipolla et al. 1997, §11) that we find the direction, at any rate for an opaque surface, as follows.

Orient the visible part of the apparent contour towards the cusp point; this makes $\mathbf{r}_u$ a *positive* multiple of $\mathbf{p}$. Choose a normal $\mathbf{n}$ at the cusp point and consider the sign of $[\mathbf{p}, \mathbf{c}_t, \mathbf{p}_t]/\mathbf{p}_t \cdot \mathbf{n}$. The chosen normal is along $\mathbf{r}_u \wedge \mathbf{r}_t$ (i.e. a *positive* multiple of this) if and only if this sign is positive. Thus the sign of H is unambiguous in the above formula.

4. Once we have the Gauss and mean curvatures at a point where the apparent contour gives a cusp we have essentially determined the second fundamental form of the surface at that point (see below). Thus by following cusps we can recover a surface strip along the cusp generator curve, together with the second fundamental form of the surface along that strip.

Think of a surface in 'special Monge form', $z = f(x, y)$ with f, f_x, f_y all vanishing at $x = y = 0$, so that the tangent plane to the surface at the origin is the plane $z = 0$. Let one asymptotic direction be along the x-axis. Then the surface has the form

$$z = \frac{1}{2}(2f_{xy}xy + f_{yy}y^2) + \text{h.o.t.},$$

the derivatives being evaluated at $x = y = 0$. Knowing $K = -f_{xy}^2$ and $H = f_{yy}/2$ we know the second-order terms, and hence the second fundamental form, apart from an ambiguity of sign in f_{xy}.

In fact, in our situation of working at the cusp points, we can eliminate this ambiguity: f_{xy} has the sign of $\mathbf{p}_t \cdot \mathbf{n}$, where $\mathbf{n}$ is determined as in Note 3 above. See (Cipolla et al. 1997, §12).

5. Note the interpretations of $\mathbf{p}_t \cdot \mathbf{n}$ and $\mathbf{p}_{tt} \cdot \mathbf{n}$ as the normal components of velocity and acceleration along the cusp trajectory, as in (4.17) and (4.18) above.

6. A special case of the formulae above for K and H was obtained in (Giblin and Soares 1988). It can be shown fairly readily that these special results follow from ours.

7. In fact the formulae of the above Proposition do not depend on *following* cusps, merely on *starting* at a cusp point. The instantaneous velocities can be measured for any surface curve parametrized by time t and starting at this point and the formulae then hold *at this point*.

4.11 Image velocity of a cusp point

Recall from (4.17) that we can measure $\mathbf{p}_t$ by measuring the velocity of the cusp along its trajectory in the image. Now write $\mathbf{t}$ for the tangent to the cusp, which we can define as $\mathbf{n} \wedge \mathbf{p}$. We have

$$(\mathbf{p}_t \cdot \mathbf{n})(\mathbf{c}_t \cdot \mathbf{t}) - (\mathbf{c}_t \cdot \mathbf{n})(\mathbf{p}_t \cdot \mathbf{t}) = ((\mathbf{t} \wedge \mathbf{n}) \wedge \mathbf{c}_t) \cdot \mathbf{p}_t = [\mathbf{p}, \mathbf{c}_t, \mathbf{p}_t].$$

Using the depth formula (4.5) and the formulae (4.22), (4.23) we find:

Property 4.11.1 *The components of image velocity of the cusp are given by*

$$\mathbf{p}_t \cdot \mathbf{n} = -\frac{\mathbf{c}_t \cdot \mathbf{n}}{\lambda},$$

$$\mathbf{p}_t \cdot \mathbf{t} = -\frac{\mathbf{c}_t \cdot \mathbf{t}}{\lambda} \pm \frac{\mathbf{c}_t \cdot \mathbf{n}}{\lambda^2 \sqrt{-K}},$$

where the sign, $\pm$*, is that of* $[\mathbf{p}, \mathbf{c}_t, \mathbf{p}_t]$*.*

Note that the formula for $\mathbf{p}_t \cdot \mathbf{n}$ is *the same* as we would get by following the end-point of a surface marking, rigidly attached to the surface, while the *first* term of $\mathbf{p}_t \cdot \mathbf{t}$ is the one we should expect from a surface marking. The second term represents the contribution of the surface, when we are following a cusp, which is not rigidly attached to the surface. If K is large, then this term is insignificant; the limiting case of '$K = \infty$' corresponds to that of a space curve or surface marking.

4.12 Envelopes of surfaces and apparent contours

Given a *family of surfaces* M_t, these surfaces sweep out an *envelope surface* M which is tangent to all the M_t. This can also be thought of as follows. Two surfaces M_t and $M_{t+\delta t}$ which are very close together in the family will intersect in a curve, called the 'characteristic curve' on M_t. As t varies, this curve sweeps out a surface which is the envelope.

For a simple example take M_t, for all t, to be a sphere of fixed radius r, with the centre of this sphere describing a circle of radius R in space (where $R > r$). Then the envelope is a torus surface (Figure 4.17): each sphere fits snugly inside the torus with its centre lying on the 'core circle' of the torus. More generally, if the centre describes any space curve, then the envelope is a *canal surface* or *tubular surface*.

Similarly a family of spheres of varying radius centred on a straight line l sweeps out a surface of revolution (Figure 4.18) with l as its axis. Taking l to be the z-axis, let the radius of the sphere M_t centred at $(0, 0, t)$ be $\rho(t) > 0$. Then the equation of this sphere is

$$x^2 + y^2 + (z - t)^2 = (\rho(t))^2. \tag{4.24}$$

To find the envelope, we differentiate with respect to t; compare (Bruce and Giblin 1992, Ch. 5), giving $z = t - \rho(t)\rho'(t)$. For a given t, this is the equation of a plane parallel to the x, y-plane, which intersects M_t in a circle. This circle

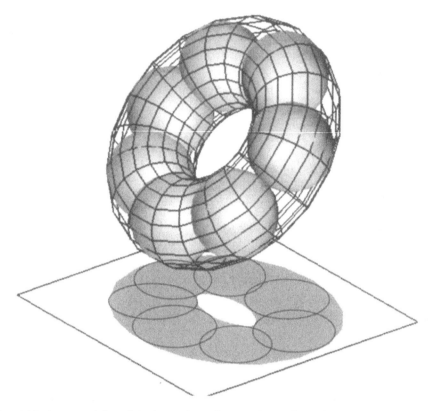

Fig. 4.17 A torus (above) is formed as the envelope of a sphere sweeping through space with its centre moving on a circle. The apparent contours of these spheres have envelope which is the apparent contour (below) of the torus.

is the characteristic curve on M_t and as t varies this circle sweeps out the surface of revolution. Substituting for z in (4.24) gives $x^2 + y^2 = \rho^2(1 - \rho'^2)$ so the radius of the characteristic circle is $\rho\sqrt{1 - \rho'^2}$, provided $\rho'^2 < 1$. Note that if $\rho' \geq 1$ or ≤ -1 then the radius of the sphere is 'changing too rapidly' and the envelope ceases to exist.

For example, if $\rho(t) = t/2$ then the radius of the characteristic circle is $\sqrt{3}t/4$, and since this circle is at height $z = 3t/4$ the envelope surface is a circular cone with half-angle at the vertex equal to $\tan^{-1}(1/\sqrt{3}) = \pi/6$.

A general result which is very useful in this situation is the following, which applies to orthogonal or perspective projection. A version of this result for orthogonal projection appeared in (Rycroft 1992).

Property 4.12.1 *Suppose that the apparent contour γ_t of each M_t is a smooth curve (free from cusps) and that the envelope surface M is a smooth*

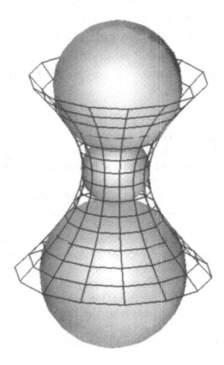

Fig. 4.18 A surface of revolution as the envelope of a family of spheres of varying radius centred on a straight line.

surface (free from singularities such as cusp edges, swallowtail points and Whitney umbrellas). Then the apparent contour γ of the envelope M coincides with the envelope E of the apparent contours γ_t.

This property is particularly attractive when considering envelopes of *spheres*. The reason for this is that the contour generator of a sphere S is *always* a circle (Figure 4.17). In the case of orthogonal projection the radius of the circle is the same as the radius of the sphere and furthermore the apparent contour is also a circle whose centre is the projection of the centre of the sphere S. For perspective projection the apparent contour of S in the image sphere will also be a circle, whose radius depends on the distance of the camera centre from S, but if the image is captured on a plane then the apparent contour of S may be a conic (ellipse, hyperbola or parabola) rather than a circle.

Thus, for orthogonal projection or for perspective projection using an image *sphere*, the apparent contour of a surface which can be described as an envelope of spheres is always an envelope of circles. For example with a canal surface the radii of the spheres are constant so for orthogonal projection the radii of the circles are constant too. In the simple example where a sphere of constant radius ρ moves along a circle C in space, giving a torus, for orthogonal projection the apparent contour is an envelope of circles of radius ρ centred on an ellipse, the latter being the projection of C to the image plane. See Figure 4.17.

Further notes on Property 4.12.1

The smoothness restrictions in this theorem are to ensure that M has a well-defined apparent contour and that the Π_t have a well-defined envelope. There is no requirement that $\Pi(M)$ or $E(\Pi_t)$ should be smooth. For example if a sphere of constant radius moves with its centre traversing a circle then M is a torus (a smooth surface), but its apparent contour will generally have cusps. Likewise the Π_t will be circles (smooth curves) but their envelope will have the same cusps.

Property 4.12.1 is really a theorem about ranks of composites of smooth maps, and belongs to singularity theory. A direct proof for perspective projection is messy, and we give here a Monge–Taylor type proof for orthogonal projection. Thus let $z = F(x, y, t)$ be the equation of a family of surfaces, where M_t is given by fixing t, and let us consider projection in the direction of the x-axis, $(1, 0, 0)$. We can think of t as being close to 0 and (x, y) close to the origin: we are considering surfaces close to M_0 in the family and points on them close to $(0,0,0)$.

The contour generator of the surface M_t is given by the equation

$$z = F, \quad F_x := \frac{\partial F}{\partial x} = 0.$$

We can solve the second of these for $x = g(y, t)$, say, provided that $F_{xx} \neq 0$ (using the implicit function theorem; see for example (Bruce and Giblin 1992, p. 68)). This condition says that we want the x-axis to be tangent to M_0 ($F_x = 0$) but we do not want $(1, 0, 0)$ to be an asymptotic direction to M_0 at the origin ($F_{xx} \neq 0$). This is satisfied provided M_0 has a smooth apparent contour, which is one of our assumptions in the statement of the theorem.

The contour generator on M_t then consists of points

$$(g(y, t), y, f(g(y, t), y, t)),$$

and the apparent contour of M_t has equation

$$z = F(g(y, t), y, t).$$

The envelope is obtained by differentiating with respect to t:

$$0 = F_x g_t + F_t, \quad \text{i.e. } F_t = 0 \text{ since } F_x = 0.$$

So the 'envelope of apparent contours' condition is $F_x = F_t = 0$.

Turning to the envelope M of the surfaces, this is given by $z = F$, $F_t = 0$. We solve the second of these for $t = h(x, y)$ say, provided $F_{tt} \neq 0$. This is precisely the condition for the envelope M to be smooth, another assumption of the theorem. Compare (Bruce and Giblin 1992, p. 115). The envelope M then has equation

$$z = F(x, y, h(x, y)),$$

and its apparent contour is given by differentiating with respect to x:

$$0 = F_x + F_t h_x, \text{ i.e. } F_x = 0 \text{ since } F_t = 0.$$

Thus the 'apparent contour of the envelope' condition is $F_t = F_x = 0$, and the two conditions coincide.

5

Reconstruction of Surfaces from Profiles

In this chapter we describe the implementation of the theory of Chapter 4 and show how to recover the geometry of a surface from an image sequence of apparent contours (profiles) from different viewpoints.

The algorithms are described in sufficient practical detail to allow the reader to implement the theory. Details are given on the localization and tracking of apparent contours; the recovery of the viewpoint geometry and camera calibration; the epipolar parametrization of the spatio-temporal family of apparent contours; and the reconstruction of surfaces. These algorithms have been used in a real-time system to recover the geometry of visible surfaces from apparent contours under known viewer motion. Examples are given.

5.1 Localization and tracking of apparent contours

A monochrome video image can be digitized into a pixel array of quantized (discrete) intensity values which can be represented by a matrix $I(u, v)$ where u, v here refer to the column and row position of the pixel respectively. A typical image is shown in Figure 5.1(a). Its size is 512×512 and the intensity value of each pixel is sampled to an accuracy of 8 bits giving 256 brightness values varying from 0 (black) to 255 (white).

The projections of surface markings, surface edges and contour generators appear as fragments of image curves across which there is an abrupt change in intensity. These image curves or contours can be extracted by first detecting the position of intensity discontinuities (*edge detection*) and then representing aggregates of edges analytically with B-splines.

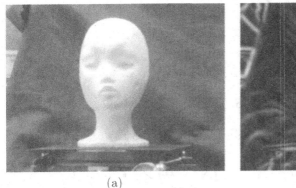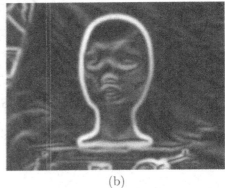

(a)   (b)

Fig. 5.1. Edge detection.

Edge detection

Edges can be detected by localizing the maxima of intensity gradients after convolution with a smoothing filter. The smoothing filter helps reduce the effect of image noise on the derivative operation used to find the intensity gradient. A typical edge detection algorithm (Canny 1986) involves the following the steps to smooth the image and to localize the maxima.

Algorithm 5.1.1 Edge detection.

(i) The image is smoothed by convolution with a smoothing filter $G_\sigma(i,j)$:

$$S(u,v) = \sum_{i=-n}^{n} \sum_{j=-n}^{n} G_\sigma(i,j) I(u-i, v-j)$$

where the filter kernel is of size $(2n+1)$ and is a discrete approximation for the Gaussian function:

$$G_\sigma(i,j) = \frac{1}{2\pi\sigma^2} \exp\left[-\left(\frac{i^2+j^2}{2\sigma^2}\right)\right].$$

(ii) The gradient, ∇S, of the smoothed image $S(u,v)$ is then computed at every pixel. Differentiation is performed using a finite-difference approximation.

$$\nabla S(u,v) = \begin{bmatrix} S(u+1,v) - S(u,v) \\ S(u,v+1) - S(u,v) \end{bmatrix}$$

Figure 5.1(b) shows $|\nabla S|$ for the image of Figure 5.1(a).

(iii) Edge elements, or *edgels*, are placed at locations where $|\nabla S|$ is a local maxima in the directions $\pm \nabla S$ and is above a threshold.

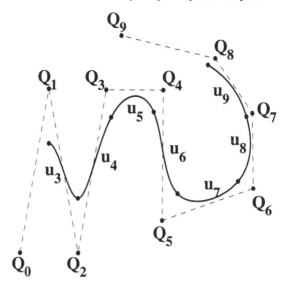

Fig. 5.2. The cubic B-spline.

The representation of the image contours as a linked chain of edge elements or edgels is not very compact and does not lend itself readily to the sub-pixel localization of the image curve and the computation of image curvature. An alternative is to automatically fit an algebraic, parametrized curve to the chain of edgels of interest. The representation is now extremely compact (only the coefficients of the curve's equation need be stored) and the smoothness and continuity of the curve are implicit.

B-spline curve representation

A natural choice for the curve parametrization is the *B-spline*, which is widely used in computer graphics (Bartels et al. 1987). A cubic B-spline is specified by $m + 1$ *control points* $\mathbf{Q}_0, \mathbf{Q}_1, \ldots, \mathbf{Q}_m$ and comprises $m - 2$ cubic polynomial curve segments $\mathbf{u}_3, \mathbf{u}_4, \ldots, \mathbf{u}_m$. The joining points between each curve segment are known as *knots*. The equation of each curve segment is

$$\mathbf{u}_i(s) = \frac{1}{6} \begin{bmatrix} s^3 & s^2 & s & 1 \end{bmatrix} \begin{bmatrix} -1 & 3 & -3 & 1 \\ 3 & -6 & 3 & 0 \\ -3 & 0 & 3 & 0 \\ 1 & 4 & 1 & 0 \end{bmatrix} \begin{bmatrix} \mathbf{Q}_{i-3} \\ \mathbf{Q}_{i-2} \\ \mathbf{Q}_{i-1} \\ \mathbf{Q}_i \end{bmatrix} \tag{5.1}$$

for $0 \le s < 1$ and $3 \le i \le m$. See Figure 5.2. B-splines are ideal for representing curves and fitting to image edges. They may be open or closed as required, and are defined with continuity properties at each point and

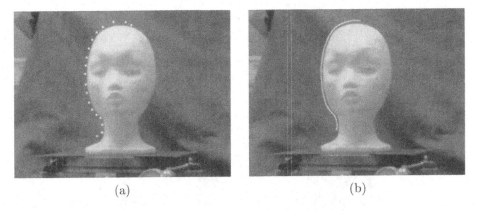

(a)   (b)

Fig. 5.3. Initialization of the B-spline snake.

knot. The flexibility of the curve increases as more control points are added: each additional control point allows one more inflexion. It is also possible to use multiple knots to reduce the continuity at knots. They also exhibit *local control*: modifying the position of one control point causes only a small part of the curve to change.

A number of methods exist to fit B-splines to image edges. An automatic scheme that selects the number of control points and their image positions is described in (Cham and Cipolla 1999). In the following we describe a simpler algorithm to localize and track image contours using a variant of *snakes* or active contours (Kass et al. 1988) which use B-splines (Cipolla and Blake 1990, Blake and Isard 1998). The snake is a computational construct, a dynamic curve, which is able to track moving and deforming image contours.

Tracking image curves with B-spline snakes

B-splines can be fitted to image edges by the following iterative algorithm:

Algorithm 5.1.2 B-spline snake.

(i) Initialize a B-spline by placing control points $\mathbf{Q}_0, \mathbf{Q}_1, \ldots, \mathbf{Q}_m$ near the image edge. An example is given in Figure 5.3.

(ii) Select a number of evenly spaced sample points, N, along each segment of the B-spline, $\mathbf{u}_i(s)$. The sample points are given by $\mathbf{u}_i(s_j)$ where $i = 3, \ldots, m$ and $j = 0, \ldots, N$. Typically $N > 10$ for each segment, $\Delta s < 0.1$ between samples.

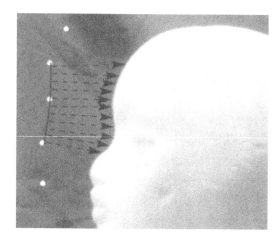

Fig. 5.4 The B-spline snake. B-spline snakes can be used to localize image contours. The control points, $\mathbf{Q}_0, \mathbf{Q}_1, \ldots, \mathbf{Q}_m$, are positioned iteratively to minimize the normal displacements (shown as arrowed vectors) between the spline segments and nearby edge features.

(iii) From each sample point search along the normal to the spline for edges in the image and calculate the distance to the nearest edge. See example in Figure 5.4.

(iv) Move the control points to minimize the sum of squares of the distances between the discrete data points of the image feature and the B-spline approximation. This is a standard least squares problem and we can compute the new control point positions (Cipolla and Blake 1992).

 (v) Repeat steps (iii) and (iv) until the algorithm has converged to produce a spline which localizes the image contour.

As the B-spline snake approaches the image contour the scale at which the edge search takes place can be reduced to enable accurate contour localization. After localization the same algorithm is used to track the image contour over the image sequence, provided the inter-frame image motion is less than the search (capture) window of the snake.

Since accurate measurements are required to compute surface geometry, care has been taken over sub-pixel resolution. At earlier stages of tracking, when coarse blurring (large scale) is used, the capture range of the snake is large but localization is poor – the snake may lag behind the contour. Once the snake has converged on to the contour, standard edge-detection techniques such as smoothing for sub-pixel resolution (Canny 1986) can be used to obtain accurate localization.

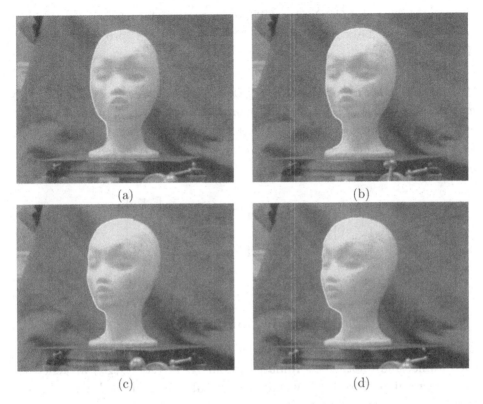

(a)   (b)

(c)   (d)

Fig. 5.5 A B-spline snake can localize and track the image contours over an image sequence.

Figure 5.5 shows a sequence of images and a B-spline snake which has been used to localize and track the apparent contour of a surface. The output of the tracking algorithm is a family of image contours, $\mathbf{u}(s,t)$, which are parametrized by the spline parameter s and indexed by the time, t, when the image was taken. In the next section we show how to normalize and parametrize this family of image contours to recover the spatio-temporal family of apparent contours in the reference coordinate system, $\mathbf{p}(s,t)$. The latter will be used to recover the geometry of the surface.

5.2 Camera model for perspective projection onto image plane

To reconstruct the surface we require the mapping from image plane pixel coordinates, $\mathbf{u}$, to visual rays in the fixed *world* coordinate system, $\mathbf{p}$. This is determined by transformations describing the position and orientation of the coordinate system attached to the camera relative to the world coordinate system; perspective (central) projection onto the image plane and the geometry of the CCD array. These three transformations are derived below and can be conveniently written as a 3×4 projection matrix (Roberts 1965).

Property 5.2.1 The projection matrix. *Under perspective projection the map between the three-dimensional world coordinates of a point (X, Y, Z) and its two-dimensional image plane pixel coordinates (u, v) can be written as a linear mapping in homogeneous coordinates and represented by a 3×4 projection matrix:*

$$
\begin{bmatrix} \zeta u \\ \zeta v \\ \zeta \end{bmatrix} = \begin{bmatrix} p_{11} & p_{12} & p_{13} & p_{14} \\ p_{21} & p_{22} & p_{23} & p_{24} \\ p_{31} & p_{32} & p_{33} & p_{34} \end{bmatrix} \begin{bmatrix} X \\ Y \\ Z \\ 1 \end{bmatrix}. \tag{5.2}
$$

Rigid-body transformation

Consider a coordinate system $\mathbf{X} = (X, Y, Z)$ attached to the world reference frame, and another coordinate system $\mathbf{X}_c = (X_c, Y_c, Z_c)$ attached to the camera at position $\mathbf{c}(t)$, where the optical axis is aligned with Z_c. See Figure 5.6. In terms of the notation of Chapter 4 and §4.3, the camera centre $\mathbf{c}$ is the origin of the $\mathbf{X}_c$ coordinate system and we write R for the geometrical rotation which has 3×3 matrix $\mathbf{R}$. The measurements in the different coordinate systems are given by

$$
\mathbf{r} = \mathbf{X} = \mathbf{c} + \lambda \mathbf{p}, \quad \mathbf{X}_c = \lambda \mathbf{q}, \quad \mathbf{p} = R\mathbf{q}.
$$

For apparent contours, $\mathbf{r}, \mathbf{X}, \mathbf{X}_c, \lambda, \mathbf{p}$ and $\mathbf{q}$ are functions of two variables s and t, while R and $\mathbf{c}$ are functions of time t alone. Recall that λ is the depth measured along the ray from $\mathbf{c}$ and the unit vector $\mathbf{p}$ is the direction (in world coordinates) of a surface point $\mathbf{r}$ from $\mathbf{c}$ while the unit vector $\mathbf{q}$ is the direction in camera coordinates of the same point.

The camera and reference coordinate systems are related by a rigid body transformation

$$
\mathbf{X} = \mathbf{R}\mathbf{X}_c + \mathbf{c} \tag{5.3}
$$
$$
\mathbf{X}_c = \mathbf{R}^\top (\mathbf{X} - \mathbf{c}) \tag{5.4}
$$

which are conveniently represented with a rotation matrix and a translation vector, **t**, by:

$$\begin{bmatrix} X_c \\ Y_c \\ Z_c \end{bmatrix} = \begin{bmatrix} r_{11} & r_{12} & r_{13} \\ r_{21} & r_{22} & r_{23} \\ r_{31} & r_{32} & r_{33} \end{bmatrix} \begin{bmatrix} X \\ Y \\ Z \end{bmatrix} + \begin{bmatrix} t_X \\ t_Y \\ t_Z \end{bmatrix} \tag{5.5}$$

where the translation vector is related to the position of the camera centre by

$$\mathbf{t} = -\mathbf{R}^\top \mathbf{c}.$$

Perspective projection onto the CCD image plane

Perspective projection onto the imaging plane followed by the conversion of image plane coordinates into CCD pixel coordinates, (u, v), can be modelled by

$$u = u_0 + \alpha_u \frac{X_c}{Z_c} \tag{5.6}$$

$$v = v_0 + \alpha_v \frac{Y_c}{Z_c} \tag{5.7}$$

where the CCD array axes are assumed aligned with the X_c and Y_c axes; (u_0, v_0) is the *principal point* (the point of intersection of the optical axis and the image plane); α_u and α_v are image scaling factors. These four parameters are known as the *internal camera parameters*. The ratio α_v/α_u is known as the aspect ratio.

Projection matrix

The relationship between image pixel coordinates and rays in Euclidean 3-space can now be expressed succinctly by introducing *homogeneous coordinates* to represent image points with 3-vectors and points in 3-space by 4-vectors, defined up to arbitrary scales (e.g. ζ). Homogeneous (projective) coordinates are often used in projective geometry and allow us to represent projective transformations as a matrix multiplications. By concatenating the matrices for the transformations described above the relationship becomes:

$$\begin{bmatrix} \zeta u \\ \zeta v \\ \zeta \end{bmatrix} = \begin{bmatrix} \alpha_u & 0 & u_0 \\ 0 & \alpha_v & v_0 \\ 0 & 0 & 1 \end{bmatrix} \begin{bmatrix} r_{11} & r_{12} & r_{13} & t_X \\ r_{21} & r_{22} & r_{23} & t_Y \\ r_{31} & r_{32} & r_{33} & t_Z \end{bmatrix} \begin{bmatrix} X \\ Y \\ Z \\ 1 \end{bmatrix}$$

or more simply as the 3×4 *projection matrix* representing the perspective projection of a point in space onto a digitized image given in Property 5.2.1

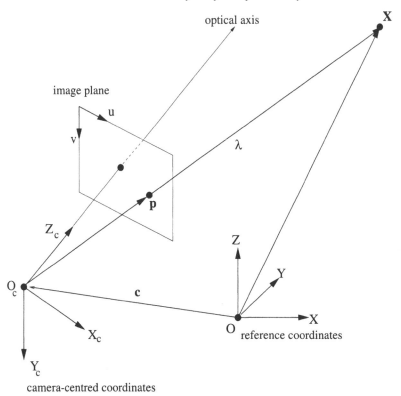

Fig. 5.6 Camera model and camera and reference coordinate systems. $\mathbf{X} = \mathbf{c} + \lambda\mathbf{p}$ and $\mathbf{X} = \mathbf{c} + \mathbf{R}\mathbf{X}_c$.

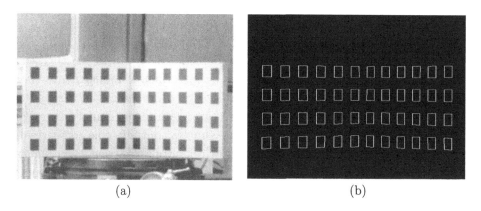

(a)   (b)

Fig. 5.7 Camera calibration. A camera is calibrated by processing an image of a calibration grid (a). The image positions of known 3D points on the grid are extracted automatically. Edge detection is followed by fitting lines to the image segments. Intersections of lines are used to localize the image features to sub-pixel accuracy (b).

where equality is defined up to an arbitrary scale:

$$\mathbf{u} = \mathbf{PX}. \tag{5.8}$$

The projection matrix, $\mathbf{P}$, is not a general 3×4 matrix. It has 11 parameters (since the overall scale does not matter) and it can be decomposed into a 3×3 upper triangular matrix of camera internal parameters called the *camera calibration matrix*, $\mathbf{K}$, and a matrix representing the rigid-body motion.

The mapping from an image point to a visual ray in 3-space is expressed in homogeneous coordinates and up to an arbitrary scale by

$$\mathbf{u} = \mathbf{Kq} \tag{5.9}$$

$$\mathbf{u} = \mathbf{KR}^\top \mathbf{p}. \tag{5.10}$$

5.3 Camera model for weak perspective and orthographic projection

A useful approximation to perspective projection occurs when the field of view is narrow or the depth variation along the line of sight is small compared with the distance from the camera to the scene. The camera model can then be simplified to *weak perspective* and (5.6) and (5.7) can be re-written as:

$$u = u_0 + \alpha_u \frac{X_c}{Z_o} \tag{5.11}$$

$$v = v_0 + \alpha_v \frac{Y_c}{Z_o}. \tag{5.12}$$

The difference with perspective projection is that all image points are scaled uniformly by Z_o, the mean distance of the features of the scene to the camera centre. Weak perspective can in fact be considered as the orthographic (parallel) projection of all points onto the plane $Z_c = Z_o$ followed by a perspective projection to give a uniform inverse-depth scaling. It can be represented by the transformation:

$$
\begin{bmatrix} u_a \\ v_a \\ 1 \end{bmatrix}
=
\begin{bmatrix} \alpha_u & 0 & u_0 \\ 0 & \alpha_v & v_0 \\ 0 & 0 & 1 \end{bmatrix}
\begin{bmatrix} r_{11} & r_{12} & r_{13} & t_X \\ r_{21} & r_{22} & r_{23} & t_Y \\ 0 & 0 & 0 & Z_o \end{bmatrix}
\begin{bmatrix} X \\ Y \\ Z \\ 1 \end{bmatrix}.
$$

If the principal point of a camera is (u_0, v_0), the variation of depth in the scene is ΔZ along the optical axis and the mean distance of the features of the scene to the camera is Z_o, then the difference of the image of a point taken from a perspective camera (u, v) and its image with the weak perspective camera, (u_a, v_a) is given by

$$u - u_a = (u - u_0)\Delta Z / Z_o \qquad (5.13)$$

$$v - v_a = (v - v_0)\Delta Z / Z_o. \qquad (5.14)$$

When the field of view is narrow, the terms $u - u_0$ and $v - v_0$ will be small. In this case, or when the depth variation of the scene is much smaller than its mean depth, e.g. $\Delta Z / Z_o < 0.1$, the error due to the weak perspective approximation is negligible.

Orthographic projection can be modelled in exactly the same way but with no scaling due to depth by setting $Z_c = f$.

5.4 Camera calibration

For reconstruction we require the camera centres, $\mathbf{c}(t)$, and the rays $\mathbf{p}(s, t)$. These can be obtained from the projection matrix for each viewpoint. *Camera calibration* is the name given to the process of recovering the projection matrix from an image of a controlled scene. For example, we might set up the camera to view the calibrated grid shown in Figure 5.7(a) and automatically extract the image positions of known 3D points (Figure 5.7(b)). Each image point, (u_i, v_i), of a known calibration point, X_i, Y_i, and Z_i, generates two equation which the elements of the projection matrix must satisfy:

$$u_i = \frac{\zeta u_i}{\zeta} = \frac{p_{11}X_i + p_{12}Y_i + p_{13}Z_i + p_{14}}{p_{31}X_i + p_{32}Y_i + p_{33}Z_i + p_{34}}$$

$$v_i = \frac{\zeta v_i}{\zeta} = \frac{p_{21}X_i + p_{22}Y_i + p_{23}Z_i + p_{24}}{p_{31}X_i + p_{32}Y_i + p_{33}Z_i + p_{34}}.$$

These equations can be rearranged to give two linear equations in the 12 unknown elements of the projection matrix. For n calibration points and their corresponding image projections we have $2n$ equations:

$$
\begin{bmatrix}
X_1 & Y_1 & Z_1 & 1 & 0 & 0 & 0 & 0 & -u_1X_1 & -u_1Y_1 & -u_1Z_1 & -u_1 \\
0 & 0 & 0 & 0 & X_1 & Y_1 & Z_1 & 1 & -v_1X_1 & -v_1Y_1 & -v_1Z_1 & -v_1 \\
\vdots & \vdots & \vdots & \vdots & \vdots & \vdots & \vdots & \vdots & \vdots & \vdots & \vdots & \vdots \\
X_n & Y_n & Z_n & 1 & 0 & 0 & 0 & 0 & -u_nX_n & -u_nY_n & -u_nZ_n & -u_n \\
0 & 0 & 0 & 0 & X_n & Y_n & Z_n & 1 & -v_nX_n & -v_nY_n & -v_nZ_n & -v_n
\end{bmatrix}
\begin{bmatrix}
p_{11} \\ p_{12} \\ p_{13} \\ p_{14} \\ p_{21} \\ p_{22} \\ p_{23} \\ p_{24} \\ p_{31} \\ p_{32} \\ p_{33} \\ p_{34}
\end{bmatrix} = \mathbf{0}.
$$

Since there are 11 unknowns (scale is arbitrary), we need to observe at least 6 reference points to recover the projection matrix and calibrate the camera.

Numerical considerations

The equations can be solved using orthogonal least squares. First, we write the equations in matrix form:

$$\mathbf{Ax} = \mathbf{0} \tag{5.15}$$

where $\mathbf{x}$ is the 12×1 vector of unknowns (the 12 elements of the projection matrix, p_{ij}), $\mathbf{A}$ is the $2n \times 12$ matrix of measurements and n is the number of observed calibration points. A linear solution (least squares) which minimizes $||\mathbf{Ax}||$ subject to $||\mathbf{x}|| = 1$ is obtained as the unit eigenvector corresponding to the smallest eigenvalue of $\mathbf{A}^\top\mathbf{A}$. Numerically this computation is performed via the *singular value decomposition* of the matrix (Strang 1988)

$$\mathbf{A} = \mathbf{U}\mathbf{\Lambda}\mathbf{V}^\top$$

where $\mathbf{\Lambda} = \mathrm{diag}(\sigma_1, \sigma_2, \ldots, \sigma_{12})$ is the diagonal matrix of singular values and the matrices $\mathbf{U}$ and $\mathbf{V}$ are orthonormal. The columns of $\mathbf{V}$ are the eigenvectors of $\mathbf{A}^\top\mathbf{A}$ and the least squares solution is given by the last column of $\mathbf{V}$ which is the singular vector with the smallest singular value σ_{12}. The least squares solution is, however, only approximate and should be used as the starting point for non-linear optimization: i.e. finding the parameters of the projection matrix, $\mathbf{P}$, that minimize the errors between measured image points, (u_i, v_i) and the projections onto the image plane of the reference points:

$$\min_{\mathbf{P}} \sum_i ||(u_i, v_i) - \mathbf{P}(X_i, Y_i, Z_i, 1)||^2.$$

Once the projection matrix has been estimated the first 3×3 submatrix, $\mathbf{KR}^\top$, can be easily decomposed by standard matrix algorithms into an upper triangular matrix, $\mathbf{K}$, and a rotation (orthonormal) matrix (known as QR decompositon) or used directly to determine the ray in space $\mathbf{p}$ and the position of the camera centre:

$$\mathbf{p} = \mathbf{RK}^{-1}\mathbf{u} \tag{5.16}$$

$$\mathbf{c} = -\mathbf{RK}^{-1}(p_{14}, p_{24}, p_{34})^\top. \tag{5.17}$$

5.5 Epipolar geometry

Epipolar geometry plays a key part in the algorithms to recover the geometry of surfaces from apparent contours. The *epipolar parametrization* of the spatio-temporal family of apparent contours, $\mathbf{p}(s,t)$, introduced in Chapter 4, requires the *epipolar geometry* between successive snapshots of an apparent contour.

We briefly review the geometry of two views and describe how to compute the epipolar geometry when the cameras are calibrated. The use of uncalibrated cameras and the recovery of the epipolar geometry from apparent contours is described in Chapter 6.

The epipolar constraint

In stereo vision the projection of a world point in two calibrated viewpoints can be used to recover the three-dimensional position by triangulation. The geometry of the two views, as shown in Figure 5.8, plays a key part in helping to find correspondences by constraining the search for correspondence from a region to a line. This matching constraint is known as the *epipolar constraint*.

The epipolar constraint arises from the fact that the two rays, $\mathbf{p}$ and $\mathbf{p}'$, to a common scene point, $\mathbf{X}$, and the optical centres of the two camera (the stereo baseline, $\mathbf{t} = \Delta\mathbf{c}$) lie in a plane called the *epipolar plane*. The intersection of the epipolar plane with each image plane defines a line called an *epipolar line*. The correspondence of an image point in the first view, $\mathbf{u}$, must lie on the epipolar line, $\mathbf{l}'$, in the other view shown in Figure 5.8. Using homogeneous coordinates to represent the coefficients of a line in the image as a 3-vector, the epipolar constraints in each view can be written as:

$$\mathbf{u} \cdot \mathbf{l} = 0 \tag{5.18}$$
$$\mathbf{u}' \cdot \mathbf{l}' = 0. \tag{5.19}$$

Each world point, $\mathbf{X}$, has its own epipolar plane. The family of epipolar planes define a *pencil* of epipolar lines which pass through a common point called the *epipole*, illustrated in Figure 5.9. The epipoles and pencil of epipolar lines in each view are known as the *epipolar geometry*. The epipolar geometry is completely determined by the relative position, $\mathbf{t}$, and relative orientation, $\mathbf{R}$, of the two views and the camera parameters of each camera, $\mathbf{K}$ and $\mathbf{K}'$ respectively. It does not depend on the 3D structure of the scene being viewed.

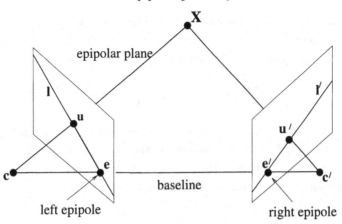

Fig. 5.8 The geometry of two views. In stereo vision an *epipolar plane* is the plane defined by a 3D point **X** and the optical centres of the two cameras. The *baseline* is the line joining the optical centres. An *epipole* is the point of intersection of the baseline with the image plane. An *epipolar line*, **l** and **l′**, is a line of intersection of the epipolar plane with an image plane. It is the image in one camera of the ray from the other camera's optical centre to the point **X**.

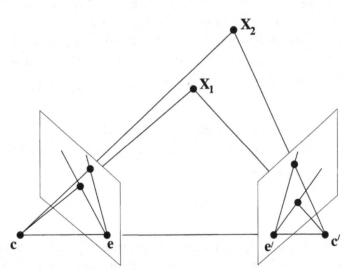

Fig. 5.9 Epipolar geometry. Each world point **X** has its own epipolar plane which rotates about the baseline. All epipolar lines intersect at the epipole.

The essential matrix

The epipolar constraint is a co-planarity constraint and can be expressed algebraically as a scalar triple product:

$$\mathbf{p}' \cdot (\mathbf{t} \wedge \mathbf{p}) = 0. \tag{5.20}$$

Without loss of generality, we can align the reference coordinate system with the second camera so that the epipolar constraint can be rewritten in terms of image positions (3-vectors in homogeneous coordinates), $\mathbf{u}$ and $\mathbf{u}'$, using (5.16):

$$\mathbf{u}'^{\top}\mathbf{K}'^{-\top}\mathbf{E}\mathbf{K}^{-1}\mathbf{u} = 0 \tag{5.21}$$

where $\mathbf{E}$ is a 3×3 matrix known as the *essential matrix* (Longuet-Higgins 1981) and is the product of a skew-symmetric or antisymmetric matrix (representing the vector product with the translation vector) and an orthonormal matrix representing the rotation between the two views:

$$\mathbf{E} = \mathbf{t} \wedge \mathbf{R} = [\mathbf{t}]_{\times}\mathbf{R}$$

where

$$[\mathbf{t}]_{\times} = \begin{bmatrix} 0 & -t_3 & t_2 \\ t_3 & 0 & -t_1 \\ -t_2 & t_1 & 0 \end{bmatrix}$$

and $\mathbf{R}$ now specifies the relative orientation between the views.

The essential matrix is of maximum rank 2. Its factorization into the product of a non-zero skew-symmetric matrix and a rotation matrix is only possible if it has two equal non-zero singular values. The other is of course equal to zero (Tsai and Huang 1984, Faugeras and Maybank 1990).

The fundamental matrix

From (5.21) we see that the epipolar geometry can be conveniently specified by introducing a matrix, $\mathbf{F}$ (Faugeras 1992)

$$\mathbf{F} = \mathbf{K}'^{-\top}\mathbf{E}\mathbf{K}^{-1}. \tag{5.22}$$

Property 5.5.1 The epipolar constraint and the fundamental matrix. *The image coordinates (projective representation using homogeneous coordinates) of all pairs of corresponding points, $\mathbf{u}_i = (u_i, v_i, 1)^{\top}$ and $\mathbf{u}'_i = (u'_i, v'_i, 1)^{\top}$, must satisfy the epipolar constraint:*

$$\mathbf{u}'^{\top}_i\mathbf{F}\mathbf{u}_i = 0 \tag{5.23}$$

or

$$\begin{bmatrix} u'_i & v'_i & 1 \end{bmatrix} \begin{bmatrix} f_{11} & f_{12} & f_{13} \\ f_{21} & f_{22} & f_{23} \\ f_{31} & f_{32} & f_{33} \end{bmatrix} \begin{bmatrix} u_i \\ v_i \\ 1 \end{bmatrix} = 0 \tag{5.24}$$

where $\mathbf{F}$ is a 3×3 real matrix of rank 2 which is defined up to an arbitrary scale and is known as the fundamental matrix.

Epipolar lines and epipoles

The epipolar geometry (see Figure 5.9) is completely determined by the fundamental matrix.

Property 5.5.2 Epipolar geometry from fundamental matrix.

(i) **Epipolar lines.**

The epipolar line (represented by a homogeneous 3-vector), $\mathbf{l}'$, corresponding to a point $\mathbf{u}$ in the other view is given by

$$\mathbf{l}' = \mathbf{Fu} \qquad (5.25)$$

and $\mathbf{u}'$ must lie on this line to satisfy the epipolar constraint:

$$\mathbf{u}' \cdot \mathbf{l}' = 0.$$

The epipolar line corresponding to $\mathbf{u}'$ is given by $\mathbf{l} = \mathbf{F}^\top \mathbf{u}'$.

(ii) **Epipoles.**

The epipole is defined as the point in each image which is common to all the epipolar lines. The left and right epipoles ($\mathbf{e}$ and $\mathbf{e}'$ in homogeneous coordinates) are therefore given by the null spaces of $\mathbf{F}$ and $\mathbf{F}^\top$ respectively

$$\mathbf{Fe} \;=\; 0 \qquad (5.26)$$
$$\mathbf{F}^\top \mathbf{e}' \;=\; 0. \qquad (5.27)$$

5.6 Epipolar geometry from projection matrices

For calibrated cameras with known projection matrices it is trivial to compute the fundamental matrix and hence obtain the epipolar geometry (epipoles and epipolar lines for each image feature). We here outline a simple method by exploiting the following result.

Property 5.6.1 Projective ambiguity. *The pair of cameras and projection matrices* $\mathbf{P}$ *and* $\mathbf{P}'$ *give rise to the same fundamental matrix as the pair of cameras and projection matrices* $\mathbf{PH}$ *and* $\mathbf{P}'\mathbf{H}$ *where* $\mathbf{H}$ *is a* 4×4 *non-singular matrix.*

A simple proof can be found in (Hartley 1992 and 1994) but follows trivially from the fact that the simultaneous transformation of the projection matrices, $\mathbf{P}$ by $\mathbf{H}$ and the 3D point coordinates, $\mathbf{X}$, by $\mathbf{H}^{-1}$ leaves the image coordinates $\mathbf{u} = \mathbf{PX}$, unchanged.

Assume we are given the projection matrices for two viewpoints, $\mathbf{P}$ and $\mathbf{P}'$. The position of the optical centre of the first camera, $\mathbf{c}$, can be computed directly from the projection matrix $\mathbf{P}$ from (5.17). In homogeneous coordinates we can represent it by a 4-vector $\mathbf{C} = (\mathbf{c}^\top 1)$ so that

$$\mathbf{PC} = \mathbf{0}$$

and its projection into the second image plane defines the epipole, $\mathbf{e}'$,

$$\mathbf{e}' = \mathbf{P}'\mathbf{C}. \tag{5.28}$$

We can also compute the pseudo-inverse, $\mathbf{P}^+$, of the projection matrix $\mathbf{P}$,

$$\mathbf{P}^+ = \mathbf{P}^\top (\mathbf{PP}^\top)^{-1}, \tag{5.29}$$

such that multiplication with the first projection matrix gives the identity matrix, $\mathbf{I}$, and multiplication with the second projection matrix gives a 3×3 matrix (a two-dimensional projective transformation), $\mathbf{M}$:

$$\mathbf{I} = \mathbf{P}\,\mathbf{P}^+ \tag{5.30}$$

$$\mathbf{M} = \mathbf{P}'\mathbf{P}^+. \tag{5.31}$$

The two projection matrices have in this way been normalized to have the special forms:

$$\mathbf{PH} = [\mathbf{I} \mid \mathbf{0}] \tag{5.32}$$

$$\mathbf{P}'\mathbf{H} = [\mathbf{M} \mid \mathbf{e}']. \tag{5.33}$$

These normalized projection matrices are known as *canonical cameras*. From Property 5.6.1 both the original projection matrices and these normalized forms have the same fundamental matrix $\mathbf{F}$ given by (see Property 6.3.1):

$$\mathbf{F} = [\mathbf{e}']_\times \mathbf{M}. \tag{5.34}$$

An example of the epipolar geometry of two discrete views computed from calibrated projection matrices using (5.28)–(5.31) and (5.34) is shown in Figure 5.10.

For uncalibrated cameras we do not have the projection matrices and hence $\mathbf{E}$, $\mathbf{K}$ and $\mathbf{K}'$ are unknown *a priori*. The fundamental matrix and epipolar geometry, however, can still be estimated from *point* and curve correspondences between the two views (see Chapter 6).

Fig. 5.10 Epipolar geometry computed from known projection matrices. Selected image points are shown in the left view with corresponding epipolar lines shown in the right view. The corresponding image feature satisfies the epipolar constraint.

5.7 Reconstruction of surfaces

Implementation of the epipolar parametrization

In the *epipolar* parametrization of the spatio-temporal image and surface, a point on an apparent contour in the first image is *matched* to a point in successive images (in an infinitesimal sense) by searching along the corresponding epipolar lines. This allows us to extract t-parameter curves ($\mathbf{u}(s_0, t)$ or $\mathbf{p}(s_0, t)$) from the spatio-temporal image. As shown in Chapter 4, depth and surface curvature are then computed from first and second-order temporal derivatives of this t-parameter spatio-temporal curve by equations (4.5) and (4.11). This requires a dense (continuous) image sequence.

In practice the epipolar parametrization and the reconstruction can be implemented in a variety of ways. In (Cipolla and Blake 1992) and (Cipolla 1995) two simple methods are described for special cases. For *pure translation* perpendicular to the optical axis and with a dense (continuous) image sequence it is possible to recover the depth and surface curvature from the first and second-order derivatives of the spatio-temporal image trajectories directly (see Figure 5.11). For *linear* motion and a minimum of three discrete views a simple numerical method was proposed to estimate the depth of the contour generators and the *osculating circle* in each epipolar plane by assuming that the curvature of the epipolar curve, $\mathbf{r}(s_0, t)$, is locally constant. See Figure 5.12. This approximation was also exploited by (Vaillant and Faugeras 1992) and (Szeliski and Weiss 1998).

We choose to implement the theory presented in Chapter 4 directly by estimating temporal derivatives from measurements in the discrete views of the apparent contours, $\mathbf{u}(s, t_0), \mathbf{u}(s, t_1), \ldots, \mathbf{u}(s, t_n)$, which are indexed by

(a) first image   last image

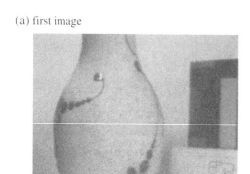   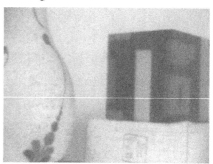

(b)

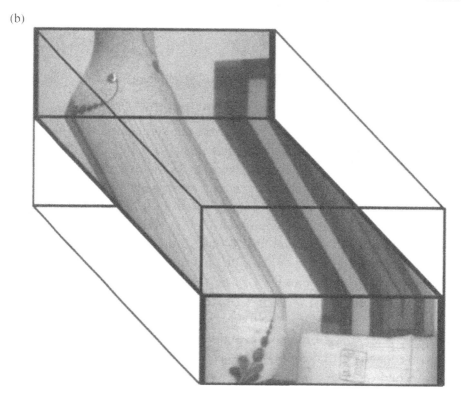

Fig. 5.11 3D spatio-temporal image. (a) The first and last image from an image sequence taken from a camera mounted on a robot arm and moving horizontally from
left to right without rotation. (b) The 3D spatio-temporal image formed from the
image sequence piled up sequentially with time. The top of the first image and the
bottom of the last image are shown along with the spatio-temporal cross-section
corresponding to the same epipolar plane. For simple viewer motions consisting
of camera translations perpendicular to the optical axis the spatio-temporal cross-
section image is formed by storing the scan-lines (epipolar lines) for a given epipolar
plane sequentially in order of time. The t-parameter curves $\mathbf{p}(s_0, t)$ are easily extracted from this spatio-temporal image and its first and second derivatives can be
used to recover depth and surface curvature respectively (Cipolla and Blake 1992).

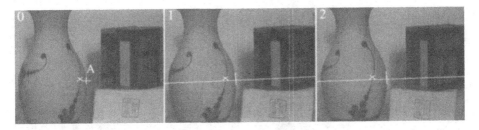

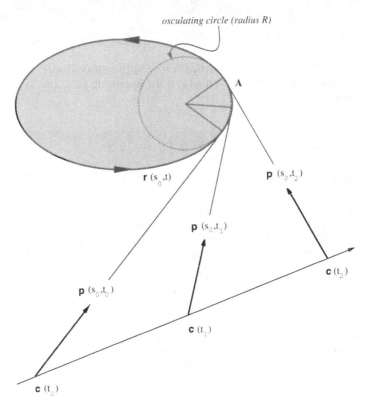

Fig. 5.12 The epipolar plane. Each view defines a tangent to the epipolar curve $\mathbf{r}(s_0, t)$. For linear camera motion and epipolar parametrization the rays and $\mathbf{r}(s_0, t)$ lie in a plane. If $\mathbf{r}(s_0, t)$ can be approximated locally by its osculating circle, it can be uniquely determined from measurements in three views, $\mathbf{p}(s_0, t_0)$, $\mathbf{p}(s_0, t_1)$ and $\mathbf{p}(s_0, t_2)$. For curvilinear motion the epipolar geometry is continuously changing and the epipolar curve is no longer planar (Cipolla and Blake 1992).

time, t_i and the corresponding camera position, $\mathbf{c}(t_i)$. Figure 5.5 shows 4 of 36 images taken by rotating an object in front of a fixed camera. This is equivalent to considering the image sequence to have been obtained by the camera rotating about the same axis of rotation, i.e. circular motion.

Fig. 5.13 In the epipolar parametrization of apparent contours, *correspondence* between points on successive snapshots of an apparent contours is set by matching along epipolar lines.

Fig. 5.14 The epipolar parametrization is degenerate at frontier points where the epipolar plane is tangent to the surface. Frontier points appear as epipolar tangencies – the epipolar lines are tangent to the apparent contour. In the vicinity of an epipolar tangency the parametrization is sensitive to errors in the epipolar geometry and the localization of the image contour. Reconstruction is therefore poor near a frontier point.

The apparent contours are extracted and tracked over the sequence using B-splines snakes.

The family of image contours is then parametrized using the known epipolar geometry obtained by first calibrating the sequence of discrete viewpoints by viewing a calibration grid as described in the previous section and illustrated in Figure 5.10. The projection matrices for each view can be used to obtain camera positions, $\mathbf{c}(t_i)$, and the epipolar geometry as described in §5.6. The epipolar geometry is then used to parametrize the image contours as follows.

Points are selected on the apparent contours in the first view, e.g. $\mathbf{u}(s_i, t_0)$,

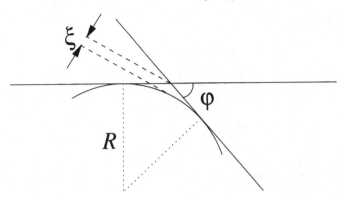

Fig. 5.15 The error ξ between the reconstructed point and the surface is related to the radius of curvature R and the angle φ between the viewing rays.

shown in Figure 5.13(a), and the calibrated epipolar geometry is used to induce a parametrization of the apparent contour in the other views, e.g. $\mathbf{u}(s_i, t_1), \ldots, \mathbf{u}(s_i, t_n)$. An example is shown in Figure 5.13(b). This requires finding the intersection of the cubic B-spline representing the apparent contour and the epipolar line. This is done analytically and multiple solutions are disambiguated by using ordering and disparity gradient constraints as in stereo vision. Particular care must be taken at an epipolar tangency (frontier point). See Figure 5.14. The known (calibrated) projection matrices for each viewpoint can then be used to convert image plane pixel coordinates, $\mathbf{u}(s_i, t_1), \ldots, \mathbf{u}(s_i, t_n)$, to rays in 3-space, $\mathbf{p}(s_i, t_1), \ldots, \mathbf{p}(s_i, t_n)$, as described in §5.2.

Recovery of depth

The depth is then estimated by a finite-difference (discrete) approximation to the infinitesimal analysis presented in (4.5). For each apparent contour point (indexed by spline parameter, s_0) in each view (indexed by time, t_i) an approximation to the depth to the contour generator can be computed from:

$$\lambda(s_0, t_i) \approx -\frac{\Delta\mathbf{c} \cdot \mathbf{n}}{\Delta\mathbf{p} \cdot \mathbf{n}} \tag{5.35}$$

where $\Delta\mathbf{c} = \mathbf{c}(t_{i+1}) - \mathbf{c}(t_i)$ and $\Delta\mathbf{p} = \mathbf{p}(s_0, t_{i+1}) - \mathbf{p}(s_0, t_i)$. The surface normal, $\mathbf{n} = \mathbf{n}(s, t_{i+1})$, is estimated directly from the apparent contour in a single view as described by Property 3.6.1.

The use of finite-differences introduces an error. Equation (5.35) is in fact equivalent to estimating the distance to the surface point by *triangulation*

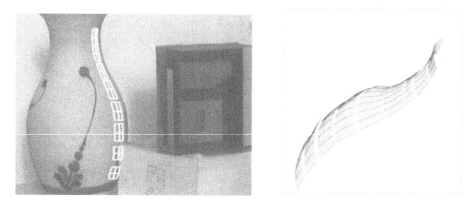

Fig. 5.16 Recovery of surface strip in vicinity of apparent contour. The surface is recovered as a family of s-parameter curves, $\mathbf{r}(s, t_i)$ – the contour generators – and t-parameter curves, $\mathbf{r}(s_0, t)$ – portions of the *osculating* circles measured in each epipolar plane. The strip is shown projected into the image of the scene from a different viewpoint and after extrapolation (Cipolla and Blake 1992).

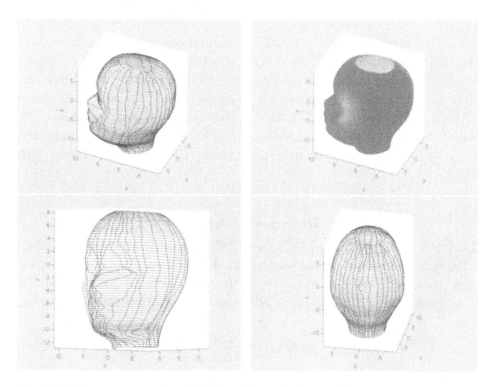

Fig. 5.17 The reconstruction of the head from 36 views of the apparent contour under circular motion. Three discrete views of the 36 reconstructed contour generators and epipolar curves are shown. The reconstructed surface is also shown shaded.

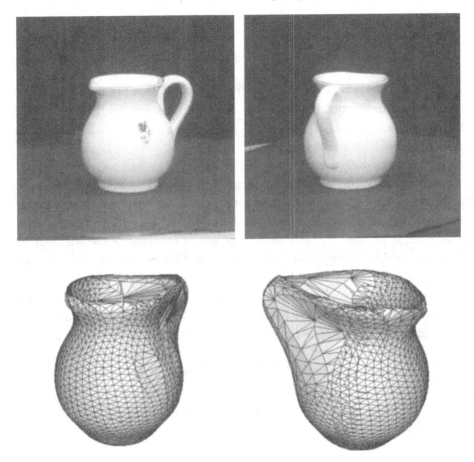

Fig. 5.18 Reconstruction of a vase using the epipolar parametrization and the method of triangulation described in (Boyer and Berger 1997).

as the intersection of two rays. This is, of course, exact in the stereo reconstruction of a fixed point from its correspondences in two discrete views but is an approximation when the views are of contour generators except in the infinitesimal limit as $\Delta \mathbf{c} \to 0$. See Figure 4.9.

The error introduced by using a finite-difference approximation can be easily quantified in the case of circular motion. See Figure 5.15. By assuming that the radius of curvature R along the epipolar curve is locally constant, the error in the recovered distance, $\Delta \lambda$, is given by:

$$\Delta \lambda = R \tan \left(\frac{\varphi}{2} \right). \tag{5.36}$$

The error ξ, which is the distance between the reconstructed point and the surface, is however given by

$$\xi = \left(\sec \left(\frac{\varphi}{2} \right) - 1 \right) R \approx \frac{\varphi^2}{8} R \qquad (5.37)$$

where φ is the angle between the viewing directions (see Figure 5.15). If the camera is far from a rotating object, φ can be approximated by the angle of rotation ω. For ω equals $10°$, the error will be 0.38% of the radius R, which will be negligible for small values of R.

Except for the degenerate cases listed in §4.6, we can use the epipolar parametrization of the family of apparent contours to recover the two families of parametric curves. The s-parameter curves are the contour generators from the different viewpoints and the t-parameter curves are the epipolar curves formed by the intersection of a pencil of epipolar planes defined by the camera centres in adjacent views. These surface curves form a *conjugate* grid, shown in Figure 5.16 and Figure 5.17.

The reconstructed surface from the image sequence of Figure 5.5 is shown in Figure 5.17 as a grid of 36 contour generators and 100 epipolar curves. The reconstruction is surprisingly accurate given that the views are discrete and not continuous. Figure 5.18 shows another example of a reconstruction using the epipolar parametrization but in which greater care is taken in computing the spatio-temporal derivatives (Boyer and Berger 1997).

6

Recovery of Viewer Motion from Profiles

In the previous chapter we described the algorithms and their practical implementation to recover the geometry of visible surfaces from the deformation of apparent contours (profiles) under *known* viewer motion. The epipolar geometry between the distinct viewpoints played an important part in the parametrization and recovery of the surface. In this chapter we describe how the epipolar geometry (and hence the camera motion) can be recovered from the deformation of apparent contours when the viewer motion is not known a priori.

The recovery of the structure and motion from point correspondences has attracted considerable attention and many practical algorithms exist to recover both the spatial configuration of the points and the viewer motion compatible with the views. These are briefly reviewed in §6.1 to §6.3 before showing how the deformation of apparent contours, and in particular frontier points, can be used to recover viewer motion. A set of working algorithms are then presented which are able to recover viewer motion and which exploit this to reconstruct surfaces. The special case of circular motion, which is often used in 3D model acquisition and hence has important practical applications, is described in greater detail.

6.1 The fundamental matrix from point correspondences

For uncalibrated cameras we do not have the projection matrices and hence the essential matrix parameters, $\mathbf{t}$ and $\mathbf{R}$, and the camera calibration parameters, $\mathbf{K}$ and $\mathbf{K}'$, are unknown a priori. The fundamental matrix, however, can be estimated from *point* correspondences between the two views. We briefly describe the algorithms used for computing the epipolar geometry from point correspondences (also reviewed in Zhang 1998) before describing the extension to curves and apparent contours.

139

From the epipolar constraint (5.24) we see that each point correspondence, $\mathbf{u}_i = (u_i, v_i, 1)^\top$ and $\mathbf{u}'_i = (u'_i, v'_i, 1)^\top$, generates one constraint on the epipolar geometry which can be expressed in terms of the elements of the fundamental matrix $\mathbf{F}$:

$$
\begin{bmatrix} u'_i & v'_i & 1 \end{bmatrix}
\begin{bmatrix}
f_{11} & f_{12} & f_{13} \\
f_{21} & f_{22} & f_{23} \\
f_{31} & f_{32} & f_{33}
\end{bmatrix}
\begin{bmatrix} u_i \\ v_i \\ 1 \end{bmatrix} = 0.
$$

For n pairs of correspondences, the constraints can be rearranged as linear equations in the 9 unknown elements of the fundamental matrix:

$$
\begin{bmatrix}
u'_1 u_1 & u'_1 v_1 & u'_1 & v'_1 u_1 & v'_1 v_1 & v'_1 & u_1 & v_1 & 1 \\
\vdots & \vdots & \vdots & \vdots & \vdots & \vdots & \vdots & \vdots & \vdots \\
u'_n u_n & u'_n v_n & u'_1 & v'_n u_n & v'_n v_n & v'_n & u_n & v_n & 1
\end{bmatrix}
\begin{bmatrix}
f_{11} \\ f_{12} \\ f_{13} \\ f_{21} \\ f_{22} \\ f_{23} \\ f_{31} \\ f_{32} \\ f_{33}
\end{bmatrix} = \mathbf{0}
$$

or in matrix form:

$$
\mathbf{Af} = \mathbf{0}
$$

where $\mathbf{A}$ is an $n \times 9$ measurement matrix, and $\mathbf{f}$ represents the elements of the fundamental matrix as a 9-vector. Given 8 or more correspondences a solution[1] can be found by least squares as the unit eigenvector ($\mathbf{f}$ is defined up to an arbitrary scale) corresponding to the minimum eigenvalue of $\mathbf{A}^\top \mathbf{A}$. A unique solution is obtained unless the points and the camera centres lie on a ruled quadric or all the points lie on a plane (Faugeras and Maybank 1990).

The computation can be poorly conditioned and it is important to precondition the image points by normalizing them to improve the condition number of $\mathbf{A}^\top \mathbf{A}$ before estimating the elements of the fundamental matrix by singular value decomposition (Hartley 1998).

---

[1] Note that the fundamental matrix has only 7 degrees of freedom since its determinant must be zero. A non-unique solution can be obtained from only 7 point correspondences and is described in (Huang and Netravali 1994).

Parametrization of the fundamental matrix

Two steps can be taken to improve the solution. The most important requires enforcing the rank 2 property of the fundamental matrix. This can
be achieved by a suitable parametrization of **F**.

The epipolar geometry between two uncalibrated views is completely determined by 7 independent parameters: the position of the epipoles in the
two views, $\mathbf{e} = (u_e, v_e, 1)^\top$ and $\mathbf{e}' = (u'_e, v'_e, 1)^\top$, and the 3 parameters of the
one-dimensional projective transformation[1] relating the pencil of epipolar
lines in view 1 to those in view 2 (Luong and Faugeras 1996),

$$\tau'_i = -\frac{h_2 \tau_i + h_1}{h_4 \tau_i + h_3} \tag{6.1}$$

where τ_i and τ'_i represent the directions (as the gradient of a line) of a pair
of corresponding epipolar lines, $\mathbf{l}_i$ and $\mathbf{l}'_i$, in the first and second images
respectively. Namely

$$\tau_i = \frac{v_i - v_e}{u_i - u_e} \tag{6.2}$$

$$\tau'_i = \frac{v'_i - v'_e}{u'_i - u'_e}. \tag{6.3}$$

The transformation of epipolar lines between views is sometimes known as
the *epipolar transformation* and is fixed by 3 pairs of epipolar line correspondences. The correspondence of any additional epipolar line is completely determined since it must preserve the cross-ratio of the 4 epipolar planes and
corresponding epipolar lines. See (Luong and Faugeras 1996) and Figure 6.1.

Substituting (6.2) and (6.3) into (6.1) for the image coordinates of a pair
of corresponding points results in the epipolar constraint and leads to the
following minimal parametrization of the fundamental matrix:

$$\mathbf{F} = \begin{bmatrix} h_1 & h_2 & -u_e h_1 - v_e h_2 \\ h_3 & h_4 & -u_e h_3 - v_e h_4 \\ -u'_e h_1 - v'_e h_3 & -u'_e h_2 - v'_e h_4 & u_e u'_e h_1 + v_e u'_e h_2 + u_e v'_e h_3 + v_e v'_e h_4 \end{bmatrix} \tag{6.4}$$

This parametrization will be exploited later when apparent contours are
used instead of point correspondences to estimate the epipolar geometry.

---

[1] This one-dimensional projective transformation (also known as a collineation or homography)
can be represented by a 2×2 matrix in homogeneous coordinates.

Optimization

Another improvement requires finding the 7 independent parameters of the fundamental matrix which minimize the distances between the image points and their epipolar lines.

Property 6.1.1 Geometric error using epipolar distances. *The geometric distance between an image point* $\mathbf{u}'$ *and the epipolar line,* $\mathbf{l}' = \mathbf{Fu}$ *is given by:*

$$\frac{(\mathbf{u}'^{\top}_i \mathbf{Fu}_i)^2}{(\mathbf{Fu}_i)^2_1 + (\mathbf{Fu}_i)^2_2} \tag{6.5}$$

A suitable cost function, C, consisting of the sum of the squared geometric distances (defined above) between image points and their epipolar lines in both images (Luong and Faugeras 1996),

$$C = \sum_i \left(\frac{1}{(\mathbf{Fu}_i)^2_1 + (\mathbf{Fu}_i)^2_2} + \frac{1}{(\mathbf{F}^{\top}\mathbf{u}'_i)^2_1 + (\mathbf{F}^{\top}\mathbf{u}'_i)^2_2} \right) (\mathbf{u}'^{\top}_i \mathbf{Fu}_i)^2$$

can be minimized by non-linear optimization techniques (Press et al. 1992).

6.2 Recovery of the projection matrices and viewer motion

As shown above it is possible to recover the epipolar geometry (via the fundamental matrix) from point correspondences in the case of uncalibrated cameras. Nevertheless we must recover the projection matrices corresponding to each viewpoint if we are to attempt reconstruction.

Factorization of the essential matrix

If the camera internal parameters, $\mathbf{K}$ and $\mathbf{K}'$, are known the viewer motion and the projection matrices are determined by the epipolar geometry. We can transform the recovered fundamental matrix into an essential matrix (5.22):

$$\mathbf{E} = \mathbf{K}'^{\top}\mathbf{FK} \tag{6.6}$$

and decompose this matrix into a skew-symmetric matrix corresponding to translation and an orthonormal matrix corresponding to the rotation between the views:

$$\mathbf{E} = [\mathbf{t}]_{\times}\mathbf{R}. \tag{6.7}$$

The latter is in fact only possible if the the essential matrix has rank 2 and two equal singular values (Tsai and Huang 1984). This property turns out

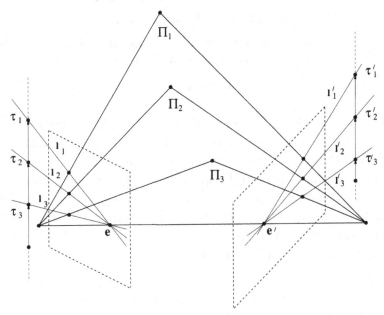

Fig. 6.1 The epipolar geometry of an uncalibrated stereo pair of images is completely specified by the image positions of the epipoles and 3 pairs of corresponding epipolar lines. The projective parameters τ and τ' represent the intersection of the epipolar line and the line at infinity. The directions in the 2 views are related by a one-dimensional projective transformation (homography).

to be very important in recovering constraints on the internal parameters of the cameras when they are uncalibrated. The difference in the two singular values can be used to refine the camera parameters. In fact, each fundamental matrix places two quadratic constraints on the internal calibration parameters (the Kruppa equations) which can be used to estimate, for example, the scale factors of the two cameras. This is known as self-calibration (Maybank and Faugeras 1992 and Hartley 1992).

The translation vector, $\mathbf{t}$, which can only be recovered up to an unknown magnitude, can be found as the unit eigenvector corresponding to the smallest eigenvalue of $\mathbf{E}\mathbf{E}^\top$ since it must satisfy

$$\mathbf{E}^\top \mathbf{t} = 0.$$

The rotation can then be obtained as the orthonormal matrix which minimizes the matrix Frobenius norm

$$||\mathbf{E} - [\mathbf{t}_\times]\mathbf{R}||^2$$

which can be solved linearly if we represent the rotation with a quaternion (Horn 1987).

Numerical considerations

An alternative numerical approach is to perform the singular value decomposition (Strang 1988) of the essential matrix (Hartley 1992):

$$\mathbf{E} = \mathbf{U\Lambda V}^\top \qquad (6.8)$$

where $\mathbf{\Lambda} = \mathrm{diag}(\sigma_1, \sigma_2, \sigma_3)$ and the matrices $\mathbf{U}$ and $\mathbf{V}$ are orthogonal. The decomposition into a translation vector and the rotation between the two views requires that $\sigma_1 = \sigma_2 \neq 0$ and $\sigma_3 = 0$. The nearest (in the sense of minimizing the Frobenius norm between the two matrices) essential matrix with the correct properties can be obtained by setting the two largest singular values to be equal to their average and the smallest one to zero (Hartley 1992). The translation and axis and angle of rotation can then be obtained directly up to arbitrary signs and unknown scale for the translation:

$$[\mathbf{t}]_\times = \mathbf{U} \begin{bmatrix} 0 & 1 & 0 \\ -1 & 0 & 0 \\ 0 & 0 & 0 \end{bmatrix} \mathbf{U}^\top \qquad (6.9)$$

$$\mathbf{R} = \mathbf{U} \begin{bmatrix} 0 & -1 & 0 \\ 1 & 0 & 0 \\ 0 & 0 & 1 \end{bmatrix} \mathbf{V}^\top. \qquad (6.10)$$

The projection matrices follow directly from the recovered translation and rotation by aligning the reference coordinate system with the first camera to give:

$$\begin{aligned} \mathbf{P} &= \mathbf{K}[\mathbf{I} \mid \mathbf{0}] \\ \mathbf{P}' &= \mathbf{K}'[\mathbf{R} \mid \mathbf{t}]. \end{aligned}$$

Four solutions are possible due to the arbitrary choice of signs for translation, $\pm\mathbf{t}$, and rotation, $\mathbf{R}$ or $\mathbf{R}^\top$. The correct solution is easily disambiguated by ensuring that reconstructed points lie in front of the cameras.

6.3 Recovery of the projection matrices for uncalibrated cameras

If the camera calibration matrices are unknown the projection matrices can not be uniquely recovered from the epipolar geometry of two views alone. In fact we will see that they can only be recovered up to an arbitrary 3D projective transformation, known as a projective ambiguity.

From (5.22) it follows that the fundamental matrix can, like the essential matrix, be factorized into a skew-symmetric matrix corresponding to translation and a 3×3 non-singular matrix (ignoring arbitrary scalings of the elements of $\mathbf{F}$):

$$
\begin{aligned}
\mathbf{F} &= \mathbf{K'}^{-\top}[\mathbf{t}]_\times \mathbf{R} \mathbf{K}^{-1} \\
&= [\mathbf{K't}]_\times \mathbf{K'} \mathbf{R} \mathbf{K}^{-1} \\
&= [\mathbf{e'}]_\times \mathbf{M}_\infty
\end{aligned}
\tag{6.11}
$$

where

$$
\mathbf{M}_\infty = \mathbf{K'} \mathbf{R} \mathbf{K}^{-1}
\tag{6.12}
$$

is a 2D projective transformation (homography) which maps points on the plane at infinity in one image to the other (Luong and Vieville 1996).

The factorization of the fundamental matrix as the product of a skew-symmetric matrix and a non-singular matrix $\mathbf{M}$ is not unique since there is a 3-parameter family of matrices $\mathbf{M}$ (which represents the 2D projective transformation between views induced by different planes) such that:

$$
\mathbf{M} = \mathbf{M}_\infty + \mathbf{e'} \mathbf{v}^\top
$$

where $\mathbf{v}$ can be arbitrarily chosen to give a different projective transformation but the same fundamental matrix (Hartley 1994 and Luong and Vieville 1996)[1].

Property 6.3.1 Factorization of the fundamental matrix. *The fundamental matrix can be factorized into a skew-symmetric matrix and a 3×3 non-singular matrix, $\mathbf{M}$:*

$$
\mathbf{F} = [\mathbf{e'}]_\times \mathbf{M}
$$

where $\mathbf{e'}$ is equivalent to the epipole in the second view:

$$
\mathbf{F}^\top \mathbf{e'} = \mathbf{0}
$$

and $\mathbf{M}$ can be chosen from the 3-parameter family (defined by the arbitrary choice of $\mathbf{v}$) of homographies given by:

$$
\mathbf{M} = [\mathbf{e'}]_\times \mathbf{F} + \mathbf{e'} \mathbf{v}^\top.
$$

---

[1] Note the relationship with the minimal parametrization introduced in (6.4). A 3-parameter family of two-dimensional projective transformations, $\mathbf{M}$, representing the transformation between views induced by points on a plane, can be recovered from the pair of epipoles and 3 pairs of corresponding epipolar lines. The epipoles must satisfy $\mathbf{e'} = \mathbf{M}\mathbf{e}$ while the epipolar lines must pass through the epipoles and satisfy $\mathbf{l}'_i = \mathbf{M}^{-\top}\mathbf{l}_i$.

Singular value decomposition of the fundamental matrix

As with the essential matrix, we can factorize the fundamental matrix into a skew-symmetric component and a non-singular matrix by analysing its singular value decomposition:

$$\mathbf{F} = \mathbf{U}\mathbf{\Lambda}\mathbf{V}^\top$$

where $\mathbf{\Lambda} = \mathrm{diag}(r, s, 0)$. The skew-symmetric component can be recovered from:

$$[\mathbf{e}']_\times = \mathbf{U} \begin{bmatrix} 0 & 1 & 0 \\ -1 & 0 & 0 \\ 0 & 0 & 0 \end{bmatrix} \mathbf{U}^\top \tag{6.13}$$

in exactly the same way as with calibrated cameras. The non-singular matrix $\mathbf{M}$ is no longer an orthogonal transformation and is not uniquely defined. As shown by Property 6.3.1, the homography (two-dimensional projective transformation) is defined up to an arbitrary choice of parameters, here described by $\{\alpha, \beta, \gamma\}$:

$$\mathbf{M} = \mathbf{U} \begin{bmatrix} 0 & -1 & 0 \\ 1 & 0 & 0 \\ 0 & 0 & 1 \end{bmatrix} \begin{bmatrix} r & 0 & 0 \\ 0 & s & 0 \\ \alpha & \beta & \gamma \end{bmatrix} \mathbf{V}^\top. \tag{6.14}$$

Canonical cameras and projective ambiguity

The factorization of the fundamental matrix can be used to compute the canonical cameras – the normalized projection matrices – given by (5.32) and (5.33)

$$\begin{aligned} \mathbf{PH} &= [\mathbf{I} \mid \mathbf{0}] \\ \mathbf{P'H} &= [\mathbf{M} \mid \mathbf{e}']. \end{aligned}$$

The real projection matrices, $\mathbf{P}$ and $\mathbf{P}'$, have only been recovered up to an arbitrary 3D projective transformation represented algebraically by a 4×4 matrix $\mathbf{H}$, and known as a projective ambiguity.

Property 6.3.2 Projective ambiguity. *A general 3D projective transformation can be represented by a non-singular 4×4 matrix, $\mathbf{H}$, of the form*

$$\mathbf{H} = \begin{bmatrix} s\mathbf{R_w} & \mathbf{t_w} \\ \mathbf{0}^\top & 1 \end{bmatrix} \begin{bmatrix} \mathbf{K}^{-1} & \mathbf{0} \\ \mathbf{0}^\top & 1 \end{bmatrix} \begin{bmatrix} \mathbf{I} & \mathbf{0} \\ \mathbf{v}^\top & 1 \end{bmatrix}. \tag{6.15}$$

The projective ambiguity is composed of the following effects. A metric transformation resulting from the rigid body motion between the coordinate system of the first camera and the reference frame and an arbitrary scaling. This can be ignored if we align the reference coordinate system with the first camera and accept that shape can only be recovered up to an arbitrary scale, s, if the distance between the two camera centres is unknown. The second component of the ambiguity results from an 3D affine transformation due to the unknown parameters of the first camera. Finally we are left with a projective transformation which transforms points on the plane $(\mathbf{v}^\top 1)\mathbf{X} = 0$ to points on the plane at infinity and results from the ambiguity of Property 6.3.2.

The ambiguity in the projection matrices is of the form above and will result in a projective ambiguity in the recovered geometry, i.e. the 3D coordinates of visible points, $\mathbf{X}$, can only be recovered up to a 3D projective transformation, $\mathbf{H}^{-1}\mathbf{X}$. This ambiguity can only be removed with additional information derived from scene constraints or knowledge of the camera parameters, $\mathbf{K}$ and $\mathbf{K}'$. In particular the ambiguity is completely removed by using the 3D position of 5 known scene points to determine the transformation $\mathbf{H}$ or $\mathbf{H}^{-1}$. Alternatively we require the internal camera parameters of the first camera and must then find the equation of the plane at infinity represented by $\mathbf{v}$ where

$$\mathbf{M} = \mathbf{K}'\mathbf{R}\mathbf{K}^{-1} + \mathbf{e}'\mathbf{v}^\top.$$

The ambiguity is removed by using knowledge of the camera parameters to fix $\mathbf{v}$ to make the homography, $\mathbf{M}$, be that induced by the plane at infinity (Hartley 1994). The rotation matrix follows.

6.4 Frontier points and epipolar tangencies

As described in Chapter 4 an important degeneracy of the epipolar parametrization occurs when an epipolar plane (spanned by the direction of translation and the visual ray) coincides with the tangent plane to the surface. This will occur at a finite set of points on the surface where the surface normal $\mathbf{n}$ is perpendicular to the direction of translation:

$$\mathbf{c}_t \cdot \mathbf{n} = 0. \tag{6.16}$$

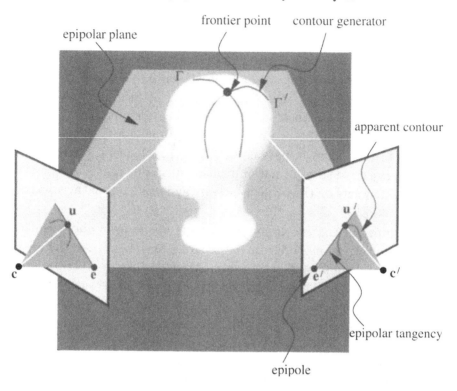

Fig. 6.2. The frontier point and epipolar tangencies in two distinct views.

The contour generator is locally stationary. In fact (see Figure 4.13) consecutive contour generators will intersect at a point on the surface called a *frontier point* (Rieger 1986 and Giblin et al. 1994)[1].

For larger discrete motions (see Figure 6.2) the contour generators defined by the discrete viewpoints also intersect at points on the surface where the epipolar plane is tangent to the surface. This is easily seen if we consider the motion to be linear. $\mathbf{c}_t$ is then a *constant* vector, and the frontier point on the surface at time t satisfies the frontier condition at subsequent times. The frontier degenerates to a point on the surface. In the discrete case the frontier points are defined by the condition

$$\Delta\mathbf{c} \cdot \mathbf{n} = 0 \qquad (6.17)$$

---

[1] In the image sphere model of Figure 4.13 the epipole $\mathbf{e}$ is the intersection of the epipolar great circle with the baseline $\mathbf{c}_1 - \mathbf{c}_2$, or with the velocity vector $\mathbf{c}_t$ in the limit as the two camera centres tend to coincidence. Thus the epipolar great circle passes through the epipole in exactly the same way as, in the image plane model adopted here, the epipolar line passes through the epipole.

where $\Delta \mathbf{c} = \mathbf{c}(t_2) - \mathbf{c}(t_1)$ and $\mathbf{n}$ is the surface normal at the point of intersection of the two contour generators.

Property 6.4.1 Epipolar tangency. *The frontier point projects to a point on the apparent contour which is an epipolar tangency, i.e. the epipolar line is tangent to the apparent contour.*

The property follows directly from the fact that the epipolar plane is also the tangent plane at a frontier point. Its projection in the two views, $\mathbf{u}(s)$ and $\mathbf{u}'(s)$, must be such that its tangent ($\mathbf{u}_s(s)$ and $\mathbf{u}'_s(s)$) passes through the respective epipole ($\mathbf{e}$ and $\mathbf{e}'$):

$$\det[\mathbf{e} \ \mathbf{u}(s_i) \ \mathbf{u}_s(s_i)] = 0 \qquad (6.18)$$

where $\mathbf{u}_s(s_i)$ represents the image contour tangent.

The surface curvature can not be recovered at these points since the epipolar parametrization fails (§4.8). However frontier points correspond to real, fixed feature points on the surface which are visible in both views. Once detected they can be used to provide a constraint on the epipolar geometry (Figure 6.3) and hence the viewer motion. In fact they can be used in the same way as points in the recovery of the epipolar geometry via the epipolar constraint

$$\mathbf{u}'(s_i)^\top \mathbf{F} \mathbf{u}(s_i) = 0. \qquad (6.19)$$

The epipoles and epipolar tangencies in each view completely determine the epipolar geometry ((Cipolla et al. 1995) and (Aström et al. 1996)).

Property 6.4.2 Epipolar tangency constraint. *Given two images, and the epipoles $\mathbf{e}$ and $\mathbf{e}'$, the set of lines through $\mathbf{e}$ which are tangent to the apparent contour, and the corresponding set of epipolar tangency lines through the epipole in the other image, are related by a one-dimensional projective transformation (since they arise from the same pencil of planes through the two camera centres).*

6.5 Recovery of motion under pure translation

Under pure translation (i.e. the rotation R of §4.3 is *constant*, or that Ω in §4.3 is zero) the epipolar geometry is completely determined by the position of the epipole in a single view. The fundamental matrix has the simple

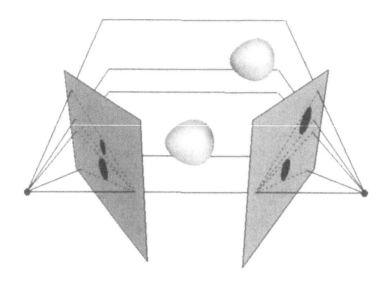

Fig. 6.3 Epipolar geometry and epipolar tangencies under arbitrary motion. The epipolar geometry is completely determined by the epipoles and 3 epipolar tangencies in each view.

skew-symmetric form:

$$\mathbf{F} = [\mathbf{e}]_\times. \tag{6.20}$$

If the camera parameters do not change the position of the epipole is the same in both views. The epipolar lines have the same directions with corresponding image points lying on the same epipolar line (i.e. are *auto-epipolar*):

$$\mathbf{e} = \mathbf{e}'$$
$$\mathbf{l} = \mathbf{l}'.$$

The key fact here is that, when there is no rotation, the projection of the frontier is simply the envelope of apparent contours in *rotated* coordinates; generally it is only the envelope when the coordinates are *unrotated*. See Property 4.8.1, and (4.8) which, when $R(t)$ is constant, states the (obvious) fact that $\mathbf{p}_t = R\mathbf{q}_t$. Note that $\mathbf{p}_s = R\mathbf{q}_s$ always, since this refers to a particular time for which R will have some particular value.

For a discrete motion we superimpose the two views and find common tangents to the two consecutive apparent contours instead of the envelope. See Figure 6.4. We refer to these informally as *bitangents* (though they are only tangent to each apparent contour once). The bitangents are in fact epipolar tangencies and hence the projection of frontier points. The

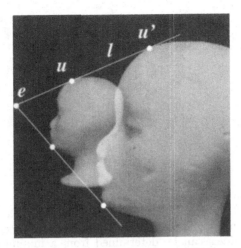

Fig. 6.4 Under pure translation the epipolar tangency point moves along the epipolar line since the position of the epipole and the direction of the epipolar lines do not change. From a minimum of two *bitangents* of the apparent contour in two views it is possible to recover the epipole, **e**.

intersection of at least two distinct tangencies (epipolar lines) is therefore sufficient to determine the position of the epipole and hence the epipolar geometry. A simple procedure to find the epipole, and hence the direction of translation, is described in (Sato and Cipolla 1998).

6.6 General motion

The solution is no longer trivial in the case of arbitrary motion with rotation. There is in fact no closed form solution since the epipoles are needed to define the epipolar tangency points and these are needed to determine the epipolar geometry.

The solution proceeds as a search and optimization problem to find the position of the epipoles in both views such that the epipolar tangencies in the first view are related to the set of epipolar tangencies in the second view by a one-dimensional projective transformation or homography (see Property 6.4.2 and (6.1)).

A suitable cost function is needed. Geometric distances are used in the estimation of the fundamental matrix from point correspondences and can also be used in the case of curves. The geometric distance is computed as the sum over all tangency points of the square of the distance between the image point and the corresponding epipolar line from the tangency point in the other view, as shown in Figure 6.5.

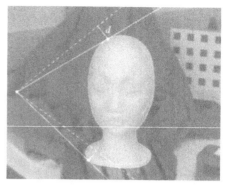

Fig. 6.5 Illustration of the cost function to be minimized in the motion estimation algorithm. From the initial guess of the epipoles the 1D projective transformation which maps epipolar lines can be determined from a minimum of 3 tangencies. Epipolar tangencies are then transferred from one image to the other. The length d is the distance from a tangency point in the first image and an epipolar line obtained by the transfer of an epipolar tangency from the second image. The distance d' is found in the same way, interchanging the roles of the images. The cost function is then the sum $\sum_i (d_i^2 + d_i'^2)$ for each matching pair i of putative epipolar tangencies.

The key to a successful implementation is to ensure that the search space is reduced and that the optimization begins from a good starting point using approximate knowledge of the camera motion or point correspondences. A minimum of 7 epipolar tangencies of features which are visible in each image are required. The solution proceeds as follows.

Algorithm 6.6.1 Motion recovery under general motion and perspective projection.

(i) Start with an initial guess or estimate of the epipoles in both views, $\mathbf{e}$ and $\mathbf{e}'$.

(ii) Compute the epipolar tangencies, $\mathbf{u}_i(\mathbf{e})$ and $\mathbf{u}'_i(\mathbf{e}')$, in both views respectively. These are points on the apparent contours with tangents passing through the epipole as defined by (6.18).

(iii) Estimate the elements of the homography (one dimensional projective transformation) between the pencil of tangencies in both views (6.1). This can be done linearly by minimizing

$$\sum_i (h_4 \tau_i \tau_i' + h_3 \tau_i' + h_2 \tau_i + h_1)^2 \qquad (6.21)$$

by least squares over all pairs $(n \geq 3)$ of correspondences, τ_i and τ_i'.

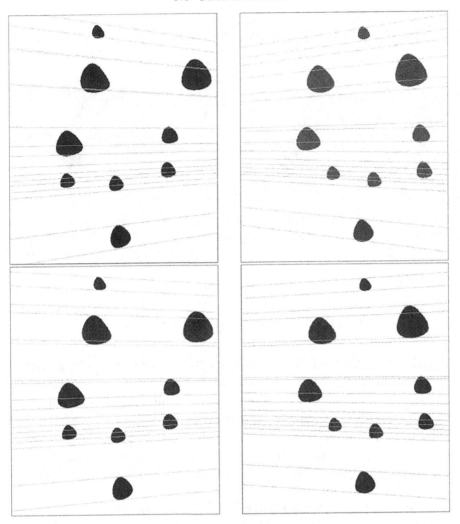

Fig. 6.6 Starting point for optimization (above). An initial guess of the position of the epipoles is used to determine epipolar tangencies in both views and the homography relating the epipolar lines. For each tangency point the corresponding epipolar line is drawn in the other view. The distances between epipolar lines and tangency points are used to search for the correct positions of the epipoles. Convergence to local minimum after 5 iterations (below). The epipolar lines are tangent to apparent contours in both views.

(iv) The fundamental matrix is now given by the parametrization of §6.1 and the cost function, i.e. sum of squared geometric distances between tangency point and corresponding epipolar line, can be computed as

Fig. 6.7 Local minimum obtained by iterative scheme to estimate the epipolar geometry from 8 epipolar tangencies in a stereo pair of a Henry Moore sculpture.

below:

$$C = \sum_i \left(\frac{1}{(\mathbf{Fu}_i)_1^2 + (\mathbf{Fu}_i)_2^2} + \frac{1}{(\mathbf{F}^T\mathbf{u}'_i)_1^2 + (\mathbf{F}^T\mathbf{u}'_i)_2^2} \right) (\mathbf{u}'^T_i\mathbf{Fu}_i)^2.$$
$$(6.22)$$

(v) Minimize the cost function by using the Levenberg-Marquardt algorithm or the conjugate gradient method (Press et al. 1992). The search space is restricted to the four coordinates of the epipoles only. This requires the first-order partial derivatives of the cost function (6.22) with respect to the coordinates of the epipoles which can be computed analytically but are more conveniently estimated by numerical techniques.

At each iteration of the algorithm, steps (ii) to (v) are repeated, and the positions of the epipoles are iteratively refined. The search is stopped when the root-mean-square distance converges to a minimum (usually less than 0.1 pixels). It is of course not guaranteed to find a unique solution and we do not know whether there is a unique solution. The only case where we know of a uniqueness theorem is that of circular motion and parallel projection (Giblin et al. 1994).

Experimental results

A number of experiments were carried out with simulated data (with noise) and known motion (Figure 6.6). The apparent contours were automatically extracted from the sequence by fitting B-splines. 5–10 iterations each for 4 different initial guesses for the position of the epipole were sufficient to find the correct solution to within a root-mean-square error of 0.1 pixel per tangency point.

Figure 6.7 shows an example with real data whose apparent contours are detected and automatically tracked using B-spline snakes. A solution is found very quickly which minimizes the geometric distances. The solution is however incorrect and corresponds to a local minimum. As with all structure from motion algorithms, a limited field of view and small variation in depths result in a solution which is sensitive to image localization errors. A more stable solution can be obtained by considering a simpler projection model (see below).

Other more practical alternatives include using a planar contour (if present in the scene) to estimate the 2D projective transformation component, $\mathbf{M}$, directly. Recall that the fundamental matrix can be factored into:

$$\mathbf{F} = [\mathbf{e}']_\times \mathbf{M}.$$

We can apply this planar projective transformation, $\mathbf{M}$, to an apparent contour in the first view. The epipolar constraint can be rewritten as:

$$\mathbf{u}'(s_i)^\top [\mathbf{e}']_\times (\mathbf{M}\mathbf{u}(s_i)) = 0$$

and the epipolar geometry between points in this rectified view, $\mathbf{M}\mathbf{u}(s)$, and the second view, $\mathbf{u}'(s)$, has now been simplified. This has, in fact, reduced the general problem to the case of pure translation and is known as *projective reduction* (Aström et al. 1999). The pure translation algorithm can now be applied to find common tangents to the pairs of apparent contours (analogous to bitangents) to determine the epipole and hence the full epipolar geometry.

Finally, analysing extended image sequences, instead of only two views, avoids convergence to a local minima and results in a more accurate and better conditioned solution for the epipolar geometry and motion (Aström and Kahl 1999).

6.7 Weak perspective

When the field of view is narrow or the depth variation is small compared with the distance from the camera to the scene, the epipoles will be far from the image centre, and the epipolar lines will be approximately parallel. This viewing geometry suggests the use of a *weak perspective* camera model. The epipolar geometry under weak perspective is known as *affine epipolar geometry* (Shapiro et al. 1995), and assumes that the epipoles will be at infinity. This reduces the degrees of freedom of the fundamental matrix which will then take the form:

$$\mathbf{F} = \begin{bmatrix} 0 & 0 & c \\ 0 & 0 & d \\ a & b & e \end{bmatrix}. \tag{6.23}$$

There are two circumstances when the *affine fundamental matrix* may be used. The first is when the weak perspective camera model can be used to describe the cameras, as described in §5.3. Another favourable situation for the use of the affine fundamental matrix is when the motion is restricted to translation orthogonal to the optical axis and rotation about the optical axis. In this case the affine fundamental matrix can be used even though the weak perspective camera model is inappropriate. It is important to notice that a rotation by a small angle around a distant axis is a good approximation for such motion.

As scale factors are not important, the affine fundamental matrix has only four degrees of freedom, and can be linearly computed from 4 point correspondences. Each epipole, being at infinity, is described by a single parameter, corresponding to its direction in the image plane. This observation suggests another parametrization for the fundamental matrix, where the directions of the epipoles are made explicit. If ϕ and ϕ' are the directions of the epipolar lines in the first and second images, the affine fundamental matrix can be expressed as

$$\mathbf{F} = \begin{bmatrix} 0 & 0 & \alpha' \sin \phi' \\ 0 & 0 & -\alpha' \cos \phi' \\ -\alpha \sin \phi & \alpha \cos \phi & \sqrt{1 - \alpha^2 - \alpha'^2} \end{bmatrix} \tag{6.24}$$

where the parameters α and α' are related to the distances between epipolar lines in each image. The geometric interpretation of the parameters α and α' can be seen in Figure 6.8. It is easy to show that they are proportional to the distance between epipolar lines, or, in the notation of Figure 6.8,

$$\begin{bmatrix} \alpha \\ \alpha' \end{bmatrix} = \frac{1}{\sqrt{(d_2 d_1' + d_1 d_2')^2 + (d_1' - d_2')^2 + (d_1 - d_2)^2}} \begin{bmatrix} d_1' - d_2' \\ d_2 - d_1 \end{bmatrix}. \tag{6.25}$$

In the affine case the epipolar tangencies will be parallel lines, with directions given by the corresponding epipole, and, as in the perspective, the epipolar tangencies will touch the apparent contours at corresponding points. Since the number of degrees of freedom of the affine fundamental matrix is 4, this will also be the minimum number of epipolar tangencies necessary for its computation.

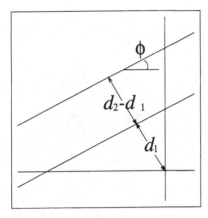 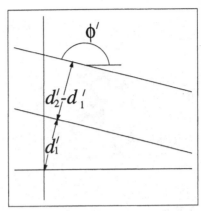

Fig. 6.8 Geometric interpretation of the parametrization of the affine fundamental matrix presented in (6.24). The orientation of the epipolar lines in each image is given by the angles ϕ and ϕ', and the parameters α and α' are proportional to the differences of distances $d_2' - d_1'$ and $d_2 - d_1$, respectively (see (6.25)).

The algorithm for computing the epipolar geometry from apparent contours under weak perspective is described as follows:

Algorithm 6.7.1 Motion recovery under weak perspective.

(i) Start with initial estimates for the directions of both epipoles, ϕ and ϕ'.

(ii) Determine tangency point correspondences $\mathbf{u}_i(\phi)$ and $\mathbf{u}_i'(\phi')$ from epipolar tangencies consistent with the directions of the epipoles.

(iii) Compute the affine fundamental matrix from the epipoles and the correspondences. This must be done by using the parametrization given in (6.24).

(iv) Minimize the sum of geometric distances from the tangency points on the contours to their corresponding epipolar lines. The search is restricted to the two directions of the epipoles, and the cost function is the same as given by (6.22).

Experimental results

The algorithm was tested on the images shown in Figure 6.7, with the directions of the epipoles initialized at $0°$. The recovered epipolar lines are shown in Figure 6.9. There is some discrepancy between the result obtained with the general motion algorithm and that obtained by the algorithm for the affine case. The epipolar geometry found by the algorithm assuming weak

Fig. 6.9 Estimated affine epipolar geometry from the apparent contours of the Moore sequence. The result differs with the one found by the general motion algorithm shown in Figure 6.7.

perspective is consistent with planar motion along the ground plane and includes an epipolar line parallel with the horizon. This is qualitatively correct for the motion used in acquiring the images.

6.8 Circular motion

Circular motion is commonly used in model acquisition. An object is placed on a turntable and a sequence of snapshots is taken from a fixed camera as the object rotates about a fixed axis. This is equivalent to a stationary object and a camera undergoing motion with its centre moving on a circle and its image plane rotating rigidly with it (compare Example 4.1.1). Figure 6.10 shows a sequence obtained by a single camera under circular motion.

The estimation of epipolar geometry under circular motion is considerably simpler than more general motions. It is possible to exploit features which remain fixed in the image over the complete sequence. In fact the epipolar geometry of two views is completely specified with 6 parameters (compared with 7 in the general motion case). The epipolar geometry for a sequence of n images can be parametrized with only $5+n$ parameters: each additional view adding only one additional degree of freedom and with 5 of the parameters corresponding to features which remain fixed over the whole image sequence, irrespective of the viewpoints (Fitzgibbon et al. 1998).

Consider circular motion with the camera internal parameters remaining fixed during the object rotation. The following relationships between corresponding features lead to a simple parametrization of the epipolar geometry and fundamental matrices (Figures 6.10 and 6.11):

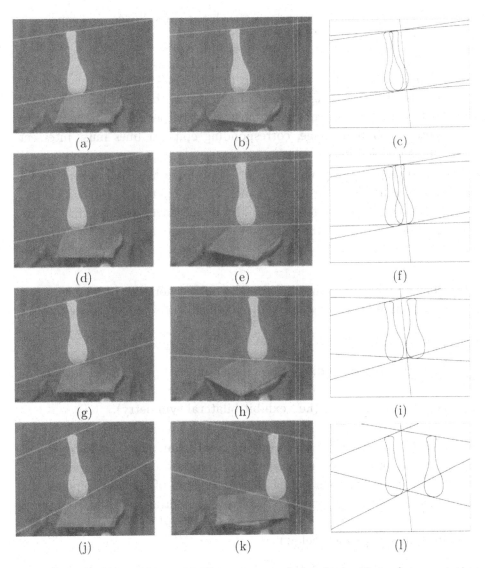

Fig. 6.10 Five images from a single camera and circular motion after a rotation of $10°, 20°, 40°$ and $80°$ are shown in (b), (e), (h) and (k). The epipolar geometry between pairs of images is shown. Epipolar tangencies are found that intersect at a common axis, lie on a common horizon (above and not shown) and which are projectively symmetric about this axis shown superimposed onto a single image in (c), (f), (i) and (l).

(i) There is no relative motion between the axis of rotation and the camera. The projection of the axis of rotation in the image, l_s, is therefore a fixed image line. Points on the projection of the axis,

$\mathbf{l}_s \cdot \mathbf{u} = 0$, have correspondences with the same image position:

$$\mathbf{u} = \mathbf{u}'.$$

(ii) Points on the projection of the axis of rotation must therefore lie on the corresponding epipolar line drawn in the same image (i.e. are auto-epipolar). If we superimpose the two pencils of epipolar lines onto a common image, corresponding epipolar lines must intersect on the projection of the axis.

(iii) The image of the plane of motion containing the camera centres, $\mathbf{l}_h$, remains fixed in the image sequence. We refer to it as the horizon. All image points on the horizon, $\mathbf{l}_h \cdot \mathbf{u} = 0$, have corresponding image points which lie on the same epipolar line, i.e. are also auto-epipolar:

$$\mathbf{l} = \mathbf{l}'.$$

The epipoles are constrained to lie on the horizon. In homogeneous coordinates a line (the horizon) is defined by two points (the epipoles)

$$\mathbf{l}_h = \mathbf{e} \wedge \mathbf{e}'.$$

(iv) The rays corresponding to pairs of epipoles superimposed onto a single image are bisected by the plane containing the camera centre and the axis of rotation (i.e. exhibit bilateral symmetry).

(v) There is a fixed point on the horizon, $\mathbf{u}_s$, which is the same for all views and depends on the orientation of the camera relative to the axis of rotation. As a consequence, the positions of the epipoles on the horizon are constrained. The cross ratio of the two epipoles, the intersection of the axis of rotation and the horizon and the fixed point on the horizon, are fixed and must correspond to bilateral symmetry in space (explained below).

All points $\mathbf{u}$ which lie on the projection of the axis or the horizon are auto-epipolar and must therefore satisfy the quadratic form:

$$\mathbf{u}^\top \mathbf{F} \mathbf{u} = 0 \qquad (6.26)$$

when $\mathbf{l}_h^\top \mathbf{u} = 0$ or $\mathbf{l}_s^\top \mathbf{u} = 0$. The condition is satisfied by any skew-symmetric matrix. The symmetric part of the fundamental matrix (up to an arbitrary scale factor) is constrained to be of the form

$$\mathbf{F} + \mathbf{F}^\top = \mathbf{l}_s \mathbf{l}_h^\top + \mathbf{l}_h \mathbf{l}_s^\top.$$

Property 6.8.1 Epipolar geometry under circular motion. *Under circular motion the fundamental matrices, $\mathbf{F}_{ij}$, relating correspondences in two views in the sequence, i and j, have a special form which can be parametrized into an anti-symmetric component which depends on a fixed vanishing point on the horizon, $\mathbf{u}_s$, and a symmetric component which depends only on the image of the axis of rotation, $\mathbf{l}_s$, and the horizon, $\mathbf{l}_h$:*

$$\mathbf{F}_{ij} = [\mathbf{u}_s]_{\times} + k_{ij} \left[\mathbf{l}_s \mathbf{l}_h^{\top} + \mathbf{l}_h \mathbf{l}_s^{\top} \right]. \tag{6.27}$$

The scaling factor, k_{ij}, depends on the angle between the two views, ϕ_{ij}, and uniquely determines the position of both epipoles once the other 5 parameters are known.

A derivation of (6.27) follows directly by considering two projection matrices parametrized for circular motion (see (6.34)). The scaling factor, k_{ij} can be shown to be equal to $\tan(\phi_{ij}/2)$. The anti-symmetric component results from symmetry properties of circular motion which will be considered below. The latter can be used to derive a simpler parametrization of the fundamental matrix.

Bilateral symmetry under perspective projection

Symmetry properties play a useful role in the recovery of epipolar geometry under circular motion. These are briefly derived below. Consider the projection of pairs of points in space which are bilaterally symmetric about the plane containing the camera centre and the axis of rotation. If the optical axis intersects the axis of rotation, the projection of point correspondences will also display bilateral symmetry about the projection of the axis of rotation, $\mathbf{l}_s$.

The symmetry transformation, $\mathbf{T}$, between corresponding points in the image, $\mathbf{u}$ and $\mathbf{u}'$:

$$\mathbf{u}' = \mathbf{T}\mathbf{u}$$

has a very special structure since it must satisfy $\mathbf{T}^2 = \mathbf{I}$ and must map points on the axis to themselves. In fact the transformation has eigenvalues $\{-1, 1, 1\}$ with the eigenvectors with the same eigenvalue defining the image of the axis of symmetry and the other corresponding to the vanishing point of the lines of symmetry (i.e. in a direction perpendicular to the axis and at infinity). See Figure 6.12(a).

The bilateral symmetry is projectively distorted if the optical axis is rotated away from the axis of rotation. Note that the components of rotation about the optical axis and perpendicular to the axis of rotation leave this

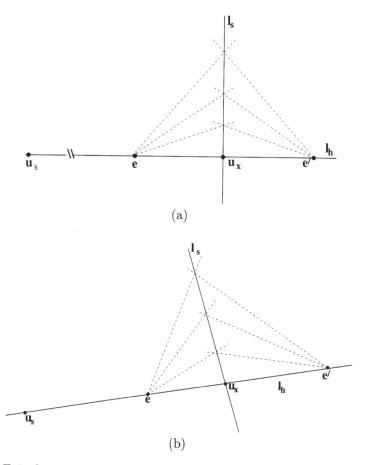

(a)

(b)

Fig. 6.11 Epipolar geometry under circular motion. The epipolar geometry of two views is completely determined by the projection of the axis of rotation, $\mathbf{l}_s$, and the position of the two epipoles. Corresponding epipolar lines intersect on the axis. Only two epipolar tangencies are required to fix the one-dimensional projective transformation between pencils of epipolar lines. The epipoles are also bilaterally symmetric about the axis when the optical axis intersects the axis of rotation (a). Rotation of the optical axis away from the axis of rotation introduces a projective distortion with lines of symmetry meeting at a vanishing point $\mathbf{u}_s$, (b). This point is a infinity in (a).

symmetry unchanged. Only the component of rotation about an axis parallel to the rotation axis will result in projective distortion. See Figure 6.12.

Under rotation about the optical centre, image points are mapped by a 2D projective transformation given by (6.12). The new transformation relating points in the image which are bilaterally symmetric in space is given by

$$\mathbf{T}_s = \mathbf{M}_\infty \mathbf{T} \mathbf{M}_\infty^{-1}$$

where $\mathbf{M}_\infty$ is the 2D projective transformation which maps image points before and after the rotation. The eigenvalues are preserved under this transformation, leading to the following property (Springer 1964).

Property 6.8.2 Planar projective symmetry transformation. *Under perspective projection, pairs of points in space which are bilaterally symmetric about the plane containing the camera centre and the axis of rotation, are related in the image by a projective symmetry transformation, $\mathbf{T}_s$, which can be represented by a 3×3 matrix with 4 degrees of freedom and eigenvalues $\{-1, 1, 1\}$ given by:*

$$\mathbf{T}_s = \mathbf{I} - 2\frac{\mathbf{u}_s \mathbf{l}_s^\top}{\mathbf{l}_s^\top \mathbf{u}_s}. \tag{6.28}$$

The transformation is known as a *planar harmonic homology* and is fixed by the image of the axis of rotation, $\mathbf{l}_s$, and the vanishing point, $\mathbf{u}_s$. The latter corresponds to the image of parallel lines of symmetry which map corresponding points and is known as the centre of the homology. $\mathbf{u}_s$ is at infinity in the special case of bilateral symmetry in the image.

The transformation must satisfy $\mathbf{T}_s^2 = \mathbf{I}$ and maps the point $\mathbf{u}_s$ and points on the axis, $\mathbf{l}_s^\top \mathbf{u} = 0$, to themselves:

$$\mathbf{T}_s \mathbf{u}_s = -\mathbf{u}_s \tag{6.29}$$
$$\mathbf{T}_s \mathbf{u} = \mathbf{u}. \tag{6.30}$$

The transformation can therefore be parametrized by (6.28).

Fundamental matrix under circular motion

The camera centres, epipoles and pencils of epipolar lines are also symmetric about the axis of rotation. See Figure 6.11. The epipoles are therefore mapped by the projective symmetry transformation

$$\mathbf{e}' = \mathbf{T}_s \mathbf{e} \tag{6.31}$$

while corresponding epipolar lines are related by

$$\mathbf{l}' = \mathbf{T}_s^{-\top} \mathbf{l} = \mathbf{T}_s^\top \mathbf{l}. \tag{6.32}$$

The projective transformation, $\mathbf{T}_s$, is in fact a special case of the 2D projective transformation (homography) between views induced by an arbitrary plane (i.e. $\mathbf{M}$ in Property 6.3.1) and can be used to define a minimal parametrization of the fundamental matrix.

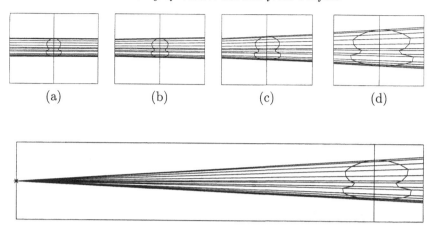

(a)   (b)   (c)   (d)

(e)

Fig. 6.12 Under perspective projection objects with a plane of symmetry which passes through the camera centre exhibit a projective symmetry. The axis and lines of symmetry are shown for different orientations of the camera relative to the object's rotation axis. If the optical axis intersects the axis of rotation the symmetry is bilateral (a). The amount of projective distortion increases with camera rotation about an axis parallel to the rotation axis of the object. The projective transformation for rotations of $20°$, $30°$ and $40°$ is shown in (b), (c) and (d) respectively. The transformation is completely determined by the axis, $\mathbf{l}_s$ and the vanishing point, $\mathbf{u}_s$, shown in (e).

Property 6.8.3 Parametrization of fundamental matrix under circular motion. *The fundamental matrix under circular motion can be parametrized by a single epipole and the planar projective symmetry transformation*

$$\mathbf{F} = [\mathbf{e}']_\times \mathbf{T}_s \qquad (6.33)$$

where

$$\mathbf{T}_s = \mathbf{I} - 2\frac{\mathbf{u}_s \mathbf{l}_s^\top}{\mathbf{l}_s^\top \mathbf{u}_s}.$$

The epipolar geometry of two views is completely determined by a single epipole, the fixed point $\mathbf{u}_s$ and the projection of the axis of rotation, $\mathbf{l}_s$. Alternatively the two epipoles, $\mathbf{e}$ and $\mathbf{e}'$, and the projection of the axis of rotation, $\mathbf{l}_s$ can be used. It has only 6 degrees of freedom.

Computation of epipolar geometry

Consider a pair of views obtained under circular motion. The key observation with apparent contours is that every epipolar tangency must be transferred to an epipolar line which remains tangent to the apparent contour in the other image. The two epipolar lines must also be related by the projective symmetry transformation and hence intersect at the projection of the axis of rotation. See Figures 6.10 and 6.11. This provides a very simple constraint for finding the epipolar tangencies in both views.

If we assume that the positions of the epipoles are known, two epipolar tangencies are sufficient to fix $\mathbf{l}_s$ and thus the epipolar geometry. The position of the epipoles is controlled by four degrees of freedom (the coordinates of the epipoles), and at least four more epipolar tangencies are required to determine the epipolar geometry of the pair of cameras. The general motion algorithm can be applied to the two images, exploiting the simplified parametrization for the fundamental matrix.

With more images better results can be obtained by exploiting the fact that the horizon, $\mathbf{l}_h$; the projection of the axis of rotation, $\mathbf{l}_s$; and the vanishing point, $\mathbf{u}_s$, remain fixed in all of the images. Each view, in fact, adds only 1 additional unknown (parameter k_{ij} in (6.27)) corresponding to the position of one of the epipoles on the horizon. Two epipolar tangencies in at least four images is sufficient to completely determine the epipolar geometry and fix the angles of rotation between the views. Results on real images are as shown in Figure 6.10.

6.9 Envelope of apparent contours under circular motion

Simpler methods exist when viewing an object that undergoes a full rotation around a fixed axis. The object sweeps out a surface of revolution. In the image the envelope of the apparent contours is in fact the image of the envelope of surfaces (a surface of revolution in this case) as described in §4.12 and (Giblin et al. 1994). If viewed by a camera pointing towards the axis of rotation, the two contour generators are a bilaterally symmetric pair with the plane of symmetry passing through the camera centre. In the image the envelope will also be symmetric about the image of the axis of rotation. See Figure 6.13.

The symmetry in the image is projectively distorted if the optical axis is rotated away from the axis of rotation (see Figure 6.12) with the two sides of the envelope being mapped by the projective symmetry transformation $\mathbf{T}_s$. The envelope can thus be used to recover the transformation $\mathbf{T}_s$. Its eigen-

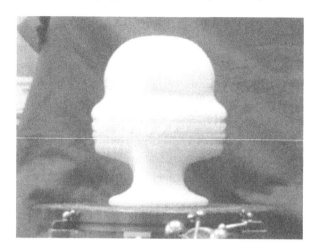

Fig. 6.13 Envelope of apparent contours under circular motion. If the optical axis intersects the axis of rotation the two sides of the envelope are bilaterally symmetric. Rotation of the optical axis away from the axis of rotation introduces a projective distortion.

vectors will determine the image of the axis of rotation, $\mathbf{l}_s$, and a vanishing point on the horizon, $\mathbf{u}_s$.

Hence the epipolar geometry is determined by only 2 parameters once this transformation is known, corresponding the position of one of the epipoles. Alternatively if the horizon is also known, then only one parameter is required to fix the epipolar geometry. This parameter corresponds to the angle between the two views or the position of one of the epipoles on the horizon.

Again the key observation with apparent contours is that every epipolar tangency must be transferred to an epipolar line which remains tangent to the apparent contour in the other image. See Figure 6.15. By exploiting symmetry properties, this provides a very simple constraint for finding the epipolar tangencies in both views. In fact only a one-parameter search is required to fully compute the epipolar geometry once the transformation $\mathbf{T}_s$ has been determined as described in the algorithm below.

Implementation

The implementation proceeds in two stages. First the projective symmetry transformation, $\mathbf{T}_s$, is estimated from the envelope of the apparent contours. Many methods exist to do this, for example, by using invariant descriptions of planar curves (Sato and Cipolla 1998). Here we choose to find the trans-

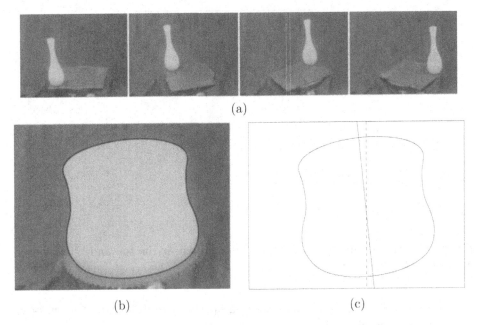

Fig. 6.14 (a) Images 1, 8, 15 and 22 in a sequence of 36 images of a rotating vase. (b) Envelope of apparent contours produced by overlapping all images in the sequence. (c) Initial guess (dashed line) and final estimation (solid line) of the image of the rotation axis.

formation by search (Cham and Cipolla 1996). The second stage involves a one-parameter search for the epipolar tangencies.

Algorithm 6.9.1 Motion recovery under circular motion.

Estimate the projective symmetry transformation, $\mathbf{T}_s$ from the envelope of apparent contours:

(i) Extract the envelope of apparent contours, $\mathbf{E}$. This can be obtained from the family of B-spline snakes used to track the apparent contour. See Figure 6.14.

(ii) Estimate the 4 parameters of the homography $\mathbf{T}_s(\mathbf{l}_s, \mathbf{u}_s)$ by sampling the envelope at N image points, $\mathbf{u}$, and finding the transformation which minimizes the sum of the squared distances between the envelope and mapped points. Initialization is performed by assuming bilateral symmetry (i.e. optical axis pointing at axis of rotation).

Search for epipolar tangencies between pairs of images with the following algorithm:

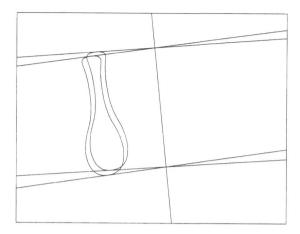

Fig. 6.15 Corresponding pair of epipolar tangents near the top and bottom of an apparent contour in two images.

(i) For each epipolar tangency assume the orientation of the epipolar line in the first view is α such that the epipolar line is $\mathbf{l}(\alpha)$.

(ii) Transfer this tangency to the other apparent contour by computing

$$\mathbf{l}'(\alpha) = \mathbf{T}_s^\top \mathbf{l}(\alpha)$$

and compute the geometric distance to the apparent contour.

(iii) Update α (one-parameter optimization problem) which minimizes the geometric distance.

Figure 6.16 shows the cost function for the top and bottom epipolar tangencies of the apparent contours of Figure 6.15. A minimum of two epipolar tangencies uniquely define the epipoles and the epipolar geometry.

An alternative to performing the one-parameter search is to map the apparent contour of one view into the other view using the projective symmetry transformation. The two epipoles have been mapped to a single point and common tangents to the pair of apparent contours (referred to as bitangents for convenience) define the epipoles uniquely. This is exactly the same method exploited under pure translation and projective reduction. Again the epipolar geometry between the apparent contour in the rectified image, $\mathbf{T}_s\mathbf{u}(s_i)$, and the second image has been reduced to the case of pure translation:

$$\mathbf{u}'(s_i)^\top [\mathbf{e}']_\times (\mathbf{T}_s\mathbf{u}(s_i)) = 0.$$

See Figure 6.17(a) and (b). Note that this computation is ill-conditioned when the apparent contours display symmetry about the projection of the

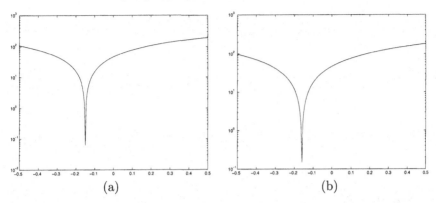

Fig. 6.16 Plot of the cost function for the pair of apparent contours shown in Figure 6.15. The cost function related to the orientation (in radians) of the epipolar lines for an epipolar tangency near the top of the apparent contour (a) and bottom (b).

axis. This is well-known to pyschophysicists who have reported a similar result in experiments on the human perception of shape from profiles (Pollick 1994).

Recovery of projection matrices

After computing the fundamental matrices, the projection matrices can be recovered for each viewpoint. If the camera internal parameters are known this is straightforward and follows the decomposition of §6.2. See Figure 6.18.

In the following we provide an alternative. Without loss of generality, we can fix the reference coordinate system to be centred at the axis of rotation, with the Z axis aligned with the axis of rotation. The X axis can be aligned with the ray defined by the intersection of the horizon and the projection of the axis of rotation. The projection matrices are then given by (Fitzgibbon et al. 1998)

$$\mathbf{P}(\phi_i) = \mathbf{KR_0} \begin{bmatrix} \cos\phi_i & \sin\phi_i & 0 & -\rho \\ -\sin\phi_i & \cos\phi_i & 0 & 0 \\ 0 & 0 & 1 & 0 \end{bmatrix} \qquad (6.34)$$

and defined up to a 2D projective transformation $\mathbf{KR_0}$ where $\mathbf{R_0}$ is the orientation of the camera relative to the reference coordinate system attached to the turntable. This transformation is completely fixed by the 3 vanishing points in the image plane corresponding to the directions of the reference coordinate system,

$$\mathbf{KR_0} = [\mathbf{u}_X \ \mathbf{u}_Y \ \mathbf{u}_Z].$$

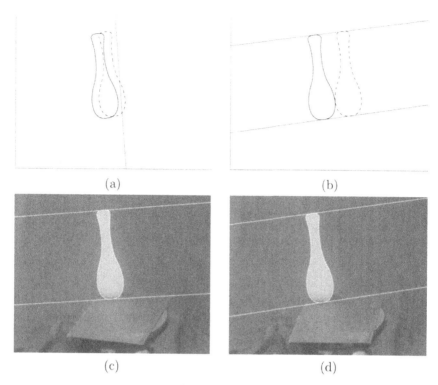

Fig. 6.17 Exploiting symmetry. The one-dimensional parameter search to find the tangencies can by avoided by exploiting the projective symmetry transformation. The original contours with symmetry axis (a). Common tangents (bitangents) to the apparent contour and transformed apparent contour from other view uniquely determine the epipolar geometry (b). The epipolar geometry for the pair of images is shown in (c) and (d).

Two of the vanishing points have already been determined directly from image measurements alone. The intersection of the horizon and the projection of the axis of rotation rotation, $\mathbf{u}_X = \mathbf{l}_h \wedge \mathbf{l}_s$, is in fact the projection of the X axis. The vanishing point corresponding to the Y axis is the fixed point, $\mathbf{u}_Y = \mathbf{u}_s$, i.e. the vanishing point of the lines of symmetry in (6.28). Note that both of these can be obtained without knowledge of internal camera parameters.

The last component of orientation requires the position of the vanishing point of lines parallel to the axis of rotation. This must lie on the projection of the axis of rotation. The direction in space is of course perpendicular to the others and can be computed up to an arbitrary sign from the other vanishing points if the camera calibration parameters are known. For an uncalibrated camera with unknown internal parameters an ambiguity remains

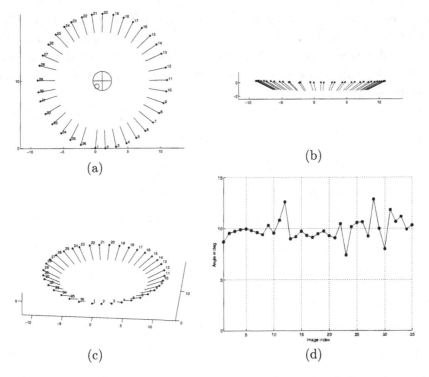

Fig. 6.18 (a)–(c) Final configuration of the estimated motion of the cameras. (d) Estimated angles of rotation.

in the orientation of the camera and leads to a 3D projective ambiguity in the reconstructed surface (Fitzgibbon et al. 1998).

The angles of rotation, ϕ_i, can be recovered from the position of the epipole in each image. Projecting the camera centre of the first viewpoint ($\phi = 0$), $\mathbf{c} = (\rho, 0, 0)$, into view i gives the epipole position:

$$\mathbf{e}'_i = \mathbf{K}\mathbf{R}_0 \begin{bmatrix} \cos\phi_i - 1 \\ \sin\phi_i \\ 0 \end{bmatrix}$$

or alternatively (up to an arbitrary scale):

$$\mathbf{e}'_i = \mathbf{u}_s - \tan\left(\frac{\phi_i}{2}\right)\mathbf{u}_X. \tag{6.35}$$

As noted before the epipoles are constrained to lie on the horizon. The arbitrary scale and angles can be recovered from a minimum of three views, even when the cameras are uncalibrated.

The epipolar geometry and the recovered projection matrices under circular motion have proven to be extremely reliable. In combination with the methods of reconstruction presented in Chapter 5, it is now possible to acquire a three-dimensional model of an arbitrary object placed on a turntable in front of a fixed camera. Both the estimation of camera motion and the reconstruction can be made to be fully automatic. Extensions to more general motions are in progress.

Afterword

We have tried to show in this book that the visual geometry of curves and surfaces is a rich field for mathematical and experimental investigation. (It has kept us busy for the last decade or so.) On the mathematical side, we have developed enough of the geometry of surfaces to show how apparent contours can, in principle, be used to reconstruct the surfaces of objects in the environment, using a calibrated camera with known motion. We hope that, in fact, the discussion of surface geometry will serve as an introduction and reference for anyone wishing to apply this powerful theory to problems in computer vision. On the experimental side, we have shown how the theory can be put into practice, even in the very difficult case of uncalibrated cameras with restricted but not fully known motion. It is, to our minds, very surprising that any useful information can be obtained from apparent contours in this situation. This brings us back to mathematical questions of uniqueness of reconstruction: could the data be consistent with two different restricted motions of a camera viewing different objects? The method we presented is iterative, and it is possible that iteration does not lead to a unique solution. Even harder is the question of whether motion and object can be recovered from apparent contours when the camera motion is not restricted, and, correspondingly, whether the answer is unique. These are problems for future investigation by ourselves or others. We hope that we have shown that there are highly practical problems to be solved here, and also that there is elegant and powerful mathematics at hand with which to attack them.

Bibliography

Aström, K. and Kahl, F. (1999). Motion estimation in image sequences using the deformation of apparent contours. *IEEE Trans. Pattern Analysis and Machine Intelligence*, 21:(2), 114–127.

Aström, K., Cipolla, R. and Giblin, P.J. (1996, 1999). Generalised epipolar constraints. *Int. Journal of Computer Vision*, 33(1):51–72. Also in *Proc. 4th European Conf. on Computer Vision*, (Cambridge). Edited by B.F. Buxton and R. Cipolla, pages 97–108, Lecture Notes in Computer Science 1065, Springer–Verlag.

Banchoff, T., Gaffney, T. and McCrory, C. (1982). *Cusps of Gauss Mappings*, Pitman Research Notes in Mathematics, volume 55.

Berger, M. and Gostiaux, B. (1988). *Differential Geometry: Manifolds, Curves and Surfaces*, Springer-Verlag Graduate Texts in Mathematics No. 115.

Bartels, R., Beatty, J. and Barsky, B. (1987). *An introduction to splines for use in computer graphics and geometric modeling*, Morgan Kaufmann.

Blake, A. and Cipolla, R. (1990). Robust estimation of surface curvature from deformation of apparent contours. In *Proc. 1st European Conference on Computer Vision*, (Antibes). Edited by O. Faugeras, pages 465–474, Lecture Notes in Computer Science 427, Springer–Verlag.

Blake, A. and Isard, M. (1998). *Active Contours: the application of techniques from graphics, vision, control theory and statistics to visual tracking of shapes in motion*, Springer-Verlag, London.

Bruce, J.W. and Fidal, D. (1989). On binary differential equations and umbilics. *Proc. Royal Soc. Edinburgh*, A111:147–168.

Bruce, J.W. and Giblin, P.J. (1984,1992). *Curves and Singularities*, Cambridge University Press, 2nd edition. (1st edition 1984.)

Bruce, J.W. and Tari, F. (1995). On binary differential equations, *Nonlinearity* 8:255–271.

Boyer, E. and Berger, M.O. (1997). 3D Surface reconstruction using occluding contours. *Int. Journal of Computer Vision*, 22(3):219–233.

Canny, J.F. (1986). A computational approach to edge detection. *IEEE Trans. Pattern Analysis and Machine Intelligence*, 8(6):679–698.

Cham, T.J. and Cipolla, R. (1996). Geometric saliency of curve correspondences and grouping of symmetric contours. In *Proc. 4th European Conf. on Computer Vision*, (Cambridge). Edited by B.F. Buxton and R. Cipolla, Lecture Notes in Computer Science 1064, Springer–Verlag, pages 385–398,

Cham, T.J. and Cipolla, R. (1999). Automated B-spline curve representation incorporating MDL and error-minimizing control point insertion strategies. *IEEE Trans. Pattern Analysis and Machine Intelligence*, 21:(1):49–53.

Cipolla, R. (1991, 1995). *Active Visual Inference of Surface Shape*. D. Phil. thesis, University of Oxford. Also as Lecture Notes in Computer Science 1016, Springer–Verlag, Heidelberg, 1995.

Cipolla, R., Aström, K. and Giblin, P.J. (1995). Motion from the frontier of curved surfaces. In *Proc. IEEE 5th Int. Conf. on Computer Vision*, (Cambridge, Mass.), pages 269–275.

Cipolla, R. and Blake, A. (1990). The dynamic analysis of apparent contours. In *Proc. IEEE 3rd Int. Conf. on Computer Vision*, (Osaka), pages 616–623.

Cipolla, R. and Blake, A. (1992). Surface shape from the deformation of apparent contours. *Int. Journal of Computer Vision*, 9(2):83–112.

Cipolla, R., Fletcher, G.J. and Giblin, P.J. (1997). Following Cusps, *Int. Journal of Computer Vision*, 23(2):115–129.

Cipolla, R. and Zisserman, A. (1992). Qualitative surface shape from deformation of image curves. *Int. Journal of Computer Vision*, 8(1):53–69.

Faugeras, O.D. (1992). What can be seen in three dimensions with an uncalibrated stereo rig? In *Proc. 2nd European Conference on Computer Vision*, (Santa Margherita Ligure). Edited by G. Sandini, pages 563–578, Lecture Notes in Computer Science 588, Springer–Verlag.

Faugeras, O.D. (1993). *Three-Dimensional Computer Vision: A Geometric Viewpoint*, MIT Press, Cambridge (Mass.).

Faugeras, O.D. (1995). Stratification of three-dimensional vision: projective, affine and metric representation. *J. Opt. Soc. America* A12:465–485.

Faugeras, O.D. and Maybank, S.J. (1990). Motion from point matches: multiplicity of solutions. *Int. Journal of Computer Vision*, 4(3):225–246.

Fitzgibbon, A., Cross, G. and Zisserman, A. (1998). Automatic 3D model construction for turn-table sequences. In *3D structure from multiple images of large-scale environments*, pages 155–170, Lecture Notes in Computer Science 1506, Springer–Verlag.

Fletcher, G. (1996). *Geometrical Problems in Computer Vision*, Ph.D. thesis, University of Liverpool.

Fletcher, G. and Giblin, P.J. (1996). Class based reconstruction techniques using singular apparent contours. In *Proc. 4th European Conf. on Computer Vision*, (Cambridge). Edited by B.F. Buxton and R. Cipolla, pages 107–116, Lecture Notes in Computer Science 1064, Springer–Verlag.

Giblin, P.J., Pollick, F.E. and Rycroft, J.E. (1994). Recovery of an unknown axis of rotation from the profiles of a rotating surface. *J. Opt. Soc. America* A11(7):1976–1984.

Giblin, P.J., Pollick, F.E. and Rycroft, J.E. (1994). Moving surfaces. *Design and Applications of Curves and Surfaces: Mathematics of Surfaces V*, Edited by R.B. Fisher, pages 433–453, Clarendon Press, Oxford,

Giblin, P.J. and Soares, M.G. (1988). On the geometry of a surface and its singular profiles. *Image and Vision Computing* 6:225–234.

Giblin, P.J. and Weiss, R. (1987). Reconstruction of surfaces from profiles. In *Proc. IEEE 1st Int. Conf. on Computer Vision* (London), pages 136–144.

Giblin, P.J. and Weiss, R. (1995). Epipolar curves on surfaces, *Image and Vision Computing*, 13(1):33–44.

Gutierrez, C. and Sotomayor, J. (1998). Lines of curvature, umbilic points and Carathéodory Conjecture, *Resenhas IME-Univ. São Paulo, Brazil* 3:291–322.

Hallinan, P., Gordon, G., Yuille, A., Giblin, P. and Mumford, D. (1999). *Two and three dimensional patterns of the face*, A.K.Peters, Natick, Massachusetts.

Hartley, R.I. (1992). Estimation of relative camera positions for uncalibrated cameras. In *Proc. 2nd European Conference on Computer Vision*, (Santa Margherita Ligure). Edited by G. Sandini, pages 579–587, Lecture Notes in Computer Science 588, Springer–Verlag.

Hartley, R.I., Gupta, R. and Chang, T. (1992). Stereo from uncalibrated cameras. In *Proc. IEEE Conf. Computer Vision and Pattern Recognition*, pages 761–764.

Hartley, R.I. (1994). Euclidean reconstruction from uncalibrated views. In *Applications of invariance in computer vision*. Edited by J. Mundy, A. Zisserman and D.A. Forsyth, pages 237–256, Lecture Notes in Computer Science 825, Springer-Verlag.

Hartley, R.I. (1997). Lines and points in three views and the trifocal tensor. *Int. Journal of Computer Vision*, 22(2):125–140.

Hartley, R.I. (1998). Minimizing algebraic error. *New Geometric Techniques in Computer Vision*. Phil. Trans. R. Soc. Lond., A356(1740):1175–1189.

Hartley, R.I. and Zisserman, A. *Multiple View Geometry in Computer Vision*. (In press), Cambridge University Press.

Horn, B.K.P. (1987). Closed-form solution of absolute orientation using unit quaternions. *J. Opt. Soc. America*, A4(4):629–642.

Huang, T.S. and Netravali, A.N. (1994). Motion and structure from feature correspondences: a review. In *Proc. IEEE*, 82(2):252–268.

Kass, M., Witkin, A. and Terzopoulos, D. (1988). Snakes: active contour models. *Int. Journal of Computer Vision*, 1(4):321–331.

Koenderink, J.J. (1984). What does the occluding contour tell us about solid shape. *Perception*, 13:321–330.

Koenderink, J.J. (1990). *Solid Shape*, MIT Press, Cambridge, Massachusetts.

Koenderink, J.J. and Van Doorn, A.J. (1976). The singularities of the visual mapping. *Biological Cybernetics*, 24:51–59.

Koenderink, J.J. and Van Doorn, A.J. (1982). The shape of smooth objects and the way contours end. *Perception*, 11:129–137.

Koenderink, J.J. and Van Doorn, A.J. (1991). Affine structure from motion. *J. Opt. Soc. America*, 8(2):377–385.

Longuet-Higgins, H.C. (1981). A computer algorithm for reconstructing a scene from two projections. *Nature*, 293:133–135.

Luong, Q.-T. and Faugeras, O.D. (1996). The fundamental matrix: theory, algorithms, and stability analysis. *Int. Journal of Computer Vision*, 17(1):43–76.

Luong, Q.-T. and Vieville, T. (1996). Canonic representations for the geometries of multiple projective views. *Computer Vision and Image Understanding*, 64(2):193–229.

Maybank, S.J. (1991). The projective geometry of ambiguous surfaces. *Phil. Trans. Royal Society, London*, 332(1623):1–47.

Maybank, S.J. and Faugeras, O.D. (1992). A theory of self-calibration of a moving camera. *Int. Journal of Computer Vision*, 8(2):123–151.

Mundy, J. and Zisserman, A. (1992). *Geometric invariance in computer vision*, MIT Press, Cambridge (Mass.).

O'Neill, B. (1966, 1997). *Elementary Differential Geometry*, Academic Press, New York.

Pollick, F.E. (1994). Perceiving shape from profiles. In *Perception and Pyschophysics*, 55(2):152–161.

Porrill, J. and Pollard, S. (1991). Curve matching and stereo calibration, *Image and Vision Computing*, 9:45–50.

Porteous, I.R. (1994). *Geometric Differentiation*, Cambridge University Press, Cambridge.

Press, W.H., Teukolsky, S.A., Vetterling, W.T. and Flannery, B.P. (1992). *Numerical Recipes in C: The Art of Scientific Computing*, 2nd edition, Cambridge University Press, Cambridge.

Rieger, J.H. (1986). Three-dimensional motion from fixed points of a deforming profile curve. *Optics Letters*, 11(3):123–125.

Rycroft, J.E. (1992). *A Geometrical Investigation into the Projections of Surfaces and Space Curves*, Ph.D. thesis, University of Liverpool.

Roberts, L.G. (1965). Machine perception of three-dimensional solids. In *Optical and electrooptical information processing*. Edited by J. Tippett, D. Berkowitz, L. Clapp, C. Koester and A. Vanderburgh, pages 159-197.

Sato, J. and Cipolla, R. (1998). Quasi-invariant parameterisations and matching of curves in images. *Int. Journal of Computer Vision*, 28(2):117–136.

Sato, J. and Cipolla, R. (1998). Affine reconstruction of curved surfaces from uncalibrated views of apparent contours. In *Proc. IEEE 6th Int. Conf. on Computer Vision*, (Bombay), pages 715–720.

Semple, J. and Kneebone, G. (1979). *Algebraic Projective Geometry*, Clarendon Press, Oxford.

Shapiro, L., Zisserman, A. and Brady, J. (1995). 3D motion recovery via affine epipolar geometry. *Int. Journal of Computer Vision*, 16(2):147–182.

Sotomayor, J. and Gutierrez, C. (1982). Structurally stable configurations of lines of principal curvature, *Astérisque* vol. 98–99, 195–215.

Springer, C. (1964). *Geometry and analysis of projective spaces*, Freeman.

Strang, G. (1988). *Linear Algebra and its Applications*, Harcourt-Brace-Jovanovich, 3rd edition.

Sullivan, S. and Ponce, J. (1998). Automatic model construction and pose estimation from photographs using triangular splines. *IEEE Trans. Pattern Analysis and Machine Intelligence*, 20(10):1091–1096.

Szeliski, R. and Weiss, R. (1998). Robust shape recovery from occluding contours using a linear smoother. *Int. Journal of Computer Vision*, 28(1):27–44.

Torr, P.H.S. and Murray, D.W. (1997). The development and comparison of robust methods for estimating the fundamental matrix. *Int. Journal of Computer Vision*, 24(3):271–300.

Tsai, R.Y. and Huang, T.S. (1984). Uniqueness and estimation of three-dimensional motion parameters of ridid objects with curved surfaces. *IEEE Trans. Pattern Analysis and Machine Intelligence*, 6(1):13–27.

Tomasi, C. and Kanade, T. (1992). Shape and motion from image streams under orthography: a factorization approach. *Int. Journal of Computer Vision*, 9(2):137–154.

Vaillant, R. and Faugeras, O.D. (1992). Using extremal boundaries for 3D object modelling. *IEEE Trans. Pattern Recognition and Machine Intelligence*, 14(2):157–173.

Zhang, Z. (1998). Determining the epipolar geometry and its uncertainty – a review. *Int. Journal of Computer Vision*, 27(2):161–195.

Index

Numbers in **bold** are definitions: numbers in *italics* refer to figures

affine
  ambiguity, 147
  fundamental matrix, 156
  transformation, 27, 147
ambiguity
  affine, 147
  direction of translation, 144
  metric, 147
  projective, **129, 130**, 145–147
  circular motion, 171
ambiguous surfaces, 140
apparent contour, 55, *56, 57*
  bitangent to, *60*, 61
  concave, 64, *64*
  convex, 64, *64*
  curvature, 62
  cusp on, 61, 62, *62*, 63, 65, 66, *67*, 73, 78, 96, 105
  cylinder, 65, 68
  ending of, 62, 96
  envelope of, 103, 150, 165
  inflexion on, 62, 66, 72
  matching, 84
  normal to, 61, 66, 73
  of curve, 70
  of envelope, *110*, 111
  orthographic projection, **55**
  parametrization, 80
  perspective projection, **58**
  reparametrization, 81
  sphere, 65, *67*
arclength, **6**, 21
area of a region, 19
aspect ratio, 121
Aström, K., 4, 149, 155
asymptotic curve, **46**, *46*
asymptotic direction, **35**, *39*, 43, 46, 62, 66, 73, 78
  condition for, 40
  line in, *49, 50*
  number of, 40
  on saddle surface, 39
  via contact, 51

auto-epipolar, *see* epipolar geometry

B-splines, *116*
  active contours, *118*
  algorithm to fit, 117
  control points, 116
  fitting to edges, 117
  knots, 116
  segments, 116
  snakes, 117
Banchoff, T.F., 46
Barsky, B., 116
Bartels, R., 116
beaks, **62**, *63*, 65, 66, 96, *99*
Beatty, J., 116
Begbie, D., *3*
Berger, M.O., 138
bilateral symmetry, 161
binormal, **21**
  discontinuous, 24, *25*
bitangent plane, *60*
bitangents
  circular motion, 166
  pure translation, 150, *151*
Blake, A., 2, 4, 58, 79, 81, 94, 107, 117, 118, 131, 132, 136
Boyer, E., 138
Brady, J., 155
Bruce, J.W., 46

calibrated camera, 85, 86
  reconstruction, 129
camera calibration, *122*, 124
  constraints from fundamental matrix, 143
  internal parameters, 121
  matrix, 123
camera centre
  as null space, 130
  from projection matrix, 125
camera model, *122*
  orthographic, 124
  perspective, 119, 121, *122*
  weak perspective, 123

camera motion
  circular, *see* circular motion
  from epipolar geometry, 142
  from essential matrix, 144
  from fundamental matrix, 145
  linear, **86**, *133*
  planar, **83**
  pure translation, **86**, 131, 149
canal surface, **109**
Canny, J., 115
canonical cameras, 130, 146
CCD array, 120, 121
Cham, T.J., 117, 167
characteristic curve, 109
characteristic point, 85
Cipolla, R., 2, 4, 58, 63, 72, 79, 81, 94, 106,
    107, 117, 118, 131, 132, 136, 149, 151,
    155, 167
circular motion, **82**, *82*, **87**, *89*, 134, 158
  axis of rotation, 165
  fixed points, 158, 160, *162*, 170
  horizon, 165
  projection matrix, 169
  projective ambiguity, 171
collineation, *see* projective transformation
cone of rays, *58*, 69, 78, 79
conjugate, **30**, 34, 74
  determination of, 31
  in epipolar parametrization, 84
  on Monge form, 41
  points on ellipse, 35
  self-, 35
  to ruling, 78
  to view direction, 61
  to visual ray, 66, 76, 77
conjugate gradient
  optimization, 154
conjugate grid, 138
contact, **48**
contour generator, 16, *50*, 55, **55**, *56*, *57*, **58**
  and coordinate grid, 96, 98
  concave, 67
  convex, 67
  cusp on, 68
  cylinder, 65, 68
  envelope of, 101, *102*, *103*
  in principal direction, 66
  of curve, 70
  singular, 62, *63*, 65, 69, 74, 96
  slips over surface, *80*
  smooth, 62, 66
  sphere, 65, 67
  tangent to, 61, 66
  two intersecting, 65, 79, *148*, 149
convolution, 115
coordinate transformations
  rigid body motion, 120
cost function
  optimization, 161
  using geometric distance, 142, 154
critical surfaces, 140

cross ratio, 141
Cross, G., 158, 169, 171
crosscap, **10**, *11*
curvature
  curve, **21**
  formulae, 22
  geodesic, *see* geodesic curvature
  line of, **46**
  normal, *see* sectional curvature
  plane curve, **22**
  principal, *see* principal curvature
  sectional, *see* sectional curvature
curve
  asymptotic, **46**
  curvature, **21**
  helix, 6
  parametrization, 5
  principal, 46
  projection of, 70
  regular, 5
  Taylor expansion, 23
  unit speed, **6**
  velocity, 5
cusp
  by projecting space curve, 23, *24*
  in tangent plane, 25
  ordinary, **61**
cusp generator curve, 105
cusp locus, 106
cylinder, *26*
  apparent contour, 65, 68
  conjugate directions, 37
  contour generator, 65, 68
  first fundamental form, 20
  normal, 12
  of rays, 78, 85
  parametrization, 10
  principal direction, 38
cylinder axis developable, 97

depth formula, **80**, **86**
  indeterminate, 103
  numerical approximation, 135
developable surface, 20, 38
developable, cylinder axis, 97
distance formula, **80**, **86**

E, F, G, 18
edge detection, 115
edgel, 115
eigenvalue
  least squares, 125, 140, 143
  relative, 32
  symmetry transformation, 161
ellipsoid, 44
  Gauss curvature, 45
elliptic point, 25, *26*, **36**
  condition for, 40
envelope
  bilateral symmetry of, 165
  characteristic point, 85

of apparent contours, 104, *110*, 111, 150, 166
of cones, 79
of contour generators, 101, *102, 103*
of cylinders, 85
of epipolar planes, 93
of planes, 20, 78
of spheres, 111, *111*
of surfaces, 109
symmetry, *166*
under circular motion, 165
epipolar constraint, 84, 126, *127*, 128, 139
coplanarity, 128
generalized, 149
epipolar curve, **90**, *91, 133*
reconstruction, 138
epipolar distance, *see* geometric distance
epipolar geometry, 92, 126, *127*
auto-epipolar, 150, 160
epipole, **129**, 141, *143*, 149, 151, 152, 171
pencil, *see* epipolar lines
under circular motion, *159*, 161, *162*, 164
under pure translation, 149, 150
weak perspective, 155, *157*
epipolar great circle, 92
epipolar lines, 129, *131*, 152
pencil, 126, *127*
under weak perspective, 156
epipolar matching, *see* epipolar constraint
epipolar parametrization, **84**, **89**
and geometry of rays, 93
degeneracies, 95
formulae assuming, 94
implementation, 131, 134
epipolar plane, *80*, **84**, *84*, **90**, *90*, 92, 126, *127*
normal to, 91
epipolar plane image, *132*
epipolar tangency, **100**, *100, 134, 148*, 149,
151, 152, 156, 157
epipolar transformation, **141**, *143*, 149, 152
essential matrix, 128, **128**
factorization, 128, 142
properties, 128, 142
Euler's formula, 43, *43*

F, *see* fundamental matrix
Faugeras, O.D., 2, 128, 131, 140, 142, 143
Fidal, D., 46
finite differences, 115, 135
first fundamental form, 18, **18**
cylinder, 20
from planar motion, 84
invariance, 19
matrix of, 19
of Monge form, 39
reparametrization, 34
special Monge form, 41
sphere, 20
Fitzgibbon, A., 158, 169, 171
flecnodal curve, 51
on surface of revolution, 52
flecnodal point, **51**, 96

condition for, 52
flecnodal scroll, 51, 96
flecnode, *50*
Fletcher, G.J., 63, 104, 106
Frobenius norm, 143, 144
frontier, 96, **97**, *102*
frontier point, 83, *134, 148*
discrete motion, 148
interpretations of, 102
projection of, 149
fundamental matrix, **128**, 139
constraints on camera parameters, 143
epipoles, 129
factorization, 130, 145
null space, 129
parametrization, 141, 164
rank, 129, 141
recovery from points, 140
relation to essential matrix, 128
under circular motion, 161, 164
under weak perspective, 156

Gaffney, T., 46
Gauss curvature, 66, 81
ellipsoid, 45
formula, **35**, 45
from apparent contours, 62
from following cusps, 107
from moving camera, 95
from planar motion, 84
hyperboloid, 45
Gauss map, **31**, 65
Gauss sphere, 31, 65
Gaussian
convolution, 115
geodesic curvature, **37**, 66
compared with curvature, 44
of curve projection, 71
geodesic inflexion, **44**
geometric distance, **142**, *152*
geometric error, *see* geometric distance
geometric proof, 78
Giblin, P.J., 2, 4, 46, 63, 79, 81, 83, 91, 93, 98,
106, 108, 148, 149, 154, 155, 165
Gordon, G., 46
Gutierrez, C., 46

Hallinan, P., 46
harmonic homology, 163
Hartley, R.I., 130, 140, 143–145, 147
homogeneous coordinates, 120, 121, 130
of a line, 126, 129
homography, *see* projective transformation
horopter, 160
constraints on fundamental matrix, 160
Huang, T.S., 128, 140
hyperbolic point, 25, *26*, **36**
condition for, 40
hyperboloid, 44
Gauss curvature, 45

I, *see* first fundamental form

II, *see* second fundamental form
image plane, **59**
  rotating, 81
image sphere, **58**
image velocity, 94
  of cusp point, 108
immersion, **7**
infinite homography, *see* plane at infinity
inflexion, **22**, 23
Isard, M., 117

Jacobian matrix, **7**

Kahl, F., 155
Kass, M., 117
Koenderink formula, **62**, **66**
  proof, 74–77
Koenderink, J.J., 2, 62, 66, 78
Kruppa equations, 143
Kruppa, E., 143

L, M, N, 28
latitude circle, 47, *47*
least squares, 125, 140, 152
  solution from singular values, 125
line of curvature, **46**
linear motion, **86**, *133*
lips, **62**, 65, 66, 96, *98*
Longuet-Higgins, H.C., 128
Luong, Q.-T., 142, 145

Maybank, S.J., 128, 140, 143
McCrory, C., 46
mean curvature
  formula, **35**, 45
  from following cusps, 107
meridian curve, 47, *47*
metric, 18
Monge form, 13
  asymptotic direction, 40
  conjugacy, 41
  elliptic point, 40
  first fundamental form, 39
  geodesic curvature, 43
  hyperbolic point, 40
  parabolic point, 40
  second fundamental form, 39
  shape operator, 40
  special, **13**, 21, 41, 72
Monge patch, **13**, *13*
Monge, G., 13
Monge–Taylor proof, 72, 74, 112
Moore, H.
  sculpture, *154*, *158*
Mumford, D., 46

near and far points, **55**, *56*, 59, 66
Netravali, A.N., 140
normal
  curvature, **32**
  derivative of, 31, 32

of plane curve, **22**
plane, *6*
principal, **21**
surface, **7**, 15
to surface, *8*
variation of, 27, 30
normal parametrization, 93
normal plane
  curve, *6*
  meeting surface, *33*
  projection to, 23, *24*
normalization
  of image data, 140
  projection matrix, *see* canonical cameras
null space
  essential matrix, 143
  fundamental matrix, 129
  projection matrix, 130

opaque surface, *60*
optical axis, 121, *122*
optical centre, **55**
optimization
  conjugate gradient, 154
orthogonal projection, **54**, 61
orthographic projection, *see* orthogonal
  projection
osculating circle, **21**, *22*, 131, *133*
osculating plane, **21**, *22*, 72

parabolic curve, **45**
  on surface of revolution, 47
parabolic point, 25, *26*, **36**, 62, 66, 73
  characterization, 36
  condition for, 40
  flat, 37, 73
paraboloid of revolution, 25
parameter plane, **7**
pencil of lines, *see* epipolar lines
perspective projection, 55, 66, 121
planar homology, 161
plane at infinity, 147
  homography, 145
points on lines
  projective representation, 126, 129
polar plane, **16**, *17*
Pollick, F., 4, 148, 154, 165, 169
Porteous, I.R., 46
principal curvature, **33**
  ellipsoid, 44
  hyperboloid, 45
  of special Monge form, 41
principal curve, **46**
  on surface of revolution, *47*
principal direction, 14, **33**, 34, *34*, *39*, 43, 46
  of special Monge form, 41
  on cylinder, 38
  on saddle surface, 39
  on sphere, 37
principal point, 121
projection

orthogonal, *see* orthogonal projection
orthographic, *see* orthogonal projection
parallel, *see* orthogonal projection
perspective, *see* perspective projection
projection matrix, **120**, 123
  calibration, 124
  circular motion, 169
  from essential matrix, 144
  normalization, *see* canonical cameras
  null space, 130
projective ambiguity, **129**, 147
projective reconstruction, 129, 130, 144, 146
projective reduction, 155, 168
projective representation
  lines, 129
  points, 121
  points on lines, 126
projective symmetry
  estimation, 167
  transformation, 161, 163
projective transformation
  estimation, 152
  one-dimensional, 141, *143*, 149, 152
  three-dimensional, 146, 147
  two-dimensional, 145, 146
pure translation, *see* camera motion
  bitangents of apparent contours, *151*
  frontier points, *151*

QR decomposition, 125
quadric surface, **16**, *17*, 44, 69
  cone of rays, 69
quaternion, 143

Rayleigh's principle, 32
reconstruction, 131
  projective, 144
Rieger, J.H., 4, 79, 148
Roberts, L.G., 120
rotated coordinates, **86**, 87, *87*, 104
rotation
  constant, 88
  estimation using quaternion, 143
  from essential matrix, 144
  infinitesimal, 88
  instantaneous axis, 88
  matrix, 120
rotation of object, 82, 88
ruled quadric, 140
Rycroft, J.E., 4, 110, 148, 154, 165

saddle surface, 25, 39, *39*, 44
Sato, J., 151, 167
scaled orthographic projection, *see* weak
  perspective
second fundamental form, **29**
  diagonal, 31
  evaluation, 29
  from following cusps, 108
  from planar motion, 84
  invariance of, 29

matrix of, **28**
of Monge form, 39
reparametrization, 34
singular, 36
special Monge form, 41
sectional curvature, **32**
  along contour generator, 62, 67, 74, 95
  along ray, 62, 66, 95
  as curvature of section, 42
  Euler formula, 43
  formula for, 32, 42
  maxima and minima, 32
self-calibration, 143
shape operator, **31**
  eigenvectors, 33
  matrix of, 31
  of Monge form, 40
Shapiro, L., 155
singular value decomposition, 125
  essential matrix, 143
  factorization of essential matrix, 144
  factorization of fundamental matrix, 146
skew-symmetric matrix
  vector product, **128**
smoothing, 115
Soares, M.G., 63, 108
Sotomayor, J., 46
spatio-temporal image, *132*
spatio-temporal surface, **100**, *101*, 103, *103*
sphere
  apparent contour, 65, 67
  cone of rays, 70
  conjugate directions, 37
  contour generator, 65, 67
  first fundamental form, 20
  latitude and longitude, *9*
  Monge form, 14
  Monge patch, *15*
  parametrization, 8
  principal direction, 37
Springer, C., 163
stereo
  baseline, 126, *127*
  geometry of, *see* epipolar geometry
  triangulation, 126, 135
stereographic projection, **8**, *9*
structure from motion, 139
surface
  graph, 20
  immersed, **7**
  implicit form, 15, 45
  intersection with tangent plane, 15
  opaque, 59, 62, 66, 107
  parametrized, **7**
  reconstruction of, 79
  rotating, 82, 88
  semi-transparent, 59
surface of revolution, 11, 47, 109, 165
  as envelope of spheres, *111*
  envelope under circular motion, 165
  flecnodal curve, 52

normal, *48*
principal curve, 47, *47*
swallowtail, 96, **96**, *97*
symmetry
    bilateral, 161, *164*, 165, *166*
    envelope of apparent contours, 165
    epipoles under circular motion, 161
    projective, 163, *164*
Szeliski, R., 131

tangent
    curve, **5**
tangent cone of rays, 58
tangent developable, 20, **38**, *38*
    cusp edge, 39
tangent plane, *8*
    bilinear form, 19
    equation, 16
    intersection with surface, 25
    meeting surface, *26*, *28*
    reconstruction of, 85
Tari, F., 46
Terzopoulos, D., 117
torsion, **21**
torus, 12, *12*, *26*, 48, 109, *110*
transformation
    rigid-body, 120, *122*
translation
    from essential matrix, 144
    sign ambiguity, 144
transverse curvature, **62**, 66, 95

triangulation, 126, 135
Tsai, R.Y., 128
tubular surface, **109**

umbilic, 46
uncalibrated camera, 144

Vaillant, R., 131
vector proof, 76, 77
velocity, 5
Vieville, T., 145
view direction, **54**
    asymptotic, 62
visual events, 96
visual ray, **54, 55**, 124
    asymptotic, 66
    closest approach, 93, *93*
    in asymptotic direction, *62*, *67*
    mapping from pixel, 123

weak perspective, 54, 123
    condition for, 124
Weingarten map, **31**
Weiss, R.S., 2, 4, 79, 81, 83, 91, 93, 98, 131
Whitney umbrella, **10**, *11*
Witkin, A., 117
world coordinates, **81**, *87*

Yuille, A., 46

Zisserman, A., 72, 155, 158, 169, 171